Dr Oliver's
"HONORABLE ROBBERS"

Oliver Akamnonu

1

TABLE OF CONTENTS:

Dedication:

To my parents, my idols, my heroes:

CAJETHAN NWANKWO AKAMNONU (Mmadukibeya)
and
REBECCA ELIABA AKAMNONU (Silver-Gold):

You did not have the benefit of a formal school education
But you had the more important education of absolute honesty,
enduring love and human kindness.
You started with nothing but worked your hands bare and
succeeded in ensuring the best education for
all your children.
You exceeded the call of duty to uplift other unrelated poor and
helpless as you would your own.
Through thick and thin, in sunshine and in rain, you were always
there for us.
I could not adequately repay you in kind while you lived.
I therefore utilize every opportunity in whatever little way I can, to
testify in script
That we are truly grateful, and that your life-long sacrifices for us
all, did not go in vain.
To you, the role models and inestimable jewels of parenthood,
To you, **Mmadukibeya** and **Silver-Gold**, this book is specially
dedicated.

Prologue

THE "HONORABLES" AND THEIR LOOT

In the same Parliament building they all sat.

In the Chambers of Parliament and government houses they daily sat

Catapulted into, or propped up in office by crime and treasury-looting

Monks in their hoods but monstrous villains in acts and hearts.

In muted tones they plotted self-enrichment and self-perpetuation

Over the microphones they pretended to work for the people

Hearts of steel but only for their loot and not the peoples' service.

It's an assemblage of a few good, the utterly bad and the outright robbers.

Society's villains and conmen had taken charge.

Like-minded evil individuals had selected their kind.

They had rigged in their comrades-in-looting into the seats of power.

From the local government level to the peak of central governance

From one cycle of rigged election to the other they replicated their kind.

A python only begets other pythons and never pious doves.

To be pious in the face of dominant evil invariably attracted peer reprisals.

Mockery has been made of education, decency and reason.

History is trashed or mocked to conceal the abnormal.

Loathsome glees exuded from the faces of the thievish *leaders*.

The Honorables would not utter a word of condemnation of evil

Their mouths were full and would never speak out against the rot.
                              "It is bad manners to talk with a mouth full of food" they chorus

It does not matter that the "food" is the common wealth of the people.

But the exploited populace still cheered the tormentors

They'll carry the hammock for crumbs from the master's table

But, they'll loathe to sacrifice some pleasures for the long-term good of their communities.

Education is lip-serviced and servitude is glamorized.

Patriotism, honor and decency are not in the lexicon of *The*

Honorables.

The treasury is robbed of billions and more is borrowed as "Sovereign Debt".

The nation's debts mount and *The Honorables'* vaults get fattened

"Belt tightening" is urged on the populace as The *Honorables'* waistlines bulge

Mindless treasury-looting knows neither limits, decency nor mercy.

And, the multitude of jobless young people wander from pillar to post

They search for any available opportunity to escape from their degraded land

But, escape from the den of thieves is laden with dangers.

Unfulfilled young citizens swarm foreign embassies in search of elusive visas

The humiliation they are subjected to, strikes none as national disgrace.

Frustrated jobless youths dare the deserts and the seas in droves.

Many end up in the depths of the seas or in the bellies of sharks

The rich land of their birth is turned into red hot irons for their feet

The prospect of enslavement is no deterrent to their quest.

Many that stay back end up with depression of sorts and others take to crime.

The few that remain sane, merely look and sigh for fear for their lives.

Mere vocalization of dissent by them could be labeled as treason.

And trumped-up charges before willing kangaroo courts could lie in waiting

Puppets and Zombies assume the center stage

Could despondency be given a more benevolent name?

Where is the messiah that will save this land and its entrapped young?

Products of crime have mainly taken the center stage

Foreign gold-diggers collaborate and ginger them on

It is a win-win game for unpatriotic treasury looters and their sponsors.

The loot amassed from evil is passed down the generations

The source of the loot and booty soon gets largely obscured

The beneficiaries are hailed for philanthropy and the source is forgotten

But evil that remains unpunished can only beget further evils

Nemesis is beckoned upon but the damage has been done

Recourse to religion confirms itself as the undisputed "opium of the masses"

The societal dent is deep and the scars will always tell the story.

The society that refuses to sanitize itself invariably sits on a tinder box

The docile poor tragically invariably hold the short end of the stick.

They are hamstrung by ignorance and so, remain impotent of positive action

And the crooked *Honorable* and his cronies daily bestride our world.

Mr. Robber, *The Honorable* grins and dances hilariously in the sun

He is fully assured of the necessary loyalty and is solidly in control

Politics becomes the most lucrative job as *The Honorable* runs the treasury

None challenges him as his victims are too scared or are mere pawns

Parliament building becomes a mere circus of sorts

And a great and industrious people get reduced to *yes-men* and zombies.
Oliver Akamnonu
Massachusetts, USA, February 23, 2020

"THE HONORABLE", THE TRENDY TITLE FOR "MR. ROBBER"

Yes, you have criminalized and tarnished the image of a once-respected nation

You have demonized the saints and canonized the sinners

You have cast doubts about existence of standards for right and wrong

You have derided morality and polluted the once-respected arms of government

You have mindlessly looted the natural resources of an otherwise richly-endowed nation

You have pauperized the populace watching with glee as your fellow citizens turned beggars
You have bastardized the polity and destroyed the foundations of a nation's financial stability
You have eliminated the middle class enthroning the super-rich and a miserable super-poor

You are addressed by your minions as "THE HONORABLE"
But, to all intents and purposes, and before a discerning international community
You, "THE HONORABLE", are ridiculed as a mere ROBBER.

Chapter 1

THE YOUNG ELITE AND HIS DAY AT SCHOOL

The Mercedes SUV that brought fourteen-year-old Adegoke to school had just pulled up at the school gate. Kenneth, the personal assistant to Mr. Martin Suleiman occupied the passenger's seat at the front row.
Kenneth's boss, Martin Suleiman was widely known as Chief Suleiman in business and social circles. His son Adegoke occupied the rear seat of the car. Kenneth immediately alighted from the car and opened the backseat door for the young occupant Adegoke. The service which was routine for the boss was invariably extended to the young son Adegoke.

"Bye, Ade. See you later in the afternoon," Kenneth greeted. Adegoke had often protested the door being opened for him, but Kenneth was so used to rushing out of the car to open the car door for Chief Suleiman that he always, without thinking about it, extended the services to Adegoke, the son of Chief Suleiman. Adegoke was in his penultimate year in high school. He was an average student by academic standards. He did not often read much even though whenever he read, he scored above the class average.
The top ten students in the penultimate class were often encouraged by the school authorities to attempt the university matriculation examinations in their penultimate year without having to reach the final year. It was found that many of the latter group of students often did better than many of the students who took the matriculation exams from their final year.
Adegoke did not belong to that category of students in the top ten. The class teachers indeed would not, under any circumstances, have considered him for the accelerated class, which, each year, was a special privilege for the consistently top ten students in the penultimate high school class alone.

Martin Omenka, who was widely known as Chief Suleiman was by nature a very humble and kind-hearted man. He believed in hard work. He had great faith in his son, Adegoke, whom all members of the family fondly called Ade. Ade was Mr. Martin Omenka Suleiman's only son. Mr. Martin, as Chief Suleiman was sometimes fondly called for short, had two other children, two daughters from a previous marriage. He was a highly disciplined man, and despite his fabulous wealth from his chains of companies that ostensibly ranged from distributorships to manufacturing, he resisted the temptation to marry more wives, which his assumed religion allowed him to do. He had started off as Martin Amannaya Omenka, the pious and soft-spoken altar boy. But later he changed his religion and his surname for socio-economic reasons. He however retained his original first name of Martin when it was expedient to do so, otherwise he preferred to be addressed simply as Chief Suleiman. Polygamy was allowed by Chief Suleiman's new religion and the accepted practice in his country which was essentially 50% Christian and 50% Muslim. Most enlightened people in Chief Suleiman's circles would, however, not take advantage of the matrimonial indulgence. Many, however, would have one official wife and have many concubines scattered over many different cities and sometimes even in the same city.
In the latter situation, even though there was no formal marriage between such concubines and the wealthy unofficial polygamists, the children of the multiple infidelities would bear their father's surname.

Ade was on the shy side. He was usually a very polite boy, and anybody who had ever come across him would readily be charmed by his pleasant manners. The same however, was not the case with most of Ade's other elitist friends. The latter whose parents were wealthy were vain, boastful, disrespectful, and downright dishonest. Ade initially was a loner. He did not have many friends, and being virtually an only child, he was often lonely and spent a good part of his time at home watching the television and playing video games.

"How was your day at school today?" Kenneth asked Ade as the latter went back into the car, whose door was held ajar by Kenneth.

"Not bad, only that it looks like the teachers are pushing us too hard," Ade replied, holding the door of the car in a modest effort not to give the impression that Kenneth was his servant. Some of his classmates occasionally teased him by calling him names. They would call him Prince Charles Ade, in obvious reference to Britain's Royal Family. Ade did not take too kindly to that allusion and often tried to prevent actions that would suggest anything in that direction.

"I don't like those advanced math classes, and it looks as if the math teacher is always trying to pick on me. He always directs the very first questions in the math classes to me. He also appears to look too frequently in my direction whenever he is in for the advanced math class." Ade furtively complained to Kenneth.

Ade was obviously not wrong in his observation. Chief Suleiman had privately consulted the advanced math teacher and had requested him to pay special attention to Ade during the advanced math classes. That request was not without some unsolicited inducement of monthly cash gifts to the math teacher. Even though the latter never requested for the gifts, the economic hard times and the regular delay in payment of teachers' salaries, coupled with the relatively poor salary structure of the nation's teachers, made a rejection of the gifts impossible.

Mr. Rufus, the advanced math teacher, however, always tried to conceal the special attention he had been suborned to pay to Ade. Yet he was often visibly worried when Ade did not appear to be measuring up in the course.

Mr. Rufus would obviously want to justify his pay by seeing to it that Ade did well in the advanced math courses. He wished all the time that Ade would score highly and even get selected as one of those that would graduate from high school in the accelerated stream. That would justify the additional monthly pay which he received from Chief Suleiman, a sum that, though described by Chief Suleiman as "a token amount," was indeed more than the monthly salary of Mr. Rufus.

Before Ade returned to the palatial mansion where his father Chief Suleiman lived with his little family and a houseful of aides and security men, the table was already set for lunch for him.
Ade's schoolbag was collected by Dauda, one of the newly engaged stewards. The latter also tried to collect another small zipped-up plastic bag that Ade held in his left hand.
"Thanks, but I want to hold this one," Ade protested. He did not want to part with the small plastic bag. It contained his personal electronic gadgets: his sophisticated video game, his cell phone, his iPad, and his small but powerful digital camera.
As he headed for the exquisitely draped dining room, he had already "wired" himself up with all kinds of gadgets—earphones, speakers, microphones, etc. His mother had a very big and successful drapery store in the center of the city. She also had an airline agency business, which was doing well, as it catered to the big and mighty in the society.

Chapter 2

ADE "THE SUPER-STUDENT"

Topet High School was about the most elitist of the high schools in Karuja, the nation's capital. Virtually every child of each cabinet minister or legislator, (people who were generally addressed as *The Honorables*), as well as the top people in the military, commerce, and civil service attended Topet High School. The school consequently charged higher tuition fees and could afford to hire very high-quality teachers.

The results of the common entrance examinations and other competitive examinations often had students from "Topet High", coming tops. Most of the students at "Topet High" also had the advantage of having private teachers who coached them at home after school hours.
Because of the higher incentives, good and dedicated teachers from other high schools were often attracted to "Topet High". They considered it an honor to be invited to do even part-time teaching in the school.

Chief Suleiman was in a hurry to see Ade graduate from high school and enter college.
He had approached the headmaster to obtain the latter's opinion about getting Ade into the accelerated stream so that he could enter college ahead of the normal schedule.
Mr. Kazeem, the headmaster, was a very principled man. It did not take long for Chief Suleiman to find out that Mr. Kazeem would not fall even for his money. Chief Suleiman, therefore, decided to get around the issue by inviting his old beneficiary, Mr. Rufus, Ade's class teacher, who was already on his payroll.

Chief Suleiman organized a party in his house and invited Mr. Rufus. He also extended invitations through Mr. Rufus to "any other four teachers of Rufus's choice" to the highbrow party. The five teachers from Topet, thus, invited to the party, along with their spouses, were at their best. They all wore their Sunday best to the party. Their spouses were also at their very best, and some of the wives wore headgears that easily obliterated the views of as many as three people sitting behind them.

Mr. Rufus himself even had to rent a suit from the local dry cleaner who occasionally rented out dresses that had overstayed in his custody and were assumed abandoned. Such dresses were rented out to people who could not afford to make their own gorgeous dresses for parties. The rented dresses often needed to be returned the same day to minimize the chances of their owners turning up and not finding their dresses. If an owner turned up on the morning that the dress was rented out, he would be told to call back later in the day. Frantic efforts would, in that situation, be made to search for the renter to persuade him or her to return the loaned dress earlier than expected. Part of the paid fees could be reimbursed to ensure early return.

Mr. Rufus had rented a pigtailed Elizabethan suit to the party. He did not own a car. Even though he was literally making double salary, he was building a big house in his village so as to be very relevant among the people of his age grade. So much money was going into the building that Mr. Rufus could not purchase a car. The car companies in Konganoga did not sell on credit or on hire purchase. Full payment was necessary for all purchases, whether it was for a house or for a car, furniture or, indeed, for anything being sold.

It had rained heavily the previous night, and the roads were muddy in a good part of the distance to Chief Suleiman's residence, which was an expansive complex at the outskirts of the city.

Mr. Rufus and his wife had chartered motorcycle taxis, which, because of the bad roads, had largely replaced conventional taxis as the means of local transportation.

Mr. Rufus had set out one hour ahead of the scheduled party time even though the expected time the journey would take was merely twenty to thirty minutes. He did not want to be late since he expected that the high and mighty in the society would be at the party.

He also wanted to make sure that he took up a choice position at the table. Besides, he wanted to ensure that he was handy to receive each of the other four teachers whom he had selected to attend Chief Suleiman's party. He wanted to show them too that he was familiar with "the mansion on the hill," as Chief Suleiman's exquisite mansion was usually called.

Mr. Rufus had dismounted about a hundred yards to the mansion to tarry awhile for the scheduled time of the party to arrive. As the couple dismounted, Mr. Rufus noticed some heaviness on his fairly large-sized coat.

As he turned around to see what was dragging him down from behind, he found lumps of mud dropping from the pigtail of the hired Elizabethan coat. Unbeknown to Mr. Rufus, the pigtail of his dress protruded behind the back wheel of the motorcycle taxi as they drove along the muddy road leading to the mansion on the hill. The pigtail of the coat gathered lumps of mud that stretched the entire length of the road.

"Damn it!" Mr. Rufus exclaimed repeatedly as he gazed for some minutes at the very embarrassing situation. There were no public taps around, and there was no way the situation could be immediately salvaged.

A stagnant pool of water by the roadside came handy. It was the only water that the couple could lay hands on to try to wash off the accumulated mud.

It was a saving grace for a very embarrassing anticlimax to many hours of dressing up, but not quite the climax yet.

As the couple was busy scrapping off the mud and washing off the soiled coat, a car heading for the party drove by and did more havoc on the already-embattled Mr. Rufus.

The car drove into another nearby water-filled pothole and splashed a massive spray of brown mud water on the couple as they were doing the final stages of the coat cleanup.

This time, it was not only Mr. Rufus that was soiled. Mr. and Mrs. Rufus were now thoroughly "baptized" with dirty mud water. It looked as if the couple was destined not to attend the party.

Mrs. Rufus suggested that the couple should get back home and forgo the party. But Mr. Rufus felt that Chief Suleiman might get so disappointed with him if he was absent that he might cut off his monthly allowance from the math tutorials. Besides, he did not want to have Chief Suleiman find more favor with any of the other four teachers that he was to introduce to him that day, especially the "sharp-eyed" Mr. Okoro, who Mr. Rufus felt might be only too willing to take over his job.

Mr. Okoro also taught math in addition to physics, which was his major.

"Mr. Okoro is very smart. He will be at the party. He teaches Math and Physics and he will definitely introduce himself to Chief Suleiman if I am absent from the party. He could become a new favorite of Chief Suleiman", Mr. Rufus explained to his wife in trying to convince the latter on why they must proceed to the party in spite of the soiled dress misfortune.

Mr. and Mrs. Rufus, therefore, decided to head straight to the party before the house would get full.

"We will have our backs against the wall as much as it is possible throughout the duration of the party. That way, I can hide the soiled pig-tail of my coat" Mr. Rufus continued.

(Mr. Rufus' pig-tailed coat gathered a lot of mud. Another passing car splashed more mud on him from the surrounding pot-hole.)

Only four people had come in for the party by the time Mr. Rufus and his wife got to the mansion, and so they were able, immediately after greeting their host, to take position at the backseat where they effectively hid their stained backsides for the duration of the party.

When it was time to introduce the other four teachers, Mr. Rufus removed his coat and hung it on his seat, pretending to be feeling too hot in the heavily air-conditioned large living room. When the party was over, the couple made sure that they stayed back till most of the guests had left. Earlier suggestions from three of the other teachers that they would all leave together were rejected by Mr. and Mrs. Rufus.

Mr. Rufus successfully introduced each of the four teachers to Chief Suleiman. He, at the insistence of Chief Suleiman, introduced each of the teachers separately and left the room after each introduction. That way an atmosphere for confidentiality was created. Mr. Rufus would have very much wanted to see all but was in no position to have an idea how much money Chief Suleiman doled out to each teacher. But From his vantage position at the back of the large living room closest to the doorway however, he could see each of the teachers leaving the room beaming with a broad smile after discussions with Chief Suleiman.

The inducement money given out by Chief Suleiman to each of the teachers must have been mouthwatering. Consequently, it did not take much trouble for Ade to *qualify* for the group of students that was to take the common entrance exams with the accelerated stream as was submitted to the examination council by Topet High School.
The lure of lucre was about to ruin a painfully and laboriously built culture of integrity and excellence, which was the trademark of Topet High School, Konganoga's noblest and best.

It looked as if the teachers that attended Chief Suleiman's party had taken an oath of secrecy in their conspiracy to push in an unqualified candidate into a program that had hitherto been the pride of Topet High School—a program that had earned the school and the teachers the admiration and respect of other schools.
The fear, however, remained in the teachers—not that they would go to hell for the sins of bribe-taking that they had committed but that Ade might not perform up to the expected standards and pass well enough to enter college. If he failed, then questions might be asked, and investigations might come up as to how he got into the program in the first instance since most other teachers knew that he was not a top student. Besides, the Principal for Academics, who had previously been approached and who had refused to be corrupted, might beam his searchlight on the events that led up to Ade's selection, if the latter did not measure up academically. Chief Suleiman had assured the teachers, when one of them raised the issue with him, that the teachers needed not to worry about

Ade's performance in the university matriculation exams if only he was admitted into the accelerated stream which would be allowed to join the final-year students to sit in the matriculation exams.

"If only you can get Ade into the accelerated stream, you can leave the issue of his success in the College Entrance Examinations to me." Chief Suleiman told the teachers. Even when the teachers did not know how Chief Suleiman would pull it through, they were nonetheless reassured.

"These Big Men, these Honorables know themselves. They know how to meet other *Honorables* and get things their own ways. Chief Suleiman is no *common-man*. He will get his son into whatever institution he so wishes." Mr. Rufus assured Mr. Okoro when the latter appeared to be panicky during a discussion on the issue with Mr. Rufus.

Chief. Suleiman was to live up to his promise as subsequent events were to unfold. He knew the system that obtained in Konganoga. He exploited every situation and the moral depravity in the system to the fullest.

To diffuse any tensions and to put everybody in a relaxed mood just before the exams, he anonymously sponsored a lavish "send-off party," which was usually held yearly from contributions from individual students. For the first time in the school's history, students did not have to contribute money for the year's end send-off party, courtesy of an anonymous sponsor, who, indeed, was Chief Suleiman.

In the hilarity and back-slapping that followed the party, few got to ask too many questions.

Chapter 3

THE CHIEF OF THE GAME DISPLAYS HIS CHARM

Chief Suleiman extended his dragnets for search for his son's college admission far and wide. He paid private investigators to fish out the relevant people that he needed to meet to ensure that his son, Ade, secured high scores in the university matriculation examinations.

Ade had approached his father for money about a week to the common entrance exams.
Students were collecting money with which they would bribe invigilators during the exams to overlook any and all indiscretions in the exams.

Others were making arrangements about other people who resembled them, people who were in higher institutions and who were willing and able to pose as the genuine candidates to sit in the exams for the academically poor candidates. Others were busy arranging for groups of people who would stay outside of the halls and have the question papers slipped out for them, and they would jointly do the shading of the exam scripts and slip back answer sheets to the candidates for a fee.
The suborned invigilators and the other security agencies, who would have also been suborned, would look the other way while the cheating went on. There were no security cameras anywhere nearby.

Chief Suleiman had advised Ade not to worry about any of the cheating arrangements.
"Don't bother to buy any *expos*." He told Ade.
"But how will I pass the exams, dad? Everybody does it. Everybody cheats. Even the smartest of my classmates still contribute money for the invigilators and the helpers otherwise the dull students

who pay money for *expos* will outscore them." Ade lamented as his father appeared disinterested about the idea of cheating in the matriculation exams.

The *expos* were smuggled examination questions which would start selling in various schools and study centers ahead of the proposed examination dates.

Several versions of these *expos* would usually be available, each one claiming to be the original *mgbo* (authentic smuggled question paper that would have the questions staggered). Very often most of the circulating question papers were fake.

Ade was so moody that his father did not want to give him money "to do what other students were doing." Chief Suleiman had his plans that he deemed superior to whatever plans his son and his friends were hatching. He was a thoroughbred Konganogan. He knew how the system worked. He grew up in the system, and he was practicing in the system. He was not a politician. But he sponsored politicians. He was like *the godfather* of the *Honorables*. Where thieving politicians were addressed as *Honorables*, Chief Suleiman was a super *Honorable*. He remained cool even in the face of agitation from both his son and his wife.

"Mariama, do not bother your head about Ade's academic success. I will go to the *river-source* of the university admission machinery. There, I will press the buttons, and the desired results will come tumbling in." Chief Suleiman uncharacteristically boasted to his wife as the latter appeared to empathize with her son Ade.

Then, turning to Ade, Chief Suleiman reassured the doubtful young man:

"Don't worry about all those gimmicks, Ade. Just ensure that you continue to read as hard as you can. My assurance to you is that you will pass the university matriculation examinations with flying colors and that you will enter the university and study to become a *dokita*" (medical doctor).

MARIAMA WOULD OFFER TO RECEIVE THE PUNISHMENT IN PLACE OF ADE.

(1 *In Ade's day and age, corporal punishment of erring minors was permissible. But Mariama would stretch out her hand in Ade's defense.*)

"But everybody else is contributing money for the invigilators. I will lose out if my friends pay and I don't pay. They will all pass the exams, and I will be left out. Even the son of the headmaster has contributed his own money," a worried Ade lamented to his father.

"I have given you my word, Ade. You will be a medical student by this time next year. It is an assurance that I have given to you and your mother, and I will ensure that this materializes."

Ade was not convinced.

When Mariama, Ade's mother, got home from the shop that night, she found Ade sullen and looking very downcast.

Mariama was a very amiable mother, and she was very passionate against anything that brought gloominess on the face of her only child, Ade. She would go to any lengths to satisfy Ade's demands.

Chief Suleiman too greatly loved his son. But unlike Mariama who often found it difficult to discipline Ade, Chief Suleiman was a great disciplinarian. When Ade was younger, Chief Suleiman had a long stick that he called *reformer*. He would use reformer to deliver six lashes on the bare buttocks of Ade whenever the latter misbehaved badly. Misbehaving badly could range from stealing money from her mother's wallet to play the big boy at school to leaving the house without informing anybody of his whereabouts and coming back late at night.

In any of such situations, reformer would lie on the dining table, waiting for Ade anytime he came back. The term "child abuse" was unknown to *reformer* in Chief Suleiman's home.

On many occasions, Mariama would come to Ade's defense. She would offer to receive the six lashes meant for Ade on her palm instead of Ade being whipped. The offer and its rejection by Chief Suleiman was a constant source of friction in the family, especially during the weekends when Ade would not go to school and would be home engaging in mischief-making. Chief Suleiman loved his wife dearly and would not be so mean as to touch her with a stick, especially when the offence was committed by somebody else. After each of such interventions from Mariama, Ade would be spared the ordeal from *reformer*.

"Papa has refused to give me the two-hundred-dollar *mgbo* contribution, and the final date for contributions is tomorrow. Everybody else in my circle of friends has paid except me. The other students taunt me and say that my father is a rich miser," Ade had tearfully told his mother.

"I will give you the money before you leave for school tomorrow, but you must not tell your father about it. This little matter should not make you unhappy," Mariama told her son.

Topet High School was a designated center for the university matriculation examination. Ade's circle of friends in question were the students whose center for the examination was "Topet High", as the school's name was usually abbreviated.

Ade had arrived early enough for the examination. The candidates who collected money had agreed among themselves that the sign that they would use to identify themselves to the invigilators was the touching of the left ala of their noses with the index finger of the left hand. While doing that, the candidate would tilt his or her head to the right side. That way, the invigilator, who would have been loaded with a good amount of the contributed cash, would immediately know that the particular candidate was a contributor and would cooperate with him or her.

Every contributor was taught the sign, and if there was a need to change the sign, all the contributors and invigilators would be informed accordingly. It was a kind of fraternity albeit on a very temporary basis. It made for understanding and cooperation among all the contributors—a cooperation that would often blossom with time for evil in the future lives of the contributors.

The chief invigilator soon arrived. He was accompanied by two armed police officers. Two other men wheeled in boxes of examination material and off-loaded them on the large table placed at the center of the large school assembly hall. Everything appeared so serene and so ordered.

A visitor or a newcomer to the system would believe that all the participants in the day's activities—candidates, invigilators, and security personnel—were innocent and pious.
But deep within each of the participants in the nefarious activities of the day, they knew that it was all pretense.

Fake examination questions started circulating weeks prior to the examinations. The genuine examination questions leaked as soon as they were delivered at "secured posts" a day prior to the examination.

The security personnel who were to guard the question papers knew that the officers who set the examinations had had their cut by selling some of the examination questions. They, therefore, would "cooperate with the candidates" so as to have their own cut from the examination center end.

The chief invigilator and the assistants also understood the game. The lone *born-again* invigilator, who, for the sake of her religion and her conscience would not want to participate, dared not talk much in the face of a badly corrupted system. She was outnumbered, and where an entire system from top to bottom was corrupted, who would she complain to? The best that she could do was to stand still for a few seconds before she entered the hall and say her prayers silently and beg God to give her the strength to survive the ordeal and come out with her soul and body intact. If she tried to keep her eyes too wide open and see all that she was not supposed to see, she might be blinded before the examination either literally or even physically by physical assault from the candidates for her obstructing the course of cheating. Her best option was therefore to see no evil and do no evil.

There was free flow of information in the hall among the contributors. A few of the faces on the identity cards that were presented at the door before admission of candidates were not the same faces that would actually sit in the examinations. But the invigilating officer would not go so far as to pry too deeply into such matters as identifying photos.

The non-contributors were only a handful, and they dared not raise a whimper in the face of the overwhelming number of contributors. In any case, who would they report to? Everybody that they would have reported to was already suborned one way or the other. The uniformed officer who collected his "own share" at the center would have to account to the senior officer who posted him out. If he did not, he would, in the future, be denied such lucrative postings. He would consequently pine away in the office and wear tattered uniform since he would not be supplied official uniform—the funds for uniform having been embezzled at source. Everybody appeared to be in the loop. And so, none being a saint, none was in a position to complain about their *Honorable* parliamentary representative, the Honorable Ministers or even the chief executive in the government House or State House making away with their joint commonwealth. The Big Boss and his men and women are *Honorable* Robbers. The legislators who loot the treasuries at all tiers of governance, too, are mostly *Honorable* Robbers and conmen! They are all "*The Honorables*"! But who among us, the governed is a saint at any level?

The examinations over, the candidates would slap their hands and jubilate.
"Old boy, the thing worked well," one told the other.
The friends would gather under a shade to congratulate themselves for a job well-done.
A few others who only bought *mgbo* (leaked question papers) and had diligently studied the purported questions gathered at another spot under a tree shade.
"Old boy, the thing no work-o. Looks like those men from headquarters sell us fake." This latter group was not as well organized as the contributors and did not have enough money to contribute for a free flow of pre-shaded scripts, and cooperation with information and impostor assistance.

Chief Suleiman was not aware that his wife had paid for *cooperation* with invigilators.
He did not want to go that low. He had his own plans, which were superior and neater than mere cheating at the examination hall.
He had decided to address the issue from *isi mmiri*, the source of

the river. He commissioned an agent to contact the offices of the Universities Matriculation Board, UMB, and purchase marks for his son.

Before the results of the examination would be released, well-heeled agents would approach the staff of the universities matriculation and negotiate to have marks added to their clients by manipulation of the computers. This would be done for a huge fee.

Initially, every mark to be added attracted a fee of one thousand dollars. The rush soon became much, and Chief Suleiman's agent came back to him to report that the prize of each mark to be added had been increased to two thousand dollars. A candidate who scored an aggregate of 150 and wanted a score of 200 would need to pay two thousand dollars for each additional score, that is 100,000 dollars for the 50 marks that would be added.

It was an elite club. Only the multimillionaires who wanted their children to be assured admission into the courses of their choice could afford to pay such fees. Chief Suleiman was told that a score of 390 and above, out of a possible 400 would certainly secure a place for medical school for his son, Ade.

"But I want make my son get maximum score," Chief Suleiman said.

"But maximum score may be suspicious, sir," the agent advised.

"Then make him get 399 instead of 400." Chief Suleiman bellowed.

"Sir, a score of 399 out of a possible 400 will still raise eyebrows." Let's keep it at 390." The agent suggested.

"And how much that one go cost?" Chief Suleiman again inquired in his broken English.

"That will be dependent on what your son originally scored and what new score you want him to have, including, of course, my agency fee of fifty thousand dollars."

"Which one be the average score?" Chief Suleiman asked.

"The average score was usually 180." The agent replied.

Chief Suleiman immediately made for his wallet and pulled out a check book which he leaned forward and signed.

"Here's a check for four hundred and eighty thousand dollars! Four hundred and thirty thousand dollars for my son's assured medical school position and fifty thousand dollars for your commission!"

"I assume that my son will make about the average score of 180 marks. I want make you add whatever marks be necessary, make him get near maximum. You hear?" I want make him become *dokita*. If that amount no do, report back to me and I go double am."

As the agent opened his mouth in amazement, Chief Suleiman again said:

"I hope you know say, this one it be deal. I no want long stories for this result. Wise people don't play foul game with Chief Suleiman. You must deliver or there go be big trouble!" He then again looked the agent straight in the face and shouted: "Deal?"

The obviously frightened agent without any hesitation replied: "Deal, Chief."

To everybody's amazement, Ade scored a whopping 392 out of a possible maximum score of 400!

It was the news of the city. Chief Suleiman was very proud even though he knew how the score came about. His wife, Mariama, was very jubilant. Chief Suleiman did not tell anybody what deal he had with the agent and the collaborating officials at the University Matriculation Board (UMB). He was a very shrewd businessman, and secrecy was his watchword. He did not take anybody into confidence, not even his wife, Mariama.

When, therefore, the results of the University Matriculation Board examinations were released, both Chief Suleiman and his wife, Mariama, each silently claimed credit for the success. One had provided the money for contribution for bribe money to the invigilators. The other had paid money to the agent for purchase of extra marks at the Matriculation Board offices.

Most of the other candidates in Topet High, however, scored around average. It did not take long before the news of the deal between the students and the invigilators spread among the incoming class of high school seniors. It was more of a seven-day wonder as it did not really last long. Nobody seemed to care. Everybody seemed to accept "cooperation" as normal.

The story of the cooperation quickly paled into irrelevance when the results of the exams were released, and both those who cooperated and those who did not pay for the cooperation scored just about the national average. Obviously, the cooperation had not made much of a difference in the score of the other students. Apart from Ade, whose score was eye-popping, only a few candidates from the school scored above 200. Ade's score of 392 out of a possible maximum of 400 was very exceptional even by national standards. It was the highest in the history of the examination body's annual exams. There was no provision for review of results. Even if there was, the reviewers were already the same people that Chief Suleiman had suborned.

Chapter 4

THE PROUD MEDICAL STUDENT

Ade's white lab coat was of very superior material. He had ten white lab coats as opposed to the two or three often owned by most other premedical students, as students in the first year of the six-year medical school program were called.

Ade's coat was always very neat and sparklingly white as he did not have to wear the same lab coat longer than a full day. He would even occasionally change his lab coat in between lab work if he had cause to get to his car. He was one of the few medical students who owned cars in the medical school system, which covered six straight years and one year of internship before a three- to five-year specialization program.

The first year in the medical school system consisted principally of an intensive training in physics, chemistry (inorganic, organic, and physical), zoology, and general studies, which included statistics. There were also courses of fewer course-hours in statistics, applied math, psychology, etc.

Ade was more inclined to the arts subjects, especially history and literature. He got into medicine more because of his parents' desires than out of a genuine wish to practice medicine.

Ade was not a very studious student. Although basically of average intelligence, his devotion to his studies was often hampered by luxurious lifestyle and too much attention to movies rather than his books. He lacked nothing and hangers-on from other disciplines made it impossible for him to cope with the stringent academic demands on the medical student.

It was soon time for the semester exams. The university's rule required all prospective medical students to score a minimum of 50 percent pass or higher in each of the subjects in their first year

to qualify to continue with medicine. If they did not, they would have to drop out of medicine and, at best, seek admission into any of the science subjects in which they might have excelled.
Earlier on, after the University Matriculation Board had posted the students with exceptionally high scores to their first choices of institutions, many of the respective institutions had had to set special qualifying exams for the candidates who were posted to them by the University Matriculations Board. The need for them to set the special exams arose from the many poor-quality fraudulently-admitted candidates whom the UMB had persistently posted to the universities. Many of the posted candidates were said to have scored highly in the UMB examinations but were found to know next to nothing. If they performed poorly in the internally organized qualifying exams, they were booted out of the university. It was a subtle display of loss of confidence by the universities on the UMB. But nobody cared. Money was the name of the game.

Chief Suleiman had again swung into action and ensured that Ade's score in the university's internal examination was padded so well that there was no way that he would be booted out for poor performance.

When Chief Suleiman learned of the proposed internal qualifying examinations, he realized that Ade might not make the screening exams.
He had therefore again commissioned a secretary in the admissions department of the university to have Ade's score marked up for a fee. Ade was thus able to escape the axe that fell on more than 30 percent of his classmates.
But as the actual studies kicked off with multiple faculties and departments and nearly daily tests and performance scoring on demonstrations on models, it was impossible for Chief Suleiman to follow his son's day-to-day scores and assessments.

The medical students in the university saw themselves as the cream of the university community. They and the law and architecture students saw themselves as the potentially most viable in terms of job opportunities and emoluments. They were the most in numerical strength in a club of the university known as "Up-School".

The students in the "Up-School" were revered by most of the other students in the university campus. The club that they belonged to held once-a-month meetings and social gatherings even though most of the medical students scarcely had time to attend those parties. Even when they attended, they left very early to get back to the anatomy dissecting rooms, the physiology laboratories, and the wards and theaters.

They were often choked up with the volume of work, and many of them would be seen coming back with their heavy anatomy book, Grey's Anatomy as late in the night as 2:00 AM when many of the other students in other faculties would be coming back from Saturday-night parties.

Often, too, the medical students scarcely had time to participate in student rallies. The latter were largely dominated by the students in the humanities. When there were student demonstrations and political seminars and rallies, the students in the humanities, especially those in political science, theater arts, and sociology, would be seen all over the place—on treetops, on window tops, and on car tops—carrying banners and chanting slogans, having fun and feeling free, expressing their feelings, and, in more ways than one, impacting on the society.

While these would be going on, the medical students would be holed up in the anatomy labs, dissecting for one little nerve or searching for the anatomical course of one tiny blood vessel. It was often said that the medical students passed through the university but that the university did not pass through them. They hardly ever disputed these assertions. Many of them often came out of college more introverted than when they entered.

Even with the medical students being introverted and near reclusive, many of the occupants of the all-female hostels outside of the discipline would want to befriend them. Conversely, many of the girls among them found it more difficult to make friends with the boys outside of the medical profession.
They were often too busy to cultivate meaningful relationships, except perhaps with people in their discipline or people with other motives for befriending reclusive individuals who had little time for anything else but their books.

Most of the medical students were diligent and extremely studious people and were people at the top of their classes in their respective high schools.
Ade did not fit into any of these categories. He did not have the academic attributes of the average medical student. Much as he was not lazy, he was not a studious person. He was rather easygoing and loved parties and fun. He was not loquacious, but he had no particular liking for extensive reading. He loved watching movies and spent a lot of time on video games.
He had lots of money from his parents to sustain a lifestyle of big spending. He had lots of the latest electronic gadgets—an electric guitar, electronic piano, several mobile phones including the latest version of i-phones, and the most expensive forms of digital cameras and video recorders.
While other students were paired in the students' hostel, Ade paid for a full apartment of two bedrooms in the "married couples' section" of the hostel.

One room was stocked full with electronic gadgets, and these spilled into the living room.
Oftentimes Ade would prefer to have lectures taped out for him while he reclined in a sofa in the exquisite comfort of his apartment.

Even attendance to some of the mandatory practical and

demonstration sessions were a burden to him.

Even as a student he had an expensive convertible sports car, which he often drove around the university compound at speeds above the allowed speed limits. He would also occasionally drop his own car and borrow one of his mother's cars and drive around town with his friends.

He did not have any steady girlfriend. He changed girlfriends as frequently as he changed his wardrobe.

He would not be described as a serious-minded student or a very reliable friend, but many of his friends still tolerated him on account of his apparently great generosity. He would often throw fabulous parties and invite the top-ranking students in his class, as well as some of his teachers and faculty members.

Many of these initially honored his invitations, but when these became very frequent and it was noticed that Ade was often at the bottom of the class, many of these faculty members stopped coming.

Ade rejected invitations to consult with his academic adviser and gradually became a loner in his class. But many other friends from other faculties readily thronged in search of his friendship—more for what he would provide rather than out of genuine desire to be his friend.

It was no surprise that Ade repeatedly failed the class tests and quizzes. His position and eligibility for the course nose-dived. By the time the end of year examination was held and the final results for the first year were compiled, Ade could not make the minimum scores required for him to continue in the medical school.

Chapter 5

CHAMBERS 146B

Chief Suleiman was not following up with his young son's educational progress. He merely supplied the funds and kept living under the illusion that his son was studying medicine and that he, Chief Martin Omenka Suleiman, would soon be the proud father of a medical doctor.

Meanwhile, Ade was booted out of the medical course. Indeed, he did not make the grades to fit into any of the single-course pre-med disciplines.

Under such circumstances, the university always gave a second chance to the individual to repeat the courses and, thereafter, fit in into any other department where the individual did best, but not medicine.

Ade, therefore, was offered a second chance to repeat the first-year science courses. He happened to be the only one in his class who did not pass even a single course that would have enabled him to have an automatic switch to one of the single science courses. He was to join the freshmen, but unlike other freshmen, he would not have the option of continuing with medicine even if he later passed all the courses.

He kept remaining in the *Up-School* facility. He still retained his big apartment, still drove his beautiful car, and still posed as a medical student before the girls and before most of his friends—except those who knew the full facts. He avoided the latter and would often become antagonistic whenever any of them asked him anything about his academic plans even when such questions were in good faith.

Ade was not the humble type of student. He did not want to be seen with the freshmen attending the courses, which he needed in order to remain enrolled in the university.

He continued with his weekend parties and, indeed, gradually graduated into attending the midweek parties too.

It did not take long before he was attracted into membership of a notorious underground club of shady students who went by the name of *"The Chambers"*.

The Chambers was an unregistered club of students who carried out a number of antisocial activities for another larger club of the same name both within the university community and outside in the city.

The members were known as cult members by the university authorities and by the general public. They called themselves by numbers and alphabets with the word chambers as a prefix.

Ade was Chambers 146B. Each new "Chambers" had a senior guide who was a senior *Chambers* and who bore the same number as the junior chambers but had the alphabet A attached to his or her name.

The senior chambers (Chambers A) was taken to be the spiritual guide to the junior chambers (*Chambers* B). Most *Chambers* members were academically poor students who aimed at disrupting as much academic and normal social activity in the campus as was possible. They had male and female members.

Chambers 146A was a female member. The female chambers were known to be more aggressive and often moved against female students who were said to disgrace their gender.

Udeaku, who was *"Chambers 146A"*, was a pretty and fragile-looking second year political science student. She was designated as Ade's mentor. She had been introduced into the Club at the end of her first academic year by one of her male classmates. The latter had convinced Udeaku that membership of the secret cult was the only way she could ward off some prying professors who would not let her rest.

"Membership of The Chambers is one sure way of avoiding sexual harassment and even of ascertaining higher grades." Udeaku was told. Her advisers appeared to have been proved right. And

Udeaku grew to become a ferocious *Chambers* member even in spite of her fragile looks.

The Chambers members were an underground movement that was once banned by the university authority as an undesirable antisocial organization whose activities ran contrary to the principles on which the university was founded.
It was neither registered by the Office of Students' Affairs, which registered student's clubs, nor was it an affiliate of any registered student organization inside the campus. The Chambers members claimed they fought against injustices in the general society and, more so, in the university campus. They received unofficial reports from aggrieved students and, occasionally, members of the public about alleged injustices from faculty members or other highly placed members of the public. They occasionally issued warnings for amends from the "oppressors," failing which Chambers would be compelled to institute retribution. Often there were no warnings, and retribution was meted instantly by way of character assassination or even subtle physical harassment of concerned individuals. Often Chambers members would compose and chant unsavory songs with the names of targeted individuals. At other times they would cartoon targeted individuals or put up graffiti with images of targeted individuals. They were a nuisance which no staff member or student would want to come up against.

The Chambers was said to have been founded in the early days of the university by well-meaning members of the academic community to eradicate social vices like discrimination against certain sections of the academic community and to stamp out corruption and sexual harassment against students. It was then hailed by the students and staff alike. Over the years influential members of the public were inducted into the club as patrons. These patrons provided the financial muscle with which the club functioned.
With time however the patrons were to start playing more commanding roles in the Chambers to the extent that they more

or less usurped the executive functions of the organization. With time they began to utilize the services of the club members especially the poorer student members for carrying out their dirty jobs.

It was elitist and noble to be addressed as a member of the Chambers. Over the years, however, as the organization was infiltrated and taken over by social misfits and never-do-wells it started blackmailing and terrorizing the academic community to the extent that it had to be banned. The ban placed on the Chambers did not, however, eradicate it.
It merely went underground and became more dangerous.
With its ban and going underground, only societal outlaws and misfits in the university community remained as members. Often people would be required to pay to report a case to the Chambers. Then the person or group reported would be required to pay a higher amount of money "to be spared retribution" from the Chambers.

Payment required could range from a few hundred dollars to many thousands of dollars. Sometimes retribution would be spared only on condition of certain demands from the Chambers being met. In extreme cases, a demand could be made on a university professor to ensure that a member of the Chambers or a client who had paid money to the Chambers was awarded unmerited high grades in an examination. The exam mark-padding aspect of the request did not come often, but it was one of the hopes that lured academically weak students into the cult. By the time that they would discover that that aspect of demands did not come often and did not get easily fulfilled, it would have become too late to opt out of the cult. Over time *The Senior Chambers*, an extra campus arm of the organization gained strength and went national. It attracted the rich and powerful who used the name of the organization to prosper, favor and support one another and perpetrate societal ills. The Senior Chambers with monumental resources and with the high and mighty in the society as members, easily took over the identity of the organization and the student wing of the organization inexorably became subservient to it.

Ade was called by Udeaku about 11:30 PM.
It was time for the two young people to set out for "The Shrine"— the secret Regional Headquarters of the Chambers and their meeting place. Udeaku the political science sophomore was to introduce Ade to the latter's inaugural meeting at the General Assembly of the Chambers.
"The Shrine" as the General Assembly chambers was called, was an obscure-looking house built with red and black bricks on the inside but lined on the outside with red aluminum corrugated metal sheets as walls. It had wrought iron pipes as pillars. Looking small and inconsequential from the roadside It was fairly expansive further in. It was located in a desolate grassland area some eight miles outside the university town. Only a pathway that could barely fully accommodate the tires of a small car led to the shrine from the road. The diversion from the major road to the shrine was so insignificant that a new visitor to the shrine could easily pass the pathway without noticing it. The frontage of the corrugated iron sheet building was also very insignificant and commonplace.
The inside of the building was a long open space with only a wooden table made from whole tree trunks that were nailed together. Ten seats made from cylindrical sawed tree trunks were arranged in a semicircular manner behind the wooden table. There were only four portioned cubicles. Two served as rooms where the few documents and relics of the organization were stored. The other two passed for ramshackle offices for the officers of the organization. Nothing was built for comfort. Indeed, it appeared as if deliberate attempts were made not to make for comfort in any of the structures except for the two toilets, one designated for male and the other for female members.
A wooden pole on which was suspended what looked like real human skull and crossbones were the most prominent structure in the otherwise bare hall. Apart from a sophisticated-looking public

41

address system, there were no other tables, chairs, or other sophisticated structures in the hall. It was a far cry from the head quarters of an organization to which some of the high and mighty in the society belonged.

Apart from the ten officers of the cult who sat on tree trunks, all others, male and female, sat cross-legged on the bare floor.
The expansive front yard of the ramshackle building could take nearly eighty cars. There was more and better-maintained parking space behind the building. But the parking spaces were neither paved nor marked. They were usually purposely roughly cleared of grass so as not to attract undue attention from passers-by during the day.
There was hardly ever shortage of parking space in the headquarters of the shrine.

Ade soon arrived at the headquarters of the Chambers along with his sponsor, Udeaku.
It was to be his initiation night into the group which most students in the campus hated but at the same time dreaded. It was a group that the school authority and the law enforcement knew about, had outlawed but had still appeared incapable of stamping out.
The Chambers was a group that had, at various times, harassed students and faculty alike into submission on issues ranging from protests over tuition fee hikes to curtailing of student liberty. It was a group that was both adored, despised and dreaded at the same time—adored for helping to curtail apparent excesses and abuse of power on the part of the authority, and dreaded on account of the frequent subtle blackmail, which members of the group employed in obtaining their demands. Those that despised The Chambers to their faces often paid a big price. Some more sinister activities of the group with the connivance of some highly-placed members of the public on the highways and in people's homes at the dead of the night were less publicized.
The Chambers had also been known to occasionally visit terror and mayhem on both the student population and the public over

issues as trivial as the refusal to grant assembly rights to certain other clubs in the campus.

In the college campuses members of the group were officially known as "Cult Members." A tag of being a cult member often raised revulsion against any individual from decent members of the public who invariably associate cult membership with evil. At the same time, the same tag sometimes created safe passage for the wearer in certain situations since people would generally not want to have anything to do openly with known cult members. Therefore, people who claimed to be cult members were allowed to have their way when they jumped the queue or when they took more than their due share in publicly owned facilities like parking lots.

Besides, the law enforcement officers often appeared to be unduly soft on known cult members when they committed certain relatively minor offences for which other people would be immediately nabbed. Such kid-glove treatment against offending cult members often raised accusations of police complicity with cult members.

Ade and fifteen other initiates for the semester were assembled by one side at the state Headquarters Building, as the rag-tag *Chambers'* house was called. The building looked anything but one that would qualify for a Headquarters for decent human beings or for a respectable organization. It certainly would only qualify for headquarters for Hell or inhabitants of Hell or the abode of the Devil.

But what it lacked in its looks, the building made up for with the caliber of the occupants inside as Ade was to witness when his blindfolded eyes were unfolded after he and his fellow initiates were led in a single file into the very dimly lit hall.

The sixteen recruits, who were called "Initiates", were led in a single file into the hall—each with a thickly woven black cloth tied over his or her face. They were eleven men and five women in all. They held one another with the left hand placed on the shoulder of the person in front as they filed in. Each was given a wooden dagger, which was held upright by each *Initiate*.

A warden, who was an elected official of the *Chambers*, led the way. He alone was not blindfolded.

When they entered the hall, the *Initiates* were lined up in a single file facing the wooden tree-trunk table. There was dead silence, and the stillness was only broken by the sound of crickets and other night insects from the nearby bush.

After the last person had entered, there was a sudden burst of weird singing by the entire members, each of whom was crouching on the cemented floor without shoes. Each of those crouching was holding a short metal dagger, which was rhythmically raised above the head, as in a stabbing motion as the song burst out spontaneously from every lip:

"All hail the Chambers as they come
The kings of the earth, future angels of heaven
All hail faithful Chambers as they march
The earth is yours and heaven is sure

All hail, all hail, all in earnest hail
Princes of the earth, and queens of heaven
All hail, all hail the heirs of heaven
Princesses of heaven and none to flee

All hail, all hail the valiant and the mighty
The blood will flow and the heads will roll
All hail, all hail the kings and the queens
The crown will come but the blood will flow

(The initiates were lined up before the executive members and sworn to oath of secrecy.)

The three-verse marching song was both weird and melodious at the same time. Emanating from men and women of varying age-groups ranging from the teenage group to men and women in their fifties and sixties, some voices were shrill, some others were croaky. The uniformity lay in the dressing of the singers, which was uniformly black, gownlike, and with red strip of cloth for belts. Each person also wore a black beret. It was difficult to distinguish the males from the females.

The serenity was marvelous and enchanting.

Soon after the initiates entered the hall, a single deep note was struck from a pot like bell that hung ungainly at the rear entrance to the makeshift building, which on the outside could easily pass for a large abandoned farmhouse.

45

"All rise! The supreme commander and the council!"
Another round of weird singing followed. This time, all the occupants of the room were on their feet. The daggers were no longer thrust into the air. Each dagger was held vertically over the lips of each member in a hushed sign.

On prompting from the warden who ushered in the Initiates, each Initiate also held his or her wooden dagger over his or her lips. As the new round of singing went on, the singers stamped the heels of their right feet on the concrete floor. The entire ramshackle building appeared to vibrate at the spontaneous stamping of feet. The singing ended as spontaneously as it had started, and all the executive council members sat down on the wooden tree trunks after the Supreme Commander had taken his seat.
The Warden again shouted in his deep, sonorous voice, "All sit!"

As the Chambers again took their crouching sitting positions, the Supreme Commander again called on the Warden to introduce the sponsors of the initiates. These sponsors, in turn, introduced their candidates. The initiates were introduced, not by names but by numbers.
Ade's sponsor, Udeaku, introduced him. "Chambers 146B, nineteen years old, medical student, well-heeled, straight, light smoker, light drinker, has never seen prison walls, has never seen blood, real green-horn, will need heavy tutoring."
As was the case with each of the other initiates, there was some clapping for Ade. But there were a few sighs and hisses as if some in the crowd felt a bit of pity for another innocent soul that was about to be corrupted, another clean hand that was about to be soiled with blood.
The introduction was accompanied by mandatory statement of the age, occupation, sexual orientation, and brief social history of the individual.
Ade was the only person in that group of initiates who was introduced as a medical student.

There were usually not many medical students among the Chambers. The apparent emergence of a medical student as one of the initiates that night was received with great approval. It apparently showed that the order was getting more widely accepted and was acquiring greater professional diversity.

Ade was no longer a medical student. But he still introduced himself as a medical student because that was the status in which he entered the university. He did not want to look a failure by being known to have dropped out of the program.
After the introduction of the initiates was done with, the Supreme Commander cleared his throat and, in a loud voice, declared, "If here and now there is any Chambers who, for any reason, opposes the acceptance into our fold of any of these blindfolded men and women standing before us, let him or her speak now or forever hold his or her peace."
There was momentary silence. No thought appeared to have been given to the fact that the actual names of the initiates were not given and hence it was difficult to fully associate any of the numbers with any name.
"In the absence of any opposition, I hereby call on Chambers here present to declare their intent to admit these cobs," the Supreme Commander continued.

Shouts of "Admit, admit, admit" rented the air. When the mass-hysteria chorus of "Admit" had died down, the warden then declared in one loud voice, "Admit!"
The order was given in such a manner as from one overlord who conveys to a faraway overseeing-god the decision of the former, about his subjects down on earth.
Then the Supreme Commander continued, "Chancellor, the oath!"

A tall and lanky young man of about twenty-eight years immediately sprang to his feet.
He placed his own dagger on the wooden table and spread out his palms to the supreme commander. The latter placed his red-

47

colored dagger on the Chancellor's palms, and the latter walked straight towards the initiates, the "cobs". The latter had been made to form a semicircle facing the Supreme Commander.
The Chancellor held out the supreme commander's dagger which he had collected and ordered the initiates each to place their wooden daggers on the shoulders of the people standing to the left of them.
A billboard on a wheeled stand with the oath boldly written on the billboard was rolled close by within reading distance of the initiates.
The initiate, standing at the center and closest to the Supreme Commander, was then ordered to place the tip of his dagger on the Supreme Commander's dagger and recite the oath of allegiance after the Chancellor. As in the case of Ade, it was as follows:

"I, Chambers 146B, hereby pledge total loyalty to the Supreme Commander and the Chambers Fraternity which he represents.
I will be obedient in action even unto death.
I will maintain total secrecy even unto death.
I will not abandon The Chambers midstream in sickness or in health under penalty of death
I will not stand idly by and see my fellow Chambers suffer poverty, oppression or deprivation
I will not withhold any part of collections, extortions or other monetary or material proceeds under penalty of death.
I will hold other Chambers and the patrons as brothers and sisters. The interest of every Chambers brother or sister will be viewed as my personal interest.
These declarations I make willingly and upon my honor and under penalty of assured death."
The Initiates took their turns in alternate left and right of the center until the last Initiate.

Soon after the oath-taking was made by the last Initiate, the Supreme Commander again ordered, "Unleash the colts!"

Thereupon, the warden proceeded to each of the initiates and undid the blindfolding. The full lights in the hall were now turned on, and there was wild rejoicing with embracing and shouts of "welcome, Comrade," and "welcome Comrade Chambers".

A long trolley whose top was covered with black cloth was then wheeled in, and after the covering cloth was removed, metal daggers from the trolley were distributed to the new Chambers in exchange for the wooden daggers, which each had hitherto held. Each new Chambers then greeted the supreme commander by lightly hitting the latter's dagger on either side with his own metal dagger while shouting, "Hail, Supreme Commander!" It was a fairly gruesome sight as it conveyed the imagery of potential savagery and violence. But the Initiates appeared to savor the symbolic show of strength and power.

Chapter 6

THE SURPRISE MEMBERSHIPS

Ade had become initiated into full membership of *The Chambers*. He and his newly initiated colleagues, having taken the oath of "total loyalty and absolute secrecy", were now entitled to be introduced to the other members and patrons of the organization. As they were now unmasked, the initiates took their positions on the floor of the assembly.

A third round of the anthem "All Hail the Chambers" was sung after the new members were given scripted versions of it so that they would join in the song.

When the singing of the anthem was done with, the chief scribe proceeded to introduce the old members. It was a most surprising admixture of who was who in the academic community, the general public, and even the local, regional and central governments.

The second in administrative command in the university was there. The second in command in the Department of Public Safety was there.

The third in command in the state administration was there. The president of the student's union government of the university was there.

The greatest shock was to come for the young Ade.
After the introduction of the members present, the chief scribe cleared his throat and announced thus,
"As the older members among us know, our patrons are not required to attend our initiation ceremonies. Nevertheless, the following patrons send their regards and best wishes: Chief The

Honorable Idi Afamefuna Odukoya from Karuja, Patron and Supreme Commander plenipotentiary, Chief The Honorable Martin Omenka Suleiman, Distinguished Patron, and Chief Zakaraya Bikaa, Patron."

Ade was not sure he heard the names right. "Did I hear Chief Martin Omenka Suleiman as Distinguished Patron?" Ade soliloquized.
"Could it be a coincidence of names or could it actually be my dad?" He asked himself again. Ade leaned slightly towards his right and in a whisper asked the member standing by his side: "Did the scribe say Chief Omenka Suleiman?" The answer was spontaneous: "Yes, the millionaire chief with the beautiful mansion on the hill. I understand that he is our Distinguished Patron."
Obviously, the Member did not know that the famous Chief Suleiman's son was the person standing by his side. Ade almost collapsed.

"Chief Martin Omenka Amannaya Suleiman, my own father, a patron of The Chambers?"
Ade almost began to tremble. But he struggled to control himself. He then again soliloquized: "My dad a Distinguished Patron of this notorious cult which I had very reluctantly joined, purely out of need to raise my ego and to be able to overcome the shame which would come with loss of my status as a medical student? Could this be a dream?"
Ade surreptitiously pinched his right ear. He wanted to convince himself that he was fully awake and not dreaming. It hurt. It was real.
"What on earth would have induced my dad to join this notorious organization?" Ade queried himself.
"And dad is such a strict disciplinarian. And he is known and addressed not just as a Chief but as Chief the Honorable. And he sponsors and creates other *Honorables* in our country's highest legislative Houses."

Ade remained in denial even after the confirmation by his colleague, one of the senior comrades who Ade and the new Chambers had mixed up with on the floor.
"Could it be a name coincidence for another Chief Suleiman? Could there be some other Chief Martin Omenka Suleiman in town?" Ade soliloquized.

Ade paused for a while. He took a deep breath.
"On the other hand, could there be other gains in this organization, which I did not know about?
Dad is a shrewd businessman. Something beneficial must have induced him to get associated with this group. And he is not just an ordinary member. He is a patron! We will see." Ade momentarily concluded.

The Chambers who Ade had sought clarification from, noticed that the new Chambers appeared to be deep in thought at the confirmation of the status of the patron that the younger comrade had surreptitiously inquired about. The older Chambers felt that he needed to reassure the younger comrade.
Therefore, turning to Ade the older Chambers quietly assured:
"The patrons of *The Chambers* are usually the richest men in any community. Chambers members make things happen in any societal setting. They uplift their members. They help younger members become rich and famous. They are the *Honorables* and they create other *Honorables* in the executive and legislative chambers of governance. They help our society to grow by encouraging the members to industrialize and create jobs. Most importantly they protect younger Chambers when the latter get into trouble. They are invariably the *movers and shakers* of society and I am happy to belong here." The senior Chambers again looked at Ade. The latter still did not appear to be convinced. He was still trying to come to terms with his loving father being a leading member of the society which he, Ade, had witnessed commit many atrocities in the college campus. He knew that

the senior Chambers were the people who financed most of the evil activities in campus. And they always bailed out the criminals in times of need.

Again, he was once told that the patrons were the people who bought for peanuts the materials stolen or snatched by the lower cadre members of the notorious group.

"What on earth would have attracted Chief Suleiman my father to parley with cult members? What did he hope to benefit from his membership, and what did he not stand to lose by a public knowledge of his association with the group?" Ade again soliloquized.

Ade had never known his father to be a man of frivolities. He had never known him to take steps only because of the ease of taking them. He had always associated his father with sternness and determination to stand up for what he wanted. He had always known him to stand up for what was right, at least so he thought. He was not yet convinced that it was the same Chief Suleiman, the disciplinarian who was his father.

At the conclusion of the initiation process Ade walked up and took a closer look at the portraits of the ten patrons of the Chambers nationwide. These, though beautifully rimmed photo frames, were hung precariously by strings on makeshift tripod stands.

It was unmistakable! Standing there in his full *Chambers* regalia was the unmistakable photo of Chief Martin Omenka Amannaya Suleiman as number two in the National hierarchy of the patrons. He was beaming with smiles—smiles that appeared to mock Ade for the reverence and confidence that he had, all his life, reposed in his father.

The number one portrait in the list of patrons would have shocked Ade more than the number two if it were not for the relationship that the number two bore to Ade.

For there, with the same stern looks on his face and the same disarming composure that characterized the portraits that hung on the walls of the nation's highest courts, was the unmistakable face of the chief judicial officer of Konganoga, The Honorable Chief Justice Titus Torro!

Ade did not go any further. He did not wish to see more. He was already feeling faint with disgust even as a nineteen year medical school dropout.

The portraits were shown to the initiates only after they had taken the oaths of dedication and secrecy for life. It was a way of convincing any wavering initiates that they were in safe hands. It was a way of letting them know that they were not alone. They could murder and plunder. They could loot and boot. They could devour an innocent society in confidence and savor the glory. They would know and truly cherish that the ultimate grim hands of the law would have little power over them.

Ade's initial anger and revulsion were soon to subside and melt into confidence, satisfaction, joy, and a sense of ultimate fulfillment.

It was the sense of fulfillment that, at last, he had joined the club of the rich and mighty, *"the movers and shakers* of society"—the club that would give him ultimate protection and accommodation. Ade felt fulfilled.

"Now the ultimate has arrived. Now the ambition for the stethoscope is gone. The Chambers is the in thing. And I will make the best of it", Ade said to himself.

The general oath-taking was over with, but the full initiation was not yet done. Individual initiates were now called into a dingy cubicle located at the rear end of the building for the final ritual.

At the entrance to the ritual cubicle—a ramshackle room with bare floor and four sliced tree trunks for a table—hung a real human skull suspended from the roof by a single copper cable. Around the tree-trunk tables were ten wooden seats made, as was in the case of the seats in the hall, from whole tree trunks. At the center of the tree-trunk table laid a plate carved out from wood and with a cover also made from wood. A glass jar with cotton wool and spirit were the only conventional materials visible from anywhere. A thick needlelike metal material lay close to the glass jar.

The warden was again ready at the entrance to the cubicle where the chief scribe was seated at the center seat. As each initiate was summoned, he would mention his code number and recite the password, which the sponsor of each candidate would have taught him or her: "Here I come, a prince of the earth" or "Here I come, a princess of the earth." As the password was recited, the warden would let in the new *Chambers,* who would then proceed to the scribe for the final ritual of the night.

The exchange of blood of comradeship was performed by the chief scribe. He stabbed the right shoulder of each comrade with the large needlelike object after cleaning it with spirit and flaming its tip over a Bunsen burner, which was stationed on the floor beside the wooden table. He would then proceed to draw some drops of blood.
The drawn blood would be mixed with concoctions from the wooden plate, and each comrade would be required to lick the blood that had been mixed with the concoctions. Each would also have some bit of it rubbed into the point from where the blood was drawn. The concoction appeared to contain some hot pepper since it was very hot to the taste and gave a sharp peppery pain as it was rubbed into the wound. After that was done, the chief scribe would congratulate the new comrade and welcome him or her to the full membership of the club.
Broad smiles beamed on the faces of the new *Chambers*. The medical risks inherent in the procedure did not appear to be very significant to the members. The radiant smiles easily testified to their pride and contentment. The following few weeks would then witness the full teaching of some of the activities for which the cult members were notorious.

Chapter 7

LEARNING OF THE ART

Before the final dispersal of the new *Chambers,* they were distributed into subunits of five members each. Each subunit was headed by a coach who was an older *Chambers*. Members of each subunit were coached in several antisocial activities ranging from car snatching to kidnapping. Others were coached in the art of torture, while others were coached in the art of breaking and entering.

Each group had special training in the use of small arms, and they were taught to shoot to kill their victims. They were coached on how to mug their victims and in the art of strangulation. As the teaching progressed, the chambers were always reminded that once they took an aim with their gun, they must fire. They were further taught that when they fired, they should shoot not to maim but to kill. Mercy and dialogue were not in the vocabulary of *The Chambers.*

The training exercises were so rigorous and professionally organized that Ade kept wondering how most of the organizers were able to gather all the experience that they exhibited, considering that most of those among them whom he knew were not very serious-minded people. One of the trainers whom Ade knew from high school was Nkem. The latter had dropped out of high school and was regarded for a long time as a never-do-well before he suddenly appeared to "have arrived", a popular slang for suddenly becoming prosperous. Nkem had started driving around in cozy cars. He started dating the most beautiful girls in town. Everybody wondered from where Nkem made all the money. He only owned a small video-renting outfit in an obscure part of the town. Ade saw Nkem as one of the sponsors at the initiation ceremony. He came to understand where all Nkem's money was coming from! He remembered what the older

Chambers who he had made enquiries from, had told him: "Chambers members make things happen in any societal setting. They uplift their members. They help younger members become rich and famous."

Prior to his discovery that his own father was one of the patrons of the Chambers, Ade had always felt guilty and apprehensive about joining the organization. He was always conscious of his father's constant warning to him to beware of bad groups and gangs. He always saw his father as a rich and morally upright law-abiding citizen. He always saw him as a big disciplinarian who succeeded in business purely by a dint of hard work.

He always had guilty conscience whenever he went out drinking at night and came back late. Even when his father did not reproach him, he always felt that he was doing something wrong. He always felt that the unseen hands of his father were following him every moment of the day. He adored his father and saw him as an embodiment of piety interwoven with success. Those feelings instilled a good measure of restraint on Ade. Indeed, he would have joined the Chambers in his first term in school since he was persistently lured into the group by one of his neighbors in the hall of residence.

Members of *The Chambers* often targeted known sons and daughters of wealthy individuals in town, believing that these would indirectly attract more funds and protection from their parents into the organization.
On Ade's initiation night as a member of the Chambers, all the feeling of adoration for his father fell apart. But with Ade and his father, Chief Suleiman, both in the organization, it was double success for the notorious gang.
Chief Suleiman obviously was not aware that his son had joined the organization. He was not usually at the meetings. He only attended meetings when there was something ceremonial or unusually important, just like most patrons.

Ade had seen much more than he needed to see in one night during the initiation process. He could now see why it was almost impossible to track down the cult members or to wipe out the cult as an organization. The very people who were entrusted with the duty of tracking down the members of the group were themselves members or patrons of the organization. They were *The Honorables*. And, *The Honorables* were above the law. They were like sacred cows except when they crossed paths with the Honorable par excellence, His Excellency, the Governor or Mr. President! In the latter case the letters of the law will be read out loud and clear. And the full weight of the law will descend on the Honorable. Where sufficient criminality is not established, retroactive laws can still be enacted. And even at that, the oath of secrecy which often ended with the words "even unto death" would still seal their lips. They would never reveal to the hewers of wood and drawers of water the whole truth about how and wherefore a nation that was blessed above all other, had become so bastardized and economically stripped naked.

The Chambers, as an organization, was very wealthy. They made their steady money from extortion and blackmail. Their members approached businesses in town and told them to contribute or donate certain sums of money in exchange for protection from the group.
When such businesses failed to play ball, the group would pretend to ignore them for a while but would come back later to foment trouble or robbery on the business.
Even lecturers and some prominent students were often targeted. They were required to pay certain monthly tithes to the organization in order to be guaranteed safe passage everywhere in campus. Where they failed to comply, they would be spared for a while but would ultimately be either attacked or violated one way or another, often in circumstances that might not lay the suspicion on the cult. Students who were academically poor often turned to the cult for assistance, not in studying harder or learning better

but in getting the lecturers to augment their scores to ensure they remained in campus. A few lily-livered lecturers often complied silently to avoid trouble either by blackmail or by other forms of targeting.

Many of the honest and upright lecturers, however, would successfully avoid getting into the traps of the gang members by encouraging the affected students who resorted to cult assistance to study harder or by lowering standards to accommodate the affected students.
A few of the very obstinate professors occasionally got physically attacked. Two were stabbed at various times even after they had reported threats to their persons both to the school authority and to the law enforcement agencies.
Many were not aware that the very persons they were reporting to were themselves members or patrons of the Chambers, the dreaded cult of the university community.

For a while, after Ade had become a full member of the Chambers, it occurred to him that he would have retained his position in the medical school if he had found out about the Chambers early enough. He felt that since he had the money, he could easily have employed the services of the organization to augment his scores in the class exams to continue as a medical student. But he realized too late.
Besides, Ade later realized that with the multitude of tests, practical exams, dissections, and *vivas* (oral quiz) conducted almost on a daily basis in the medical school; it would have been an uphill task forcing his way all through the six years of the medical school career plus the one year of compulsory houseman ship. He realized that the chances were that he would, one way or the other, have been pulled off at one stage or another.

With time, Ade felt that he was beginning to enjoy the life on the fast lane. He began to imagine how boring it would have been for him to daily remain in the isolation of the consulting rooms, perhaps looking through an endless replication of diseases and other ailments.

Life for him was already sweet on the fast lane, and he never lacked money. He never lacked friends. There was never a dull moment for him.

Training sessions and discussions were held once a week. Wednesdays were known to all Chambers as "Member's Night". Discussions and training sessions were held in different locations by the different subunits.

After the first three months of training and certification, it was time for the new *Chambers* to put their training to practice. The latter were assigned into different units: housebreaking, mugging, kidnapping, car snatching, blackmailing, public relations, finance management, and documentation units, respectively.

It was discovered that Ade started driving very early in life. He was therefore assigned to the car-snatching unit. The leader of his unit was Iyabo, a petite and innocent-looking second year sociology student.

Ade had always been apprehensive of car snatchers on the highways, especially whenever he drove out alone at night. Again, he had been the male chauvinistic type of teenager who somehow believed that men would always be in charge. When, therefore, Iyabo was placed in charge of Ade's sixteen-member car-snatching group, Ade initially was apprehensive about the viability and the effectiveness of the group.

But among the members of *The Chambers*, gender was a non-issue. It was indeed believed within the group that the girls were more resolute and often were higher achievers.

The first formal planning meeting of the car-snatching group was held in the headquarters building—the ramshackle batcher like structure—which was located in the forest with only a track road barely wide enough to accommodate the tires of a small car leading to it.

During the rehearsal, Ade was amazed at Iyabo's dexterity with guns. He was amazed at how the shy-looking girl, whom he always saw in a skimpy dress in campus, took complete control of instructions and assignment of roles.

It did not take Iyabo more than a first introduction to memorize the names of all the members of the men and women assigned to her. Her eyes sparkled and her eyeballs moved so sharply from one person to another as she issued the orders that Ade wondered whether it was the same shy-looking Iyabo that he knew.
"For Friday's operation, five men will lead the attack. Five other men will be in support car. Three men will be in reserve car in command headquarters as reserve. I coordinate all action from my command car with two men—one on the wheels and one as reserve. Oshinowo, Chambers 86A, leads the assault. Ifeora, Chambers 101A, you are at the steering. Adaora, Chambers 122A, you fire first shot and order all occupants of any intercepted vehicle out. Ade, Chambers 146B, you search all occupants, dispossess them ensuring that all wallets and cell phones are taken, and you take control of the vehicle!" Iyabo paused for a while as if to check how well her commands were sinking in.

She then in a stern voice continued, "No one resists or disobeys orders, no one gets shot.
Resistance or disobedience of orders, you shoot and kill. You don't shoot to maim; you shoot to kill. You don't shoot to kill one, you shoot to kill all. No traces must be left behind, and you never abandon your men. If one is to die, all must fight to death. Chambers don't run away! Chambers never abandon their men. Your 'crack' will be distributed well before any operation. No crack must be in your pockets, every grain must be used up. It is a do-or-die game. You either die or you do. Any questions?" Iyabo's voice was so emphatic and distinct and her assignment of roles was very definite and precise. She was smartly dressed in deep blue jeans with a slim-fitting light blue blouse to match. Apart from the butt of a pistol that was lightly sticking out from her braziers and

showing on close inspection in between two buttons of her blouse, there was nothing in her that would suggest that she was a well-armed highway robber. If she were to pose as a passenger in a bus or train, a randy gentleman might easily having made passes at her.

Ade looked at his team leader again and wondered aloud whether it was the same petite and fragile-looking Iyabo whose beautiful straight legs he used to spend useful time admiring.

"Truly, the hood does not make the monk." Ade muttered.

"Is this truly the same Iyabo?" Ade asked himself.

Of course, it was the same Iyabo, just like it was the same Udeaku in the latter's group. But it was an Iyabo charged up with drugs to the extent that life and death meant very little to her at that point in time.

Again, clad in her very tight-fitting jeans Iyabo never used "she" or "girls" even when she was addressing the three ladies in the group. All references were about he, him, or men, never she, her, or women. Use of the words shoot or kill came off her so readily that she obviously must have been fully charged with double dose of *crack* even before the address to his team members that day.

Ade could not help admiring Iyabo's courage even when the product of the displayed courage was misguided and nefarious. He felt he was already in the midst of action. All sense of societal decency and morality had disappeared from him. After all, his own father who he had always adored and looked up to had been shown to be a Distinguished Patron of the notorious organization. The young Ade could hardly wait for the actual scene in the field.

Chapter 8

THE BAPTISM OF FIRE

Ade and the other members of his attack team had just set off from the north gate of the university where they were assembled. Ade's flashy car was one of the cars in use, but false plate numbers had been affixed to it.

As dictated by Iyabo, the team leader, Ifeora, a stout and stern-looking political science sophomore, was at the wheels. Oshinowo, a tall and heavily built sociology junior, was on the passenger's seat. Ade and two girls, one of whom was Bimbo, the operations supervisor, were seated at the rear. Bimbo and Nnenna, the second girl in the team, were dressed as middle-aged women for disguise in a second car.

Nnenna's role was to convey the second car in the operation whose mandate was to snatch and deliver any two new or relatively new Mercedes-Benz cars for the day—without fail.

Two routes had been assigned to the group for coverage. The backup group would equally patrol the two routes and remain in radio contact with the assault team in case they encountered any problems or needed assistance. The third group, the reserve group, would remain at the snatched vehicle delivery site to receive the snatched vehicle for immediate defacing and to arrange immediate color change or dismantling as a backup in case the primary receiving site should fail or prove unusable.

Iyabo, the overall leader of the team, would remain holed up in a safe location and receive reports and direct actions as she deemed appropriate. She would also be ready to swing into action with her chauffeur and assistant, even at short notice.

Each member of the assault team was armed with a pistol, a dagger, and twenty rounds of ammunition. Oshinowo, the assault leader, was additionally armed with a semiautomatic gun and a supply of fifty rounds of ammunition.

The designated routes for the day were the Kuveri-Konisa Road and the Kuveri-Kababa Road.

It was 7:30 AM, and the commuters and businessmen, as well as passengers traveling to the nearby airport, had flooded the road. Assorted brands of vehicles were on the road, but the orders were clear: two new or relatively new Mercedes-Benz cars.

The definite specification of the wanted brand of car obviated the temptation to simply pounce on and impound two dilapidated cars from two wretched commuters.

At 7:45 AM, the first radio message came through the receiver that was temporarily affixed to Ade's car.

"Chambers 144A, where are you located, over?" It was Iyabo's voice. There was no mistaking the precision.

Bimbo, the operations supervisor, picked up the call. "Leader, Kuveri-Konisa is the area, over," Bimbo replied briskly.

"Chambers 144A, traffic situation, OK? Over." Iyabo voice came on again.

"Everything OK. Nothing to worry. Over."

"OK, reach me if needed, over."

"Nothing to worry, Over," Bimbo concluded.

The beautiful red sports car cruised on, dodging the potholes once in a while and bumping into others once in a while.

At exactly 7:56 AM, Ifeora exclaimed, "Here comes one, 86A, get ready."

Coming on from the opposite direction and equally slowing down periodically to avoid the potholes, was a white-colored Mercedes-Benz 230E that looked relatively new.

Ifeora slowed down more and cleared to the side of the road as he prepared to make a U-turn. As the car in question got closer, Bimbo took a close look and shouted, "That's not good enough, forget it!"

Ifeora veered back to the road. Soon after he veered back into the road the team sighted another approaching glittering ash-colored Mercedes-Benz S-class convertible.

"Here comes my baby!" Ifeora again shouted.
This time, he didn't wait for orders from the operations supervisor. He cleared a little to the side of the road and did an immediate U-turn ahead of the approach of the oncoming car.
"Chambers 86A, prepare!" Bimbo shouted.
"One-four-six B, get ready! Grab and head straight to point A. All arms ready!"
 Bimbo continued.
"One-zero-one A, overtake and block!"

As the ash-colored Mercedes drove past, Ifeora immediately gave chase, overtook, and effectively blocked it as it cleared to the side of the bush in an effort to avoid hitting the rear of the offending vehicle.

In a lightning move, Oshinowo, Ade, Bimbo, and Nnenna all opened the doors and jumped out of the vehicle, wielding their guns and pointing the nozzles at the occupants of the Mercedes car.
Bimbo fired two shots into the air, and those shots sent other approaching drivers into quick U-turns. "Everybody out! Driver don't put off the engine! Put up your hands above your heads!"

Simultaneously, the four assailants who had immediately taken up positions on all four doors pulled open the doors and forced out the five occupants of the Mercedes-Benz car.
Ade immediately took up the driver's seat. His companions shut back the doors, and he zoomed off with the car back in the direction of Kuveri.
Bimbo continued, "Everybody, lie flat on your belly. Face down

everybody! Hands behind your backs!"

As Ifeora stayed back in the assault vehicle, with the engine running, the other assailants ran a quick search on their five victims who were all lying prone by the dusty roadside.
After emptying the pockets of their victims, Bimbo also collected the wedding rings worn by three of the men in the car. She also took the shoes and bangles worn by the young lady who sat in the middle back seat of the car.
In less than three minutes, the whole operation was over.
Bimbo again fired two more shots into the air, and before she entered back into her car, she barked a final order, "Don't run or raise your heads for the next five minutes or else I can still shoot from a distance."
In another few seconds, the red sports car with a fake registration number was on its way through the village roads off the Kuveri-Kababa Road for completion of the assignment.

("Don't raise up your heads for the next five minutes otherwise I can still fire from a distance!" The victims were ordered.

The driver and occupants of the Mercedes S-class car had escaped physically unhurt. But the driver of an approaching cream-colored Mercedes-Benz 280 car was not quite so lucky.

He was alone in the car and had been overtaken by the robbers' car. He had attempted to escape despite the shots that were fired into the air by the heavily drugged Bimbo.

As the driver still tried to maneuver his way away from the besieging vehicle, Bimbo fired again, this time directly into the car through the partially wound-down window. He hit the driver in the head, and the car swerved and came crashing into a heap of sand that was dumped by the roadside.

As they had done during the snatching of the earlier car and in conformity with their training, the assailants dashed out, pulled out the bleeding victim from the driver's seat, and flung him off the vehicle unto the edge of the road. Nnenna jumped into the driver's seat and made off with the vehicle again to point A, as had been previously described to her.

The hapless driver of the second snatched Mercedes-Benz car did not as much as utter a cry. He was shot point-blank at close range. He was dead in minutes.

The driver's seat was covered with blood, but that did not bother Nnenna.

She was already soaked in drugs and did not mind being also soaked in the victim's pool of blood.

Bimbo, the operations supervisor, and Oshinowo, the assault leader, immediately dashed back into their car and were driven off from the scene by Ifeora who ensured that the engine of their car was left on while the operation lasted so that there would be no fear of the car failing to start after the assault.

In a matter of minutes, the second and final task for the day had been accomplished.

As if she had timed the operation, Iyabo, the team leader, was soon on the radiophone. "One-four-four A, situation report! Is everything OK? Over."

"Leader, this is 144A. Mission accomplished! Over."

"Mission accomplished? One or two accomplished? Over."

"Leader, two accomplished. Both goods are on way to point A. Over."

"Good job!. All Chambers OK? Any in-house casualty? Over."

"No in-house casualty. All Chambers OK. Over."

"One-four-four A, bravo. Over."

"Thanks, Leader! Heading back to base. Over and over."

The mission had been accomplished. Two cars had been successfully snatched. There were no "911 Emergency services" to call. Its equivalent existed but the operators would not respond to distress calls. No, they were busy at designated check points on busy and *lucrative* highways. They were busy collecting "tithes" from hapless commuters. And their leaders would look the other way. They too were very busy. They were very busy counting the daily "returns" from subordinate officers who they had posted to the highways. Thereafter they would build eye-popping mansions for themselves. They would be conferred with big chieftaincy titles by various autonomous communities. And they would join the ranks of "The Honorables". They would build big hotels, financed by banks which they had set up from questionable sources. And nobody would raise a whimper. Any who raised an eyebrow or sought to find out the source of the wealth might be endangering his or her life. If he or she escaped the hit men, they might end up with trumped up libel suits. And the suborned judiciary would find them liable. Konganoga was booming. Yes, it was booming with loot.

A breadwinner of a family had been deprived of his life and was lying dead on the roadside. A wife and two sons were waiting at home for the return of a loved one.
They would have to wait forever because someone had fulfilled a mission.
The champagne glasses would cling later in the evening at some dingy bar in Kuveri.
But the moans will come from two young sons and a woman that had been widowed or suddenly left fatherless. *Chambers* had been made richer by two Mercedes-Benz cars, and the patrons who invariably bought the refurbished cars would be richer, bolder, and filthier. They were ruthless robbers in private. But they would in public still be addressed as "The Honorable."

Chapter 9

POINTS A and B

Only Ifeora and Nnenna, the designated drivers for the day's operation, were given directives as to where the snatched vehicles would be deposited. The points were designated as points A and B.

Point A was not a definite location and was shifted as the need arose to avoid detection or revelation should the Chambers driver get apprehended.

From point A, another set of drivers would pick up the vehicles to point B, another site unknown to the initial drivers who would not be allowed to meet with the drivers at point A. That way, identification of the drivers from point A to point B would be impossible for the drivers from crime site to point A.

As it happened at that particular instance, the driver, who was to pick up the vehicle which Ade would have dropped at point A, had not arrived. It was risky to leave a snatched vehicle at point A, which was "not a secured site."

The order, therefore, arrived to Ade through the latter's cell phone. "Officer 146B, proceed with delivery of goods to point B." A terse description of point B was thereafter given to Ade. No house number or street name was given. Only a description of the turns and bends and landmarks.
Finally, as Ade took the turns and corners as he was directed on the phone, he could see even from a distance the imposing building with the flower lawns and large compound and imposing metal gate that he was very familiar with and which he thought he knew so well.

Could point B, the hideout of snatched cars, be so closely located to the famous head office of a man he respected so well and had until recently come to associate with honor and great achievement—his own father?

Just as Ade took the last turn and got close to the front gate of his father's giant head office building, he was told to turn in and drive slowly through the rear gate of the building.
Ade was flabbergasted. Once within the premises, the final stern order came. "Drive straight to the back gate!"
The order was followed by a quick second order: "Your code is C146B1. Quote that code into the microphone and wait for the automated gate to open for you."

Ade did as he was told. His curiosity and anxiety knew no bounds. He had visited his father's office dozens of times but had never ever known that there was a rear gate not to talk of an underground parking garage with codes.

(Dozens of exotic cars were being repainted and altered in the underground robbers' den.)

Soon after he quoted his code, Ade was prompted to repeat the code. As soon as he did so, the gate swung open for him.

Ade's sight was to behold a sight that so unnerved him that he almost swooned.
There, underground and beneath, what appeared as an innocuous office complex laid a very vibrant car-refurbishing industry.

Indeed, it was more than a car-refurbishing industry. It was a car-remanufacturing industry. Any car that went in there would come out in a couple of hours with a color, a plate number, and engine and chassis numbers, other than what they went in with. It would be the same car but with a completely different identity. Panel beaters were there. Spray painters were there. Hundreds of plate numbers of vehicles, obviously faked ones, were there. Even dismantled engines were there.

It was a very vast warehouse. Scores of workers were there—all in blue overall dresses.
Everybody appeared busy. Hardly anybody appeared to take notice of the entry of another car that would be worked on— another stolen car that would need to be turned into a new car with completely different particulars and only in a matter of hours.

A middle-aged bespectacled man approached Ade's car s soon after it was parked into an empty slot to which Ade had been directed.
The man neither spoke to Ade nor did he show any signs of panic or surprise at the arrival of the vehicle. He appeared to be very used to different cars being driven in periodically and handed over to him.

Ade switched off the engine as soon as he moved the car into the parking slot.

"Leave the engine on!" the bespectacled man ordered.

Ade quickly complied and turned on the engine.

"Thanks, and have a good day," the man said again as he entered the car and pulled open the bonnet.

As Ade stood gazing at the man, six other men moved in with spanners, metal brushes, and other gadgets. They appeared set to start immediate work on the car. Their speed and dexterity were amazing.

Right before Ade, all the parts of the car that had any identification marks were dismantled. The plate number was the first to go. The front and rear windscreens that had the registration number of the car scratched on them, were dismantled.

Ade would have liked to see more, but one bulky man who the workers simply addressed as Oga, walked up to Ade and said to him, "Your ID please!"

Ade impulsively replied, "Ade!" A hard look of surprise from the man, made Ade immediately remember that he was not supposed to be addressed as Ade. He immediately corrected himself and said, "146B."

The man brought out a device that looked like a cell phone and keyed in the code and then added, "Ade Suleiman. Mission accomplished. Good! Now, get going! Your job is done! See the cashier and get going. We don't allow loitering in here!"

Despite his grave disappointment at the realization that the underground of his father's office premises was indeed a robber's den, Ade was impressed with the coordination about information regarding his mission. He was also disappointed that there appeared to be little more information to him soon after he delivered the car. He appeared to be blacked out of events immediately after he delivered the car. He felt that he had been used and was about to be discarded. He, nevertheless, fancied that it might be part of the strategy to ensure that information did not leak from that point on until the car had been thoroughly defaced and moved out.

There were more than fifty cars of different makes. But most were in the category of the expensive and luxury brands: SUVs, convertibles, and sports cars. Two limousines were parked at the far end of the expansive garage and workshop. One was being re-sprayed with a different color, and the side mirrors of the second car were being fixed.
It was a beehive of activity.

Ade kept wondering within himself whether he was indeed seeing right, that the underground bunker where all that was going on was the premises of the man he had, all his life, come to regard as the epitome of uprightness—his own father.
Ade approached one of the men fixing a new rear windscreen to the car which he drove in a few minutes earlier, and asked him for the way to the cashier's office. The man did not talk to him. He merely pointed him to the direction where the two limousines were stationed. Everybody appeared too busy even to talk. It was possible they were under strict instructions not to talk to any strangers.

Ade walked up to where he was directed and asked another man. Again, the second man did not utter a word in reply but kept applying the thick glue with which he was fixing the rear windscreen of the car.
When the man noticed that the inquirer did not go away, he then pointed him in another direction, which happened to be the same direction from which Ade came. It was obviously a move to get Ade out of his way. Ade was both confused and a little furious.
"Why would nobody want to talk to me? Why would nobody want to direct me especially after the huge risk that I had taken to snatch the car and to deliver it successfully?" Ade complained to himself.
During the course of his wait, Ade had seen two other cars drive

in: a large BMW car and another Mercedes Benz S class.
The drivers of the cars were quickly attended to and escorted out
of the underground bunker. They appeared quite familiar with the
environment. But Ade for some reason remained apparently
ignored except for the numerous security cameras that dotted
every five to six feet intervals in the massive factory.
It was nearly about one and a half hours after he delivered the car
that a young man approached Ade and said, "146B, right?"
Ade heaved a sigh of relief and replied, "Right."

The young man then said, "My name is Idrisu or simply Idi. I am
here to direct you to the accounts department. Please follow me."
The young man then led Ade through a narrow tunnel that was
dimly lit, which led across the street into a two-storied building
that housed a grocery store. As the two young men climbed the
spiral staircase that led out of the tunnel, the young man tried to
engage Ade in conversation.
"I hope all is well," the young man started.

"Everything is OK," Ade replied.
"Do you care for cigarettes?
"No, thanks."
"You live in town?"
"Yes, I do, and what about you?"
"I was only recently transferred from the Kokoja branch. I haven't
yet found accommodation, and so I still live in the hotel."
The young man was smartly dressed in suit and spoke very good
English.
Ade picked up interest and wanted to know more. "How is the
Kokoja branch?"
"Oh, very busy. We receive goods from as far away as Karuja."
Ade did not want to give out the impression that he was a novice
in the business.
"Oh really? The cars from Karuja must all be exotic. Being the
national capital, Karuja cars must be really exotic and much
newer."

"Unfortunately, no! Security is very tight in Karuja. All those ministers and big government officials go with armed escorts, and it is risky business targeting them. We have lost quite a number of our men who tried to take some of those cars. Many of the expensive cars there also belong to these rich retired generals and retired top police officers. All those men are fully armed all the time, you know."

Idrisu paused for a while and continued.
"So, you see, business is not as good in Karuja and cities around it as people think. We even had to shut down one of our big offices in Karuja recently. We almost got busted. If it were not for the fact that the retired deputy chief of police is one of our members, our big boss would have been in trouble. Indeed, the big boss had to suddenly flee the country and had not been back for nearly a year. It was because of his long absence that the other patrons met and elected this new patron as the overall boss.

"I was one of the personal assistants to the erstwhile big boss, and it was after the election of this new big boss, Chief Omenka Suleiman, that I was transferred to this wretched Kuveri to train out people who were already assisting Chief Suleiman since they will be assuming much more important and risky roles."

Another wave of shock came over Ade at the double mention of his father's name.
But he controlled his emotions and replied, "Oh Chief Suleiman, I have heard of him, but I have not met him. What kind of man is he?"
"I have really only met with him two times since my arrival here. I have not been long in contact with him, but I understand he is a very hardworking man and that he is quite disciplined."
"Hmm, quite disciplined? Could there really be a quite disciplined man or woman in this business?" Ade added rather frankly.
"Yes, of course. Every business has its share of disciplined people. You know that some of us, robbers and cult members, steal even

from our fellow robbers. But even among robbers, there could be villains and saints. I was a sociology sophomore before I dropped out and began this job full-time.

I remember that one of my professors, who was one of the local chiefs in my campus chapter, was so mean that he used to date some of our female members. That kind of practice, as you know, is strictly against the principles of our organization nationwide and even internationally. 202AA was a very mean man. He would never augment a member's score even by one mark in his sociology course exams. It was because of his activities that people like me dropped out of the course and finally out of college."

Idrisu paused for a while and held his palm over his lips as if he was urging himself not to talk too much to a virtual stranger. But he looked at Ade and appeared to feel convinced that he could trust the latter. And so, he continued:

"Can I trust you, Chambers, …. What's the name again?"

"Ade is the name, Chambers 146B for sure, Idi!" Ade answered smartly and off-handedly.

"Yes, Ade! We of course eventually took care of the mad professor. His bones must be blaming his soul, if he had one, for letting them get interred before the age of forty in a shallow unmarked grave in the jungle. Yes, in the jungle! That was where we finally gave him a befitting burial in a shallow grave as a reward for his meanness."

Idrisu spoke so very casually about "taking care" of people as if it was a compliment or a heroic act. Killing people and burying them in shallow graves no longer meant much for him. His gentle looks easily gave a lie to what must be a hardened and demonic soul. Ade would have liked to hear more, especially about Chief Suleiman. But further discussion was cut short by the approach of some visitors.

Idi, immediately directed Ade to the cashier who had already got instructions to "disburse the sum of two thousand dollars to Chambers 146B upon identification."

It was a good day for Ade—a very rewarding and enlightening day even for a spoilt child who had hitherto had no monetary problems. But the troubling information about the elevation of his revered dad to the post of Supreme Commander of the notorious secret society *The Chambers*, weighed heavily on Ade.

Chapter 10

A FATHER, THE SON, AND THE UNHOLY CLUB

Ade received information that he would be one of the ushers in a patron's party of *The Chambers.*
After he learned of his father's deep involvement in the sponsorship of the Chambers cult, Ade had not had full peace of mind again. He could not reconcile himself to the realization that his father was involved in that kind of business. He took to heavy drinking and often soaked himself in liquor and drugs so as to remain "high" and think less about the realities of his life.

Initially, even after he had joined the Chambers, Ade still felt a sense of pride and dignity at the realization that his father was a highly respected man in the community and that his mother was no less respectable.
Now he had realized that there were people out there who knew more than he did—that Chief Suleiman was, after all, not a saint. His colleagues in the league of patrons of the Chambers knew more about the activities, which were not honorable. The people in the underground stolen-vehicle depot knew who they worked for. Even Idrisu, who came from far-off Kokoja, knew the full details of *The Right Honorable* Chief Martin Omenka Suleiman's involvement.

The knowledge of each other's extent of involvement by father and son in the ignoble society was initially not shared by both people. Chief Suleiman, though highly placed in the hierarchy of the organization, was not involved in the day-to-day running of the organization. He operated at a much higher level than his son. He was in the AA class, the main beneficiaries of the ignoble activities of the organization. He was therefore not in the know about the roll call of the membership, especially the much junior membership.

The likes of Ade only got the crumbs after doing the dirty jobs. They got protection from prosecution. They got a couple of thousands of dollars. They got the big names and respect borne out of fear from the besieged population. It was more of dread than respect. Apart from the foregoing, they got nothing more. And they got the big bad image because they were the people in the forefront. They were right in the eye of the storm. They might easily get killed if operations went sour. But when a successful snatching got done, as was the case with Ade, the latter got only two thousand dollars but the former got the megabucks. And soon after the *goods* were delivered, they got treated with near ignominy. The cult leadership got almost all the benefits.

Ade arrived the headquarters about 11:00 PM for the usher's assignment that had been given to him on the Patrons' Night event.
The reception for the distinguished guest, who was the former Distinguished Patron now the National leader of the Chambers, was slated for twelve midnight.

Ade was selected as an usher and was simply assigned a duty as Chambers 146B. He knew neither the details nor who were being expected.
He only hoped that his father, whom he had never seen around the headquarters and who did not know of his son's membership, would not come. It was bad enough that he already knew that his father was a kingpin of the organization. It would be more mutually devastating if both parties got to know of each other's involvement.

By twelve midnight, the invitees started streaming in. The inside of the ramshackle headquarters had had a thorough makeover. While the outside deliberately still wore the look of an abandoned old batcher, the inside was completely transformed into a very elegant and fully decorated hall with carpeted dancing floor, exquisitely decorated high table, and neatly arranged chairs. The brick walls on the inside were professionally draped with beautiful roof-to-floor draperies and the asbestos-covered ceiling board was also exquisitely made over with draperies and chandeliers.

The place looked so different after it was decorated that when Ade arrived to the premises, he had to walk in and out a number of times to confirm that he was in the correct place.
Ade, along with nine other newly recruited members of the Chambers, were fully clad in the ceremonial attire of the organization with bow tie and novice's green beret. They had been busy ushering in the dignitaries as they arrived.
The high table was almost fully occupied. The seat of the chief celebrant, "Nnukwu Mmanwu" ("the big masquerade") for the night, was one of the two that were still vacant.

(As Ade unexpectedly meets with his father at the initiation night, a greatly-shocked Chief Suleiman stands almost frozen. He immediately covers his mouth with his left hand with a fixed gaze on his son.)

81

At 12:06 AM, as Ade and three other ushers who manned the VIP's entrance door returned to the door to lead in yet another VIP, behold, there standing tall and in complete black suit and with the characteristic black beret and cross bones emblem of the Chambers, stood the man whom Ade had, for the twenty years of his life, regarded as the epitome of all modesty, discipline, and candor.

There, before Ade, under the full glare of the glamour and the glittering chandeliers, stood the indomitable Chief Martin Omenka Suleiman, his own father.

It was a meeting that both father and son would have given anything to avoid. It was one meeting too many.

Ade had had the knowledge that his father was a patron of the notorious club for some time. He knew that for the first time on the night of his initiation.

While he was still reeling over the burden of that discovery, he was rattled and completely unnerved by Idrisu's information about the elevation of his apparently innocent and highly disciplined father and company chief executive. But Ade did not know that his father was the person being honored for the night since the recruits were not given full information as to whom to expect or what functions they would perform prior to the chief celebrant's arrival.

Ade immediately recognized his father even before he got face-to-face with him. His gait was unmistakable, and the ever-present smile that often beguiled the inward toughness and doggedness could never be missed by anyone who had had the pleasure or, as Ade would see it, the misfortune of having been living with Chief Suleiman for nearly twenty years.

Ade's first instinct was to pull back and disappear among the rest of the ushers and participants at the party. He would have liked to

be spared the ordeal of having to meet with his father under those circumstances. This would have saved him the embarrassment and, more so, saved more embarrassment to his father.
"in as much as Dad has fallen short of the reverence and trust that he had hitherto enjoyed from me I still acknowledge that he has done for me, all that a responsible and caring father could do for a son that he loves" Ade muttered to himself. Even in the midst of indulgence in drugs and crime, Ade still had the rare moment of soberness to revere Chief Suleiman his dad.

Chief Suleiman, on his part, had not the slightest knowledge that his only son, whom he had endeavored to train to be a highly respectable physician and had gone out of his way to spend a lot of money to buy placement in the medical school, was to be the young newly recruited usher who would escort him to the high table on the night of the crowning of his glory as a patron of the club that boasted the high and mighty not just in Kuveri but also in Karuja and beyond, a club that he had helped nurture and from which he had benefited immensely for more than two decades, howbeit, a club of notorious criminals.

Ade, in one split moment, mustered the courage and approached his father, and instead of offering the signature greeting of the Chambers, he stretched out his hand in a handshake and addressed his father in his traditional title greeting:
"Oshimiri Ndewo! Jookwa!" (The sea that never dries, greetings! May you live long).
Oshimiri (The sea that never dries), was the highfaluting title which was conferred on Chief Omenka Suleiman by his native community. So much was his wealth and influence and so much was his supposed philanthropy, hat the community felt happy and obligated to confer the big title on him. None knew that the immensely-revered Chief who was also addressed as The Honorable, was donating to the community with one hand and was criminally grabbing back from the same and adjacent communities with the other hand.

In the opinion of most people in his Community the title "Oshimiri" was very well deserved in view of the fabulous wealth that was associated with Chief Suleiman. But the Chief's honor and fame, which in the estimation of his only son and hitherto greatest admirer, became punctured on the night of Ade's initiation into the odious club of the Chambers.

Chief Suleiman sprang back at the greeting and the sight of the unmistakable smartly-attired young man who offered the greeting. For a split second the senior Suleiman covered his lips with the palm of his right hand, ostensibly in an effort to avoid uttering a shout of surprise.
His eyes almost seemed to pop out of their sockets with amazement.
"Ade, my son what are you doing here?" Chief Suleiman muttered in utter consternation. His lips quivered as he spoke those words. His legs almost gave way. But the voice of the warden announcing the entry of the chief guest of honor perhaps ushered the adrenaline rush that helped the chief to remain on his feet.
"Chambers, The Distinguished Patron and to the glory of all, the incoming Supreme Commander, Chief the Honorable Martin Omenka Amannaya Suleiman. All rise!"
The announcement prevented what might have been a scene between father and son as Chief Suleiman had no option than to step forward to the podium led by his beloved and only son Chambers 146B Ade Suleiman.

As Chief Suleiman was ushered into the high table his eyes had beheld what he would have most wanted to avoid. He was not any longer the same boisterous and pleasant-talking man that he was a few seconds earlier. The image of his supposedly- innocent young son standing in full cult uniform with green beret and outstretched hand in greeting could not be relinquished from his mind.

Chapter 11

A SURPRISE ADVICE OF A FATHER TO HIS SON

The guests were all fully seated. The major job of the ushers was almost done. Everybody was boisterous and excited at what was perhaps the most lavish party that *The Chambers* had ever held in the state capital city of Kuveri. It was the first time one of their own was elevated to the "enviable position" of National Patron and Supreme Commander of *The Chambers*, as described by the Chambers Warden.
Nobody in attendance had ever seen it so lavish, not even the members who had stayed the longest in the organization. Everybody was happy and excited, except for two people. One of the unhappy people was a newly recruited member—an usher— whose happiness or otherwise was not of much significance. Another was the man who ought to be the happiest person in the party since the party was being organized in his honor. The first of these two people was Mr. Ade Suleiman. The second was Chief Omenka Suleiman, alias *Chief The Honorable Oshimiri Suleiman.*

There was eating and dancing, clinging of champagne glasses. Eulogies and encomiums were poured on the *illustrious son of Kuveri* who was going to take up the position of National Patron and Supreme Commander of an organization, which, though it might be regarded as secret, was nonetheless about the most powerful and most dreaded that anybody could hope to belong to.

After the brief gate encounter with his father, Ade contemplated on whether to leave the venue immediately or not. He knew that he would not feel free and would in no way enjoy the night, not in the presence of his once revered father and certainly not with the renewed anguish and disappointment that he had felt since he drove the stolen car into his father's secret underground garage. But he knew that he could not leave the venue of the party. First,

85

he was on official duty as an usher. Second, it was against the rules of the Chambers for anybody to leave the venue of a meeting or indeed any of the organization's activities before the official closing time for whatever reason.

Even with all its illegality and savagery, the organization was extremely well organized, and it enforced the highest standards of discipline among its members.

Ade remained behind but was sullen throughout the rest of the evening.

On his part, Chief Suleiman remained calm. But he could not crack the jokes, which he was known for in situations such as was the case during that party. Those who knew him well and who might have noticed his rather reserved demeanor that night attributed his sullen demeanor to stress and the possibility of his being overburdened with the different businesses, which he was known to own ranging from major car and other vehicle dealerships to shipping, jewelry, aviation and exotic furniture distributorships. Other observers attributed Chief Suleiman's unusually calm behavior to a new refinement and detachment which they felt that his new position demanded.

But the truth was that Chief Suleiman developed a troubled soul since his unexpected meeting with his son in a meeting of a dreaded secret organization.

Despite his very shady deals, Chief Suleiman was a very good family man. His love for his wife and children was unquestionable. He wished the best of education for his son. He had his two daughters in two of the best and most expensive universities in America. He was a disciplinarian to the core, or so it seemed.

Chief Suleiman had always looked forward to the day that his son would graduate as a medical doctor. He had imagined the kind of lavish party that he would throw for his son. He had hoped to compensate for his limited educational achievements by having his son and two daughters have the highest available education in the

best of institutions anywhere in the world. He started regretting his decision not to send Ade abroad when most of his friends were bundling their sons and daughters to institutions overseas.
He had decided to have Ade train as a doctor locally because he was afraid that he might lose him to another country if he sent him overseas.

Besides, he wanted Ade to stay close to him so that with time, he could buy him a big practice and launch him into ownership of an unprecedented state-of-the-art health institution.
He had hoped to turn over most of his enormous cash assets over to Ade and then quietly extricate himself from all shady businesses and then quietly retire to a mansion on the outskirts of Karuja, the nation's capital.

When news reached him about his elevation to the post of the National Patron and Supreme Commander of *The Chambers*, he was happy and had hoped that with the new position he would be more regular in Karuja and that would facilitate his completion of the massive residential mansion he had planned for the national capital city.
He had no knowledge whatsoever that Ade was no longer in the medical school. He had kept remitting the fees and maintenance money as well as money for rent and books.
He would have dismissed as false any information that Ade would join any secret society, not to mention one as deadly as *The Chambers*. He was devastated at the sight of his son whom he had reposed so much hope and confidence in.

Chief Suleiman had a prepared speech for the party. In the text of the prepared speech, he had chronicled the history of the Chambers club and the stages that it went through from its humble beginnings as an entirely student organization to its present position of strength.
He had detailed the advantages of membership of the club and how the club had directly or indirectly helped make men and

women in high places in academics, in government, and in commerce. He documented how senators and even governors and presidents had been helped to attain their positions by the club.

He had declared in the document that the ultimate ambition of the organization was to build itself up to such a position that nobody in the country would be able to ascend to an executive position in government without the blessing of the Chambers. He had emphatically declared in the draft of the speech.

"This is the ultimate goal of our organization. This is the challenge before us. My administration will do everything in its power to actualize this. By the time I, Chief Martin Omenka Amannaya Suleiman, Oshimiri, step down from power, I shall have ensured that nobody—repeat, nobody—gets to any of those exalted positions without our positive nod. It is achievable. It is a promise from me to you."

Copies of the speech had been reproduced and handed over to the organizers as soon as Chief Suleiman got to the venue of the party.

It was time for the climax of events for the night. It was time for the guest of honor to address the gathering. Most of the evening, Chief Suleiman kept looking into the emptiness. He appeared to be admiring the beautiful draperies, the ribbons, and the beautifully colored balloons.

The master of ceremony had started introducing the guest of honor. The ushers were handed over the prepared speech, and they quickly distributed these.

"Ladies and gentlemen, I have the honor to call on the guest of honor and the National Chief Patron and Supreme Commander of our revered organization, The Right Honorable Chief Martin Omenka Amannaya Suleiman, to address the Chambers!"

The applause was thunderous. It looked as if it would never end. But like all things that had a beginning, it did end.

Chief Suleiman stood up and tapped his hand on the microphone that had been positioned in front of him. He cleared his throat and thanked the Master of Ceremonies and the organizers of the party. He also thanked "all those who, in spite of the rains and the thunder and lightning, made time to come and grace the occasion."

He then continued, but in an unusually solemn voice, "I wish also to thank the young Chambers who greeted me at the door this evening before I entered this room. I refer to the young man who called me by my name and greeted me by my native title. To that young man, I would say, 'Do as I say, not as I do.' And to that young man and others like him, I would further say that the future is bright before you and that you must not allow the temporary fantasies and mirages that daily flash before you to distract you from more noble goals and objectives. These goals and objectives are those that any caring father or, indeed, any nation that hopes to survive, must preach and practice. To that young man I will further add: the hope of your fathers and, indeed, of the nation lie squarely on you, and you must not disappoint those hopes. You must not allow those parents who have labored so much and a nation that has suffered so much to get brokenhearted by seeing you go astray."

Chief Suleiman was not reading from his prepared text. Many people had indeed not taken note of the young Chambers who ushered the new Chambers Supreme Commander into the hall. But they noticed that as Chief Suleiman uttered those last words, tears welled through his eyes. His voice trembled. He reached for his handkerchief. He had the prepared speech before him. But he was not reading from it. He was merely holding the prepared speech on his trembling fingers as he poured out the emotions from his troubled mind.

As his listeners tried frantically but unsuccessfully to fish out the paragraph where he read from in the speech, the entire hall was quiet. Only the crickets and other night insects that emitted their unsynchronized buzzes from the adjoining bushes could be heard.

Few, if any, of the hilarious participants in the event had observed Ade approach and greet his father as the latter was about to enter the hall. Even those that noticed were not aware of the relationship between father and son.

Ade was standing close to the rear door of the ramshackle building which on that spectacular night had an exquisitely decorated hall. Perhaps, he alone understood the meaning of the advice. Perhaps, he alone understood the reasons for Chief Suleiman's sense of remorse.

Ade's eyes too were filled with tears. But unlike the tears that filled Chief Suleiman's eyes, Ade's tears were tears from disappointment and betrayal from a father he had come to associate with everything that was good. He was not thinking of his own failure as a son. He was considering the failure of a father who he felt ought to have led by examples.

Chief Suleiman's address did not last long. He held the copy of the prepared speech on his trembling fingers, but he ended up not reading a word from it. He did not for once look at the eight-paged prepared speech even as the other guests continued to make fruitless efforts to check out and follow up from the page on the paper which they had with them. Many kept searching for the corresponding page until the time the speech was over.

Chief Suleiman was not reading from the paper. No, he was simply emptying his mind and his remorse.

A few of his listeners marveled at how he was reading from the paper without looking at it. Some more observant ones were quick to notice that he was indeed not reading from the paper.

A few who were closer to the high table noticed the tears and the attempt to hold them back. Some who watched for the countenance of the speaker rather than the words felt that those were tears of joy at his elevation and tears for how successful the organization that he helped nurture had grown. Some more discerning and more attentive ones knew that those were tears of some deep-seated disappointment and remorse. None, but Ade, knew that those were tears of genuine remorse occasioned by a failure to lead by example.

None, not even Ade, knew the full extent of Chief Suleiman's involvement in robberies, kidnappings, and even more heinous crimes, which included butchering of human beings and the selling of their parts to dastardly human parts traffickers. Only Suleiman knew of those details. Only he was bearing the brunt of the remorse.

Not a few of the participants at the party were happy that the speech was brief. It was brief, thank goodness, so the party could go on. But it was brief, not by design but by chance. It was a forced brevity occasioned by the deep-seated remorse of a father in mortal distress, a father who, for that brief moment, would have wished that he gave up all that he had accumulated if only to have only a moment of internal peace—internal peace that was to elude this once loving father for the rest of his life.

A thunderous applause, nonetheless, greeted Chief Suleiman's brief speech. It did not really matter who he was referring to or who he was preaching to. Most heard him, but few understood. The good times at the party must continue to roll.

Chapter 12

SINKING DEEPER INTO CRIME

Chief Suleiman, after his elevation as the national leader of the Chambers, made haste to complete his mansion in Karuja, the national capital.

Despite his remorse on the night of his reception, he was quick to convince himself that his son, Ade, was already an adult and was therefore capable of deciding what to do with his life. He reminded himself that his own father was said to have died when he was only eight years old and that, despite being raised by a single mother, he was still able to rise to the top of the society.

"I was still able to buy the top university position for my son. I was still able to buy him a car even when his friends could not own bicycles. I was able to rent him the best accommodation in campus. What is it that he needed that I have not given to him? I have made my own mark in life even if it be in what many may label as "unholy business". It is not easy to succeed even in unholy business. It is not everybody who got into this business that succeeded. It takes wits and courage to navigate the thorny terrains of criminality. Judgments about standards of right and wrong are never fully uniform. They vary greatly with individuals and societies. Smartness and brains are needed to succeed. Some who started with me were foolish and were easily caught. They were greedy and did not share their loot with people that mattered. I was wiser and made sure that every important person was carried along.
I shared my loot with all potential whistle-blowers. I settled them from top to bottom and secured their silence. Even many that condemned the activities in the churches and mosques got their share and soft-pedaled. I donated cars to some and houses to others. Many prayed for me and gave me their blessings."

Chief Suleiman paused for a while as if to catch his breath. He then in a soft sober voice continued his self-justification:

"I have given to the poor and uplifted the wretched. I have built schools and hospitals and paid the bills of the insolvent. Ten toes, bicycles and wooden trucks belong to the poor while Bentley, Mercedes and Rolls Royce cars are owned by the wealthy. I have never stolen anybody's toes, never stolen a bicycle and would never descend to the level of carting away wooden carts that belong to the poor. I steal only expensive cars and I give part of the proceeds to the poor. I should therefore not continue to entertain any remorse. Many of the very rich from whom I steal have also stolen. Therefore, stealing part of what was stolen and giving part of the proceeds to the poor, in my opinion, is the meaning of charity. It is also equity which should be commended. Thieving politicians and cheating businessmen are enemies of the people. And the enemy number one of the people's enemy is the people's friend. And that is Chief Omenka Suleiman.

I have given scholarships and donated to motherless babies' homes. I am a good family man and have endeavored to conceal my sources of wealth so that I would not corrupt the young ones."

Chief Suleiman cleared his throat loudly and then continued his soliloquizing in a softer tone:

"Ade, my son, pulled himself into this cult business. I did not bring him in. I did not even know that he was a member.

And for those who condemn me, their own sins may even be worse. They steal public funds and impoverish society. They steal funds meant for building of schools and keep millions of people illiterate. They steal money voted for hospitals and roads and send thousands to their untimely deaths. They buy big cars with the money that they steal, and my boys snatch the cars. My duty and my source of livelihood are only to buy over the cars after they have been snatched. I make sure I don't take cars that are cheap, which belong to the middle class and poorer people. The wretched of the earth do not buy Mercedes-Benz and those types of big cars which I steal. And when I resell the cars after refurbishing them, I give part of the money to the poor.

Their own sins are more who loudly condemn my actions. In any case, didn't the Holy Book say 'Do as I do not as I say'? Again, the same Holy Book says it loud and clear: 'Judge not, lest ye be judged.' So their own sins are more who my actions condemn. Their theft of public funds kills more people on the roads in one month from road accidents and unnecessary hospital deaths than I, Chief Suleiman, will ever kill in all my career in the business of car snatching, kidnapping, and robbery. Chikana! Let God judge between me and any of my critics, who is the bigger sinner." Chief Suleiman emphatically stated.

Chief Suleiman soon moved the headquarters of his business to Karuja. *Business* was "very good", contrary to what Idrisu had told Ade. There were very many big cars on the road in Karuja than there were in the provinces. Again, not all the big cars belonged to the rich retired military generals and the top politicians.

"The public servants and other businessmen and women have devised ways of stealing back some of the loot that the well-positioned officers and top politicians had embezzled. So, these public servants and businessmen and women, especially those of them who were into contracts, also now buy big cars and build big houses. They also now have plenty of loose money to pay big ransom when they or their loved ones are kidnapped. Again, many of these latter groups do not have the top security outfits, which the top retired military men and politicians have. They are therefore easier prey." Chief Suleiman said
I am therefore very delighted with my move to Karuja." The chief continued.

The new headquarters of Chief Suleiman's business empire was an improvement on the Kuveri equivalent. It had a more obscure underground entrance that was located in a very obscure site far removed from the headquarters' gate. Again, unlike the Kuveri equivalent, the underground car parks had multiple thoroughly disguised entry and exit points. The detention sites of kidnapped individuals also were a big improvement on the house-to-house movements that was utilized in other offices. Kidnapped individuals could easily, in the improved Karuja offices, be moved from one underground tunnel to another within short notice if the required ransom was not paid.

Before Chief Suleiman moved over to Karuja, he felt that it was necessary for him to tidy up his relationship with his son, Ade. Despite his shady business, Chief Suleiman did not want to jeopardize the cohesion in his family. He thought of inviting Ade for discussions with him. But he felt that the latter might have gotten so disappointed with him and his pretense that he might decide not to honor the invitation. Despite the mutual embarrassment to both father and son on the night of the party, Chief Suleiman had continued to remit money to Ade in school. The latter continued to accept the money but had stopped to acknowledge receipt.

Chief Suleiman acknowledged to himself that he had let down his son and had failed the latter's expectations, but he also believed that his son had failed in his responsibilities as a responsible son by joining the Chambers cult. He felt that both he and his son had fallen short of each other's expectations. But he was aware of the local idiom that stated that the senior man or woman must forgive.

(As Chief Suleiman loads gifts to his son's residence, he encounters his son's drug-addicted room mate who ignores him completely.)

The idiom implied that the older and more mature individual must be prepared to make amends and reparations even when any two parties had each erred.

Chief Suleiman, therefore, decided to pay a surprise visit to Ade's apartment in the university and win him over with gifts. He knew that Ade, as a high school student, was in love with electronic gadgets. He, therefore, went to town with different kinds of electronic gadgets—from high-powered computers to state-of-the-art cell phones, laptops, play stations, digital flat screen television sets, exotic telephones, photocopiers and printers, fax machines, and all that he felt that Ade might love to have. He did not tell his wife of his mission so that the latter might not start to ask many questions. He felt that it did not matter if Ade already had equivalents of some of these gadgets. "It will not hurt to have new batches and latest models." Chief Suleiman said.

When he got to the apartment where Ade used to live and for which he, Chief Suleiman, had continued to pay the high rent, he was told by the new occupant of the apartment that Ade had moved out "since he was no longer a medical student."
Chief Suleiman was still wondering what was meant by the phrase "no longer a medical student" when he got a second shock.
When he got to the new address where Ade was said to have moved to, Chief Suleiman was told that the accommodation there was "only for students," and "Ade Suleiman, since he is no longer a student, had moved out and was living in Room LL29 on the outskirts of the university."

Chief Suleiman's chauffeur explained to the former that LL29 meant "Labor Line 29" and that his friend who was a cleaner in the University president's office lived in one of those rooms. Those were single rooms with common toilet facilities constructed for artisans and very junior staff of the university. Chief Suleiman was dumbfounded. He pinched himself several times on the cheek to convince himself that it was not a nasty dream, just like his son often did.

Chief Suleiman's car could not get to the block that housed room LL29. The room was one of many in a long row of buildings, each of which had only two toilet facilities and a common kitchen for the residents of the more than fifty rooms. Only footpaths led to the row of buildings. It was not expected that the occupants would own cars.

 Room LL29 was a small ten-feet-by-ten-feet room that barely took two tiny metal beds with a narrow walkway in between. Clothes were hung on multiple nails made on the walls. A few old electronic equipment was stacked on a rack on the far end of the wall.
There, on one side of the wall hung Ade's high school graduation

photograph while on the opposite side of the wall hung another photograph of another young man who also must have seen better days, judging from the look and background of the photograph.

Ade was not in the room, but the young man whose photograph hung on the other side of the room was leaning on his bed with his back against the wall. The young man was puffing away at some wrapped material, which from its unmistakable smell, was marijuana.
The room smelled very strongly of marijuana, and the young man made no disguise of the free use of the substance.
Chief Suleiman, despite all available evidence, still could not believe his eyes and even feeling. He and his chauffeur had parked their car by the roadside and had walked up to the building.

"Is this Ade Suleiman's room?" Chief Suleiman had asked the young man.
The rude response was sharp and completely unprovoked.
"You no see him photo for wall?" (Don't you see his photograph on the wall?) The young man rudely replied.

At the end of the ensuing silence that lasted for about two minutes, Chief Suleiman's chauffeur advised his master, "Boss, make we *commot* for this place. It no safe here." (Boss, let us get away from this place. It is unsafe here.)
Before the duo could walk 150 feet away along the long corridor, there was Ade, coming from the opposite direction. He looked gaunt, roughly-dressed, unshaved and with disheveled hair. He too was smoking. As soon as he recognized his father from a distance, he dropped the stump of the partially consumed marijuana on the ground and crushed it with his shoes.

"Oshimiri jookwa," Ade greeted his father.
Despite the tremendous amount of water that had passed under the bridge, Ade had not lost the traditional reverence for the man

he had grown up to adore.

It was only then that Chief Suleiman came to realize that it was indeed all a reality. There was not much need for long questions and long explanations. The facts were too obvious for any speculations, any questions, or any answers. The replay of the saga of the prodigal son could not be more apt. But in the scene under consideration, perhaps both father and son had sinned.

"Are you no longer in school?" was not a necessary question. "Are you in cult?" did not arise; it was already confirmed. "Are you on drugs?" was tantamount to wanting to know the obvious.
The questioner and expected respondent were right there on the scene—two sinners, none was to blame the other.
There was not enough space in the room to pack the presents. The boxes were nonetheless stacked on the narrow space between the two beds. Chief Suleiman had written out a check for the sum of twenty thousand dollars for his son before he set out for the visit.

After he saw the condition of his son and in spite of the fact that the condition was fully self-inflicted, he canceled the earlier check, and right there in the tiny little room, he made out another check for the sum of one hundred thousand dollars in the name of Mr. Ade Suleiman. He also made a cash gift of two thousand dollars to Okey, Ade's marijuana-smoking roommate who had earlier been so discourteous to him. The smile on the face of the errant young man meant more to Chief Suleiman than the two word "Thank You" muttered by the recipient. The on-the-spot present to Ade was a sum that could pay the salaries of two Konganogan university professors for more than a full year. But the money was being handed down to an errant college drop-out who would at best use it to soak himself deeper into drugs. But a dishonorable *Honorable* father was perhaps only trying to buy his conscience out of the wrath of nemesis.

On his way back to his mansion, Chief Suleiman felt one large load lifted off his heart.

Even though he found his son living in near subhuman conditions, he still felt that, at least, he had played a part that a father would play for a son.

Chief Suleiman silently repeated in his mind the oft-quoted piece by Alexander Pope, that he was so fond of in his moments of disappointment with situations, which he could not help: "Honor and shame from no condition rise; Act well your part, there all the honor lies."

Chapter 13

TUTELAGE FOR THE ROLE OF "THE HONORABLE ROBBER"

Before Chief Suleiman finally left Kuveri for the national capital Karuja, he accepted that the medical school project had failed. He therefore made arrangements for Ade to be apprenticed to Chief Unafefe, one of the people whom he, Chief Suleiman, had sponsored into the federal legislature.

Chief Suleiman had considered the possibility of incorporating Ade into his business since the latter already had full knowledge that it was not anything clean. He, however, felt that even with Ade's knowledge and even with his being a member of *The Chambers*, it would not be right that he, as a father, should be the person to pull in his son into a business of crime. He felt that it would be better if it was Ade who by choice, pulled himself into any such situation.
Notwithstanding the fact that he had made a fortune in the crime business, Chief Suleiman still felt that he would choose a less ignoble business for his son. He, therefore, arranged with Chief Unafefe his friend and acolyte who was neck-deep into Konganoga politics under sponsorship of Chief Suleiman.

"Unafefe, you know say, *na* me make you *The Honorable*. (*You realize that it was I who made you The Honorable.*)
"Now do me a favor. I want make you help my son Ade become *The Honorable* too. I know say you don become small big man from all that big salary and fat allowance you people in Karuja pay yourselves for every month. But I go still pay you one million dollar make you teach Ade politics for one year. Ade him go get apprenticed to you as your parliamentary assistant for one year. That way he go learn the trade of politics. You go teach him all those lies you de tell. Teach him all the ways you de take chop politics money. That way him go get attracted and agree to

101

contest election." Chief Suleiman said. If him agree contest election, leave the rest for me. The way I make you win your seat, that same way I sure go get him win too.

"But Honorable Sir, you know say Mr. Koko already be your constituency *Honorable*. Umudioha Constituency it no get vacancy for now. And you remember say na you help put Mr. Koko as *The Honorable* for Umudioha." Unafefe quipped, reminding Chief Suleiman that there was an incumbent Constituency Representative for Umudioha Mr. Koko, who was indeed sponsored by Chief Suleiman.

Unafefe felt relieved that it was not his seat that would be threatened.

Chief Unafefe did not feel pleased being reminded that there was an incumbent Constituency Representative for Umudioha. He appeared fixated on the idea of his son taking up the position.

"Unafefe, make you leave the creation of the Umudioha parliamentary seat vacancy for me. Na me put Mr. Koko there. Na me go remove him when it *become* necessary. Once Ade learn the art of politics finish for one year, we go make sure say a vacant parliamentary seat is created for him. If the incumbent on the seat refuse to step down, we go get him out somehow. Make you leave that one for me. After that, my son go contest. And him must win. That one go be do or die game." Chief Suleiman said.

He then continued:

"Politics in Konganoga him be the most lucrative business that any one fit engage in. Konganoga politics be even more lucrative than this car-snatching and kidnapping business. Crime, even combining of car snatching and kidnapping, comes second in ease of wealth and fame. A combination of politics and crime for the same family, especially between father and son, that one go be truly awesome. For many years, me I been sponsor other people and making them *The Honorable*. Now what about making my own son *The Honorable* too?" Chief Suleiman joked to himself.

"Yes!" he continued I no know sef which kind devil come make me put Ade for that medical school. Na only big name dokita wey them de answer. How many dokita fit answer *The Honorable*.

Them de read and read till them brains scatter and them hair turn white. And even the money, them no get plenty. But come see common Unafefe who no go school like me. Common barrow pusher, motor-park tout and blind beggar fraudster him be before I put him for Konganoga parliament the other day. Come see the kind mansions wey him de build now; eye-popping mansions. For that parliament I hear say na them de fix them own salaries. I hear say the least paid of them pass all American presidents for salary. I come hear sef say Unafefe now get plenty bank account for Dubai, London and Houston for America. How many dokita fit compete with him now? They say that their wardrobe allowances alone fit pass American President annual salary. And that one which they them call constituency allowance be big money which they pocket after putting up one ramshackle shanty old corrugated roofing sheet house which them call constituency office. Allowance for food which those Honorables de chop fit pass what I, Oshimiri, make from risky car-snatching in one year!" Chief Suleiman was disparaging doctors for working so hard, answering big name but earning so little relative to him and Konganoga politicians who answer *The Honorable* and build large mansions in various big cities around the world.

The Chief appeared to be joking but he was dead serious about it and hence his decision to pay anything to have his son apprenticed in the art of Konganoga politicking, especially as the dream of medicine for his son had collapsed.

It was common knowledge that the politicians in Konganoga all of who went by the name of *"The Honorable"* daily stole millions of dollars from the coffers of the state by way of jumbo and outlandish salaries and allowances without anybody raising an eyebrow.

Chief Suleiman opted to have his son join the club where he could steal with impunity without being deemed a robber.

He felt that being an Honorable was a more accepted way of stealing billions of dollars and getting hailed by the very people from whom the money was stolen.

"The Honorable" did not have to hide his or her source of wealth notwithstanding the public knowledge of the fact that the flaunted wealth was all from public coffers. He or she would rather be hailed more loudly the harder he or she stole. There would be blames and ridicule if any *Honorable* came out cleaner and poorer after serving in any Legislative House or government office. A good name meant nothing to a Konganogan *Honorable*. Any Konganogan public office holder who advocated fiscal morality in office would incur the wrath of his colleagues. And if he came out of political officer cleaner but poorer, he would be regarded by the citizenry as a failure.

Chief Unafefe, after being sponsored by Chief Suleiman was in Konganoga central legislature for eight months and became stupendously rich. He then took the chieftaincy title of "Oyinatumba" (the chill that catches a community). He did not have much education. But Chief Suleiman had financed him through the forgery of educational documents and financial papers and paid off the electoral officers to declare him as the duly elected candidate in the parliamentary elections. His opponent had gone to the electoral tribunal. But Chief Suleiman easily bought off every body and the case by Unafefe's opponents was thrown out.

After he vacated the blind beggar business on falling out with Mr. Okon, Unafefe was, at one time, one of Chief Suleiman's thugs. Even his earlier chieftaincy title of "Udemba" (The pride of a people), was bought and paid for by Chief Suleiman.
Seeing the astronomical financial and social rise of a near-illiterate Unafefe, Chief Suleiman felt that if the types of Unafefe—whom he felt was not very intelligent—could become a legislator that his own son, who, at least went through high school and attempted medical school, could ascend to any level with the necessary support.
Having arranged with Chief Unafefe about full political tutelage for

his son, Chief Suleiman left for Karuja with a fairly clear conscience. He was determined that he would pump in whatever amount of money that was needed to make Ade very relevant in the governance of the country. But first, he wanted Ade to study the trade.

If Ade could not become a medical doctor, one million dollars could buy him a chain of doctorate degrees from many universities in Konganoga or even a foreign honorary doctorate degree, the type that were often conferred on paying candidates in five-star hotels in Konganoga from some irrelevant oversea universities.

Unafefe was, at first, reluctant to have Ade as his assistant even for a fee. His highest documented educational qualification was the primary school education where he dropped out after the fifth grade. He was barely literate. Some other false educational certificates, which he claimed, were obtained from private tuition courses.

He was known to be very reluctant to have people who were well educated as his assistants, lest his deficiencies be detected especially if such people were those who knew him well.

For three years, when Chief Unafefe was unemployed, he had faked being blind by plastering his eyelids with Vaseline petroleum jelly. He started off at the local motor park, then relocated to a street corner and later settled for the railway coaches. He patrolled the train coaches that plied between the northern and eastern parts of the country with a cane in hand and with a personal guide. He would sing hymns and quote verses from the Bible and the Koran and appeal for alms from people.

He was so fluent in the Bible verses that travelers gathered around where he preached to listen to "the blind beggar" who could quote verses from the Bible. He got plenty of donations from sympathetic passengers. From morning till night, clutching a cane and a small plate in his outstretched hands, and led by a long stick by a helper Mr. Okon, he would hold his eyelids tightly shut and sing and pray for passengers in the trains. At the dead of the night, he and his guide Mr. Okon would brush up and check into the nearest cheap hotel, only to surface again in the trains very early the following morning.

After the first two years, Unafefe had made so much money from begging that he secretly bought two plots of land and started building houses in Karuja. It was by the end of the third year that he disagreed with his guide whom he alleged had stolen his money. "The Blind Beggar" had stated that his guide stole a total of $26,300 from him. During the mediation which was being brokered by the newly-employed hotel-room cleaner, Unafefe's eyelids were already closed with the Vaseline petroleum jelly which he dutifully applied on his eyelids first thing every morning to convey a semblance of infected eyes of a poor blind beggar. It was part of Unafefe's work dress code for the duration of his alms-begging carrier.

While he quoted the amount that was stolen from him, Unafefe swore on the Bible which he clutched from morning till night except when he was in the Muslim parts of the country when he would switch to quoting from the Koran. He swore that the stolen amount that he quoted was "correct to the penny".

"I saw the money, and I counted it very well before this scoundrel stole it," Unafefe told the hotel room cleaner who was mediating between him and his guide Mr. Okon.

(Unafefe would apply Vaseline petroleum jelly on his eye-lids and feign blindness. He would patrol the railway stations and train coaches begging for alms, led along a cane by his co-fraudster, Mr. Okon).

Unafefe's friend and fake guide Mr. Okon was a former commercial wheel barrow pusher in the local motor park. His job was to help prospective passengers to ferry their heavy luggage in his wheel barrow (cart) into the commercial buses. Mr. Okon prior to his employment by "The Blind Beggar" Unafefe, had observed how lavishly the supposed blind beggar spent money at the motor park café. He had marveled at how a blind beggar could spend so lavishly ordering for delicacies at every meal, all from doing nothing but cross his legs at a street junction sing and pray and display an alms-tray.

"Me, Okon, I toil all day pushing the cart, but I no fit buy one good piece of meat for my lunch menu. But this man sits here doing nothing but singing and praying all day and collecting tray-loads of cash from people." Mr. Okon complained.

For a while Okon had contemplated stealing some of the alms that accumulated in the blind beggar's tray. On one Saturday evening when human traffic on the road had diminished and when the dollar bills had accumulated in the blind beggar's tray, Okon succumbed to the temptation which would help him change his occupation according to him, "for the better". After walking several times to-and-fro past the blind beggar's crouching position in a massive traditional dress he stopped in front of the singing beggar. He furtively bent over the latter and pretended to be donating some cash into the bowl. Using the broad dress to cover him from view of passers-by, the diminutive Mr. Okon dropped in a dollar bill and collected all the rest of the money in the bowl and walked off briskly. He had not taken more than five steps away when the supposed blind beggar Unafefe, saw what had happened and jumped up and went after Mr. Okon. He easily caught up with the thief and grabbed the latter by the collar of his shirt and almost strangulated him. A few passers-by intervened and separated the combatants. Unafefe "The Blind Beggar" did not wish to draw a crowd or create a scene which might expose him. A few people might get attracted to him and possibly identify him if he attracted too much attention to himself outside of his crouching position, tattered dress and Vaseline petroleum jelly-coated shut eye lids.

He did not let Mr. Okon completely off. Rather he dragged him by the latter's large dress away with him to a quiet corner away from the street to settle their differences away from view of the general public. It became obvious to Mr. Okon that The Blind Beggar was indeed a fraudster, a former itinerant loader in another section of the expansive motor park.

A petty small-framed thief had met a petty large-framed fraudster! A deal was quickly struck between fraudster and his attacker. The end result was that the two men would forgive each other and team up in business as an adult blind beggar and his guide who from a distance could pass for the beggar's child since Mr. Okon was really small-statured. They agreed to commute as beggar and guide along the train coaches between the North East and South

East of the country. The train stations became their mutually-agreed-upon new office! An agreement was struck that Okon would not disclose his findings about Unafefe whose guide he would become. Unafefe on his part would carry the alms bowl, sing the hymns or recite the Koran depending upon which religious location that they operated within in the highly religiously-diversified country. Unafefe would collect the alms and pay Okon one third of all daily collections.

While Mr. Okon collected and squandered his share of the proceeds daily eating pepper-soup and other delicacies in the hotels, Unafefe who could not afford to be seen in banks depositing money, or in open places where he might easily be recognized, accumulated and safeguarded his daily collections in plastic bags some of which he carried about under his pants or under his pillow at night. It was Unafefe's share of three months of alms-begging that got missing from under his pillows. Mr. Okon, in spite of his stout denial of culpability was the indisputable culprit.

The room cleaner who was mediating between the feuding friends had asked Unafefe: "You seem so sure and so precise about the amount that you lost. Are you sure of that figure?"
Before the mediator could conclude his question, Unafefe, rolling his eyeballs behind the Vaseline-paste-enmeshed eyelids, responded, "I swear to God by this Bible. I count the money and keep it in large polythene bags. I use some of the bag of the money as my pillows at night. Before I come sleep, I come look again to make sure say the money-pillows dey intact. By the time I come wake up for morning I was instead lying on top of real hotel pillows. My money pillows all of them come disappear. I don't know whether this scoundrel come drug me. It be like him come use voodoo or drugs come make me sleep off. All that money be my share of the money which I collect over a period of four months from begging. Nobody else enter this room. I be there alone with this man. But by morning, all my money was gone. I swear to God, this man Okon, him be the thief. Him be thief

109

before I come give him this job from motor park. Him come spend all him money come begin steal my own. I swear to God him be thief. Walahi!" Unafefe vigorously accused Mr. Okon of the theft of his four months of savings from his alms-begging business.

Mr. Okon, who was infuriated by the blatant and unrestrained accusation, then had the strong temptation to expose Unafefe there and then. But he felt that if he exposed Unafefe regarding his fake blindness, he too would be seen as an accomplice since it was he who led The Blind Beggar by a cane.
He, nevertheless, in a subdued tone asked Unafefe:
"Unafefe, you be blind. And so, how you come see the money?"
Unafefe then quickly remembered and corrected himself, "I feel the money for my hands."

Luckily, for Unafefe, the mediator did not immediately take notice of the insinuation. Further discussion about the issue was postponed till the following day at the request of Mr. Okon. He felt that he needed to give time to Unafefe to withdraw his accusation, failing which he would spill the beans.
After the mediator had left, Mr. Okon threatened Unafefe that he would tell the whole story of the fraudulent practices the following day.
"By tomorrow morning, the reception desk of this hotel and the whole world them go hear about your tricks. This Vaseline on your eyelids them go replace with pepper. The people who you been deceive and collect alms from, them go come after you. Them go chase you out and collect the remainder of this your polythene bag of money." Okon told Unafefe.
"Me, I get nothing to lose. I go simply get back to the motor park from where I come." Mr. Okon told Unafefe.
Throughout that night Unafefe could not sleep. Before morning he cleared the Vaseline from his eyes, put on his best clothes, and fled from the hotel room while Mr. Okon was still asleep. He left for his hometown, Umudioha. Before he left, he made sure that he gathered all the available money that he and his friend had not yet

shared, leaving his friend with the burden of settling the outstanding hotel bill all of which was in Mr. Okon's name since his partner was supposedly blind.

Unafefe went into hiding for some time and only surfaced after two months when he felt that his former guide would no longer be after him. He, thereafter, approached Chief Suleiman, and the latter offered him employment as one of his bodyguards.
Chief Suleiman later got Unafefe introduced into *The Chambers* as his special body-guard on account of his huge stature. Chief Suleiman found Unafefe quite reliable and very obedient and so he again took him into his stolen car-refurbishing business. Finally, he sponsored him into the parliament.

Chief Unafefe was also known to be a non-repentant kidnapper. He had set up his own secret kidnapping and car-snatching ring as distinct from his master's chain and was doing really well in his ignoble business. Even while he campaigned for the position of a legislator, Unafefe was still a kingpin of kidnappers and car snatchers. He crippled the electioneering campaigns of his two opponents by ensuring that all their cars were snatched and that their most vocal staffers were kidnapped or *disappeared*. He had learned the trade from Chief Suleiman. He was later to mastermind the kidnapping of the son of the lead spray painter in Chief Suleiman's garage for a ransom. The turning point was when he stole one of the stolen vehicles parked in Chief Suleiman's garage. It was at that point that Chief Suleiman was compelled to fire him from the company with the threat that if he fought back, he would have him and his entire family kidnapped by his more powerful agents.

Unafefe dropped out of school after the fifth grade. He was nowhere close to getting a college education. But he had a forged certificate which depicted him as being a college graduate. He had presented this to the screening authorities while being sponsored by Chief Suleiman in the former's bid for election as a central government legislator. With huge deposits into the coffers of the elections screeners and Returning Officers, with the backing of Chief Suleiman, he was declared cleared and returned as the winner of the elections. The courts did the rest of the job by throwing off the petition of his better educated opponent who was the true winner of the elections. Unafefe might not have the college degrees but he had inert intelligence. He was not a fool. He was thoroughly schooled in the business of stealing and kidnapping for ransom. But he knew his limitations. He knew that he would not be able to fight his former boss, Chief Suleiman. He, therefore, later came with his village chief and jars of wine and a live goat and kola nuts to plead for forgiveness from Chief Suleiman. It was after that that Chief Suleiman saw Unafefe as a smart man and took him back. He then started grooming him more seriously for politics. He proceeded at that juncture to recommend Unafefe to be sponsored to the parliament by *The Chambers*.

Sponsoring the election of Unafefe into congress was relatively easy for Chief Suleiman.
Unafefe qualified on ground of age, but he did not qualify on educational requirements.
It was relatively easy for Chief Suleiman to secure the necessary certificate from the National Examinations Body (NEB) with excellent grades for a mere fifty thousand dollars. The documents from the most prestigious high school in Unafefe's local council area were massively redone to accommodate the years during which Unafefe claimed he attended the school. A college graduation certificate was similarly procured for him.

In spite of his lack of good formal education, Unafefe was a very ambitious man. Immediately after he secured the fraudulent certificates, he started working hard on his English language usage. He had been taunted multiple times for his poor English language especially during political rallies where he tried repeatedly to impress the audience with high-sounding English words that were wrongly applied. He was nonetheless humble enough to start reading basic English language books and novels and he procured the services of the English language teacher in the nearby high school to visit three times a week to coach him. Five months into the English learning courses the Honorable-in-waiting proceeded to arrange for a doctorate degree certificate. He first got his local traditional ruler to confer on him a befitting traditional chieftaincy title. He wanted a name that would be higher than any other locally-assumed name—one that would be both prestigious and intimidating. He would have wanted to take on the title of Oshimiri, but that had earlier been taken by his mentor, Chief Suleiman.

Another intimidating name must therefore be manufactured. Eventually, the name *Oyinatumba* ("The chill that catches a community") was coined, and that became his title in what was one of the most lavish chieftaincy-installation ceremonies in the community.

Unafefe wanted to be addressed in congress not just as Congressman Chief Joshua Unafefe. That would be a little too common since too many people were already being addressed as chiefs. He wanted to be addressed as Congressman Honorable Chief Dr. Joshua Unafefe, Oyinatumba I of Umudioha Kingdom. Nobody before him had answered a name that complex and intimidating.

Unafefe reckoned that with that kind of intimidating name, if anybody ever accused him of stealing or kidnapping, his mere gaze on that person's forehead would make that person want to disappear instantly.

Unafefe thought of forging a doctorate degree certificate from a high-sounding North American University. He was however informed that a previous similar forged certificate had landed a previous high-ranking congressman in big trouble. He, therefore, opted to have an honorary doctorate certificate conferred on him in the biggest hotel in the capital city by one of the local privately-owned universities.

Unafefe was not known to be a highly religious man. But he had seen a number of people adding the title sir to their names. He had only associated the word sir with his headmaster and teachers in his primary school days. He had recently noticed that the high and mighty in the society were adding sir to their names by becoming Knights of one of the prominent Christian Churches.

In any gathering, whenever a sir entered the room, most heads would turn in the direction of the sir. If the sir came with his wife, the latter would also be addressed as lady. That was exactly the sort of thing that Unafefe wanted. He had one official wife whom he did not pay bride price for and whom he later divorced. But when he started making money, he started having many concubines located in various places. He would address these as his wives when it suited him. But finally, he settled on one of the many former concubines who was simply addressed as missus (Mrs.).

But Mrs., as a title, had become too common. Unafefe was not used to very common things since he became a young millionaire by being an Honorable congressman. He needed to secure something more exclusive for his official wife. First, he again got his traditional ruler to confer the title of Osodieme (strong pillar of the husband) conferred on his official wife.

Many other people had however recently got the traditional ruler, for a fee, to confer the same title on their wives.

Unafefe's *missus*, (Mrs.) Osodieme of Umudioha Kingdom, must therefore have a more distinctive title—at least one that was not yet too common, conferred on her.

And not too many women were as yet addressed as lady.

So Unafefe needed to become a knight in his church. But the hierarchy of the knights in his church would not admit Unafefe despite his wealth and fame. Some principled members of the organization knew a bit of Unafefe's notoriety and would not want their revered organization to be associated with him. They, therefore, politely told him that they were not accepting any new members just then.

Unafefe was not the man to be completely denied any of his desires. He immediately sought alternative sources and joined one of the much smaller churches that were sprouting like mushrooms all over his town. He joined one church, which was called "Angels on Earth Church", which had a total membership of only 142. Angels on Earth Church operated from an uncompleted corrugated roofing sheet batcher located in a swamp area near the Kuveri River. The founder was one Mr. Amos, who was a former church warden, but was expelled from his former church for embezzling church collections.

Amos was very good at preaching. The motto of his new church was "The hand of the giver will forever remain on top."

True to their motto, the congregation of Angels on Earth Church always did give to their church. But there was little to show for all that they gave. Rather, Amos, after eight months of founding his church, bought a big Volvo car for himself and started building a big house in his village. But the church remained poor, and the congregation continued to give.

Unafefe approached Pastor Amos and offered to build a five-thousand-capacity church for Angels on Earth Church. He also bought a Mercedes-Benz S-Class for Pastor Amos. He then bought a twenty-five-seater bus for the church and persuaded Amos to convert to the title of bishop and to make him, Unafefe, a knight immediately after he would have become a bishop. Pastor Amos was over-joyed especially each time he donned on his glittering bishop's robes with a red skull cap and chauffeured in a glittering Mercedes S-class car, all courtesy of Chief Unafefe.

It was a very elaborate ceremony, and people congregated from far and wide on the day that Unafefe was made the first knight of Angels on Earth Church.

Congressman Honorable Chief Dr Sir Joshua Unafefe, Oyinatumba I of Umudioha Kingdom, was the new deal in town.

Ade Suleiman, by special arrangement and a fee of one million dollars, was attached to Chief Unafefe by his father Chief Suleiman. He immediately became Personal Assistant to Congressman Honorable Chief Dr Sir Joshua Unafefe's and was officially addressed as PA to the Honorable member.

Chapter 14

ADE LEARNS THE ART AND TAKES A PLUNGE

It was a special privilege for Ade to be addressed as PA. In his reckoning, to be an "Honorable PA" to Congressman Honorable Chief Dr Sir Joshua Unafefe, Oyinatumba I of Umudioha Kingdom, was no small position. It was not a mean feat. He saw himself as an alternative central government legislator in the absence of his congressman. He indeed often gave his name as "Honorable Ade Suleiman, Honorable PA to Congressman the Honorable Chief Dr Sir Joshua Unafefe.

Ade felt very proud. He had come to accept and live with his father's profession and double life ignoble role in society. He had come to Karuja and had seen more crooked people than his father. The latter, indeed, was like a saint when compared with what Ade saw among *The Honorables* in Karuja's executive and legislative chambers. What he witnessed within a very short stay working as P.A to an *Honorable*, was beyond words; very crooked and sometimes murderous vagabonds from *the civilized world* who huddled together in government buildings and their luxury hotels silently but overtly bleeding the nation dry and insulting the intelligence and sensibilities of the populace with open display of their ill-gotten wealth.

A number of high-sounding names were doing in the nation's capital what would be deeply abhorred in any decent society elsewhere in the truly civilized world.

Konganoga was richly endowed with abundant human and all forms of liquid and solid mineral resources. But, most of the funds accruing from these resources were steadily stolen by men and women who wielded political power in the center, in the states and in the local Governments.

The little that was left was filtered away by the top civil servants and their cronies.

It was not Chief Suleiman's intention that his son, Ade, would continue what he described as "this business of stealing, killing, and playing big." He got him apprenticed to Chief Unafefe so that he would learn from the latter the art of being a successful politician. He had made this clear to Chief Unafefe on the day he was paying him for Ade's apprenticeship.

He had told Chief Unafefe,

"Look, Joshua, I made you a politician. I had earlier taught you this other trade, my own trade. If I wanted to teach this our trade to my son, I would have kept him with me. I would be able to teach him better and faster, even as I taught you. But I pay you to teach Ade how to be a successful politician, how to meet people, how to address them, how to behave in parliament. Ade will be with you for a minimum period of one year and a maximum period of three years. After that, I will sponsor him to the senate. Don't pay him; instead I will pay you one million dollars annually for teaching him. Don't even give him any allowances. Take any official allowances that may be due to him as your PA. I will pay him more than he would have gotten officially from you. But please teach him. Teach him and teach him right. Again, please don't teach him what I taught you. Rather, turn the page and teach him how to be a respectable gentleman, an honorable congressman, a legislator of the Federal Republic of Konganoga."

Chief Unafefe listened attentively to Chief Suleiman and nodded his head in apparent affirmation. Even with all his fame and wealth, *The Honorable* Unafefe was always subdued in the presence of Chief Suleiman. He both adored and dreaded Chief Suleiman not just as his mentor but also because he knew what Chief Suleiman was capable of doing to any opponent who crossed his path.

Unafefe had immense wealth, largely courtesy of the coffers of the Federal Republic of Konganoga as one of Konganoga's Honorable congressmen elite. But he knew that Chief Suleiman's wealth, influence, and goodwill far outstripped whatever he felt he had.

Unafefe also knew that though Chief Suleiman could be a kind man, he could also be ruthless. He once saw Chief Suleiman grab the tongue of one of his employees with pinchers and pull the man with the pinchers until the hapless victim dropped. The man's offence was that "he talked glibly about a car-snatching operation that he participated in."

Chief Unafefe listened attentively to Chief Suleiman's appeal. He was being paid by his mentor Chief Suleiman, to impart what he did not possess – honesty and integrity, even in their tiniest forms. When Chief Suleiman was done with his appeal, Unafefe replied, "Oshimiri, I thank you. I no go forget how you come receive me back even after I come steal from you. I even come kidnap your worker. I owe it to you to help train out your son Ade. You be like father to me and so Ade, your son, go be like brother to me. I should not even accept a penny from you to train out Ade for this politics thing. One good turn them say deserve another. But I know say you big pass that one million dollar which you want give me. I go take-am for fuel as it go be from one Papa to him son." He was at the same time rejecting and accepting payment for the job of imparting tutelage on how to become *The Honorable,* to Chief Suleiman's son Ade.

Thus Ade, a young man who was born into stupendous albeit ill-gotten wealth, the rustic marijuana-smoking former cult member, who had messed up his life and moved into a single shared room, again dressed in smart suit ready to be trained on how to bear the appellation of *The Honorable*. He had become apprenticed to another *Honorable* a much more rustic illiterate who, initially, could scarcely make one correct sentence in English, the language of the Legislative House.
Ade marched to parliament behind his boss *The Honorable Dr Joshua Unafefe*. He was once again clean-shaven and looked respectable.
He took custody of important files, and it was part of his duties to screen members of the public who wanted to have access to Hon.

Dr. Sir Joshua Unafefe, the wealthy young congressman from Umudioha.

Ade had plenty of money to spend. His wealthy father, Chief Suleiman, had placed him on a salary that was double what he was supposed to be earning from the Congress as a P.A. Also, Chief Unafefe had allowed him to claim any and all allowances due to him as a congressman's Personal Assistant.

Life was good for Ade. He did not miss the medical school or his life of hardship and drugs in the room in the shanty quarters called "Labor Line", adjacent to the university in Kuveri. He had sold his car when he was on drugs in Kuveri after he stealthily dropped out of medical school.

After Ade's first week as Personal Assistant to Chief Unafefe, however, Chief Suleiman had bought another car for Ade. The caring dad also persuaded his son to enroll into one of the correspondence courses with the University of Karuja, so passionate was Chief Suleiman about education and intellectual excellence.

After Ade had served Chief Unafefe for eight months, the latter arranged to travel overseas on a one-month tour. It was a regular practice among Konganogan congressmen and women to regularly travel overseas, especially to western countries, ostensibly for official tours. It was however generally believed that most of the oversea tours by those congress people were undertaken with the sole intent of banking away a good part of their ill-gotten wealth in western and Dubai bank vaults. A few others travelled for medical check-up while only a small number travelled for conferences and other congress-business-related reasons.

During the period of Chief Unafefe's absence, he reassigned Ade temporarily to his private business which he ran concurrently with his congress duties in Karuja. Ade was placed in charge of taking stock of the revenue that accrued daily from the different branches of Chief Unafefe's businesses.

In his capacity as stock-taker, Ade oversaw all the cash receipts and the banking of the cash and checks that accrued to the different aspects of Chief Unafefe's business. He was so enchanted with the enormous amount of money that rolled in daily that he kept imagining how sweet it would be to own such a business by himself.

It was not as flamboyant a business as dressing up smartly and walking the red carpet with his boss as a Personal Assistant to a congressman. But Ade wanted the red cash.

From what he saw Chief Unafefe's company making, he started to imagine what his father's many companies would be netting every month.

He started to imagine what he could do with all that money if even as little as a quarter of it was his own. He decided to request a permanent reassignment from the position of PA to Chief Unafefe to his temporary assignment. He preferred to be a permanent staff of that wing of Chief Unafefe's group of companies in preference to the Personal Assistant job.

Even though the request for a change ran contrary to the arrangement with Chief Suleiman, Chief Unafefe acquiesced to the request after he got a written request to that effect from Ade. He justified his acquiescing to the request by the fact that Ade was already an adult over the age of twenty-one who should be able to decide what was best for him.

When Chief Suleiman eventually learned of Ade's decision from Unafefe, he, at first, was furious with his son. He was later to accept his son's decision with a shrug.

"I have played my part as a father," he said. "If that is the way he wants to live his life, good luck to him. He may yet find that it is not so very rosy out there."

He invited his son over to his headquarters, and after discussions with him, he made out a check for a whooping fifty million dollars to him.

He further promised him another fifty million dollars after another six months if he should successfully render a good account of how

121

he managed the first fifty million. Ade knelt down before his father and asked for his blessing. He promised to use the money wisely.

"Even if I invest in businesses that may not be completely in conformity with the law, I promise to invest wisely, and I am determined to succeed. I will work assiduously to achieve my destiny in life. Even where I have not met your expectations of becoming the medical-doctor-son of a proud father, or the high-earning Karuja politician, I intend to work hard enough to be a successful businessman and ultimately take my destiny in my own hands. I still intend to get into politics which I know is your ultimate desire for me. But first, I need time to test my abilities in car importation, car distributorships and general merchandise."

Ade set out and bought vast empty plots of land on the outskirts of Karuja and Kuveri. He utilized his contacts with the people that he had met while in the services of Chief Unafefe to float two car distribution companies and a private security company that covered corporate organizations and private individuals. He initially opened one office in Karuja and another one in Kuveri.

Initially, a number of people who knew Ade in the university were skeptical about associating with a company set up by "that rascal and cult member Ade Suleiman."

One of the banks, which retained the services of Ade's security company withdrew their patronage after the first month when the manager learned of who the chairman of the security company was: Ade Suleiman—the cult member, the college dropout, and the drug user.
But Ade was undaunted. He persisted with other companies that had confidence in him. He soon opened a small institute which he called AMEND Incorporated, a Non-Governmental Organization where high school and college dropouts received counseling and help in getting back to school. AMEND Incorporated also offered scholarships to college dropouts who did well in the monthly tests

that the institute conducted.

Within the first four months of his opening shop, "Assured Security", the private incorporated company set up by Ade, had secured patronage from over 60 percent of the top ten corporate organizations in Kuveri and 15 percent of the top ten in Karuja.

Ade ensured that he employed very capable hands in each of his business ventures. He made it a habit to personally go around once every month to visit the management of all the companies covered by his security company. He wanted to ascertain customers' satisfaction and to take personal reports of all complaints. He also personally scrutinized all weekly complaint reports from every covered company.

By the fifth month, even the companies in Kuveri, which had shunned Ade's company on hearing the latter's name, had fallen in line to retain the services of "Assured Security". Initially the car distribution company did not do as well as Ade had expected. Because of the rate at which purchasers of new cars were losing their cars or even their lives courtesy of car snatchers and Chief Suleiman's Chambers members, new car purchase had been waning tremendously.

Ade employed highly-qualified personnel in all his branch offices. He had the initial cash capital which made it possible for him to attract the very best in staffing. His capital was not a loan. It was cash gift and unlike many other new businesses, no interest accrued on the starting capital. Ade had seen it all in rascality and criminality and so, one of the tasks that he gave his staff was that they must engage in constant monitoring and surveys to find out people's needs and fears. He had full-time statisticians who gave him weekly reports about the trends and proffered suggestions on ways of getting over any obstacles.

Ade believed greatly in expansion and ensuring accessibility of his services. By the sixth month of his commencement, his father did not have to invite him for a report. The report was readily visible. Ade's fame had sailed beyond the borders of Kuveri and Karuja.

Requests were coming from far and wide for patronage from "Assured Security".

Even some government establishments had sent business proposals to the company for coverage of some state and federal government establishments.

There was hardly any bank or big hotel in Kuveri and Karuja which would not want to engage the services of "Assured Security". A few competitors in the business who had some knowledge of the background of Chief Suleiman soon started spreading the rumor that the success of "Assured Security" had something to do with the past activities of Chief Suleiman, the father of the founder and president of the company. The adversaries opined that the success had something to do with the dictum, "Set a thief to catch a thief." Ironically, as the rumor spread, so did the patronage of Ade's company wax stronger.

Ade was neither ecstatic about the success nor was he deterred by the misrepresentation. He carried on and soon floated the company in the stock exchange. The floated shares sold out within the first two days.

AMEND Incorporated, the rehabilitation company set up by Ade also continued to grow. "Assured Security", by a motion sponsored by its president, Mr. Ade Suleiman, adopted a motion to set aside 10 percent of its annual profits toward the rehabilitation of organizations that aided drug addicts, and the destitute. AMEND Incorporated benefited tremendously from this fund, which continued to increase in monthly value. Ade assiduously fished out his former roommate and many members of his marijuana-users club and ensured that they benefited from AMEND, and thereafter, he secured them employment.

Chapter 15

A FATHER'S CONFESSION TO HIS SON

Chief Suleiman was not blind to the goings-on within his son's companies. Indeed, after he released the first batch of fifty million dollars to Ade, he set up a high-powered secret monitoring team that followed on Ade and monitored where the money was going. He could not feel prouder of his son when the positive results of the espionage came tumbling in. He felt very happy with his son's lawful business ventures.

Exactly six months to the date that he issued the first check for fifty million dollars to Ade, Chief Suleiman again asked Ade to come over to his office.
Ade, in the intensity of his business commitments, had even lost sight of the date of the promised amount. When he got his father's invitation, he, indeed, almost felt like rejecting further assistance. In the first place, he felt that he was doing well enough not to need further buffering. More importantly, he felt some sense of guilt that the money he was about to receive might be money secured over the blood of some innocent victims. Memories of his role in his first car-snatching exercise among other *Chambers* members flashed ceaselessly in his mind. He remembered vividly the scene of the bloodshed that featured in the operation with him as Chambers 146B. He remembered the underground stolen-car park where respraying and renovations were carried out on snatched cars. A strong sense of revulsion was welling up in him as he approached his father's office for the scheduled meeting with Chief Suleiman his revered father. He considered turning back and canceling the meeting with his father. He momentarily parked his car by the roadside and debated with himself on whether he should proceed or cancel the meeting.

After some five to ten minutes of deep rumination, Ade convinced

125

himself about the need to honor the invitation as he mused thus: "First, the promised second batch of fifty million dollars to be disbursed after this meeting is already there ready for collection by my businesses. The money may go to some dubious causes if not accepted by me for more worthy causes. I should not allow proceeds of evil to be channeled towards promotion of other evils. I should help channel these resources towards some more worthy causes.

Second, courtesy demands that I honor the invitation from my father; I can make my case during the visit.

Third, the snatched Mercedes-Benz cars from where the money might have come, more often than not, belonged to some other thieves or embezzlers in government and outside of it.

He is doing some good who steals from thieves to alleviate pain and suffering in a deeply-corrupted society." Ade surmised.

Perhaps, Ade's reasons did not justify acceptance of the illicit money. But he felt that the opportunity of honoring his father's invitation could be utilized to initiate a reform.

As Ade entered his father's office, Chief Suleiman, for the first time ever, got up and walked up to his son and embraced him. He then shook his hands and said,

"Ade, my son, I feel proud of you."

He then brought out from the drawer two checks which he had already prepared.

One of the checks was for fifty million dollars. The other was for one hundred million dollars. As he stretched out his hand to give the checks to Ade, the latter hesitated.

Chief Suleiman then, in a solemn and almost tearful voice reminiscent of the night that he encountered Ade in the Chambers meeting immediately said,

"Ade, I fully understand and totally align with the reasons for your hesitation. But I urge you to accept these checks first. You have set up AMEND Incorporated. It is like a challenge to me. I will make amends.

(Mr. Suleiman confessed candidly to his son in his office in Karuja. Tears welled up in his eyes as he spoke)

My past and present greatly haunt me, Ade. But now I want you to help me. I want to reform. You have already reformed, and I am happy and proud of that. My chief accountant Mr. Dickson who you know is very highly educated, often quotes Shakespeare to me. 'I am in blood' he often quotes, "stepped in so far, returning for me is as difficult as going over'. But I must reform, Ade. I must make amends. I want to start somewhere. I know this may be blood money. But I want through you to give it back to the society from whom it was snatched."

As Chief Suleiman still held out his hand with the checks, Ade, who himself had also started shedding tears, stretched out his hand and reluctantly accepted the checks.

Chief Suleiman again moved over to his son and embraced him again and said, "I will reform. I will make amends. I am only making a start. I have trodden the path of infamy for nearly a generation. It will be difficult for me to dismantle it all in one go. It will be extremely dangerous to do so. Too many people are involved. Many more people than you can imagine, are involved. But I will reform. And I want to tell you this, my son, even if I get killed in this process of trying to reform, I want you to carry through the effort. I make this as a promise to you and to my God. I make this as a secret promise to my wife of twenty-four years, your mother, who, you must know, is ignorant of my roles, I will reform. And I will make amends."

As he got back to his seat, Chief Suleiman continued, "The first check for fifty million dollars is a fulfillment of my earlier promise to you. Accept it even if you feel averse to it because of its source and even if you feel that you do not need it. Expand your business and redeploy your gains into more noble deeds than I did. The second check for one hundred million dollars, you will observe, is addressed to AMEND Incorporated. Please plough it into the relevant venture and use it to make amends on my behalf while I continue to wrestle with my conscience, hoping to find some peace. I will reform. I want you to continue to pray for me and, indeed, for the thousands of my collaborators nationwide. Not many of them will agree with me. Some of them will even call for my head for abandoning them. We took oaths of cooperation, secrecy and a commitment never to jump ship. But there is no way that I will continue in this path of infamy and blood. I will, on my own part, retrace my steps even at the inevitable risk to my life. I will make amends."

Chief Suleiman whose communication skills had tremendously improved over the years then paused for a while and tried to look into the eyes of his son, whose head was bent and who appeared to have his gaze fixed on the table. Chief Suleiman could not look into his son's eyes. He could not make out what the latter felt or how he felt. But he continued, "I may have disappointed your expectations as a pillar of moral rectitude. I may have, before you, preached one thing and done another. I was already enmeshed in evil even before I married your mother and had you. I tried to train you to be something which I was not, something which I would have wanted to be but which I found I could not be, something nobler, a morally upright man with a good education, one who engaged in good and lawful business. But it was too late for me. I wanted to replicate those ideals in you. That was why I swore to myself that no matter what it would take that I must ensure that you had the best education so that there would be no reason and no need for you to engage in a business of crime.

Chief Suleiman paused for a while and then continued:

"I have tried for twenty-four years to hide my real business from my family, and I am happy that I partially succeeded. That way, I have been able to bear the cross of my sins alone without implicating any other member of my family. Now that you know or since you got to know the details but have eventually reversed your own course and taken to clean business, my soul can begin to prepare to rest in peace.

My business associates will certainly not fold their arms and watch me renege. I know they will not. The stakes are too high. The stakes run into tens of billions of dollars dispersed all over the world. And, again, we took an oath of secrecy and cooperation or death. But no matter what comes my way, I feel fulfilled. I now have a clear conscience that my only son is not going the way that I did, and I thank you and congratulate you.

"Finally, Ade, if in future you get to discover about me much more than you know now, I appeal to you not to curse the memory of your father. You may, for now, have known only about the car-snatching business. My investigations reveal that that is the much that you know for now. It is good that your young mind is spared the dastardly aspects of the businesses that yielded the resources for which they gave me the title of *Oshimiri,* the tycoon, the sea that never dries.

"Even as I begin to wind down, to find my way out of the self-inflicted quagmire, I know that my conscience will continue to whip me until I atone for the hundreds of souls that, through my activities, might have perished this last-quarter century. It may not be possible for me to make full atonement, but I will not be deterred from making a start.

"Now that I know and I have evidence that you can, and have indeed started on a clean and sound path, this coming week, I will submit my notice to my group, indicating my intention to step down, not just from my role as *The Honorable National President and Supreme Commander of The Chambers* organization nationwide but, indeed, to quit completely.

"Hundreds, indeed thousands, will call for my head because at the level to which I had risen to, one never quits. But I will quit even with the certain adverse reactions that my quitting will generate. Whichever way it turns out, whether they succeed or not in their certain call for my head, it will really not matter. It is almost too late in the day to quit. But it is better late than never. I had even muted the idea of reverting fully back to my original name Martin, or disavowing my chieftaincy title and business-acquired name in the quest for peace of mind. But it all appears elusive and too late for me.

"I have been a tycoon largely from injustice, robbery, murders, and plunder, but you must not toe my path. You can still become a tycoon from clean business and with a clear conscience, and I can see you on the path to making it.

"Whatever may happen to me in the coming weeks and months, do not be afraid. Remain true to your conscience and always abide by the golden rule to do unto others what you would want others to do unto you. That way, you can never go wrong."

As Chief Suleiman spoke those last words, tears again filled his eyes. Again, like he did at the party in his honor in the regional headquarters of the *Chambers*, he reached for his handkerchief and wiped his tears. He suddenly appeared to look older than Ade had ever known him to be. His face wore a worried look, and he appeared heavily burdened in spirit. But he managed to force a

smile as he asked his son whether he wanted some soda.
"I no longer take alcohol, you know, so I stock only soda. I used to secretly consume alcohol in spite of my adopted religion whose dictates I was not abiding by. But it was all part of my self-imposed deceit. Many of my new religious brethren were very devoted to the teachings, but I knew I was only playing along starting from my change of my earlier religion. Those are probably some of the betrayals that I am paying for." Chief Suleiman told his son.

"I know," Ade replied, reluctantly responding for the first time and trying also to force a smile. He did not wish to make any formal response to his father's confessions. He felt that all that needed to be said had been said. It would serve no useful purpose revisiting sad emotions or sour past.
After Chief Suleiman's somber words, father and son tried to find something more pleasant to talk about. "How do you find shuttling between Kuveri and Karuja?" Chief Suleiman asked Ade.
"Not very pleasant, dad; always having to be in the air," Ade replied.

Chief Suleiman then added, "You may occasionally consider going by road. The problem is that the roads are so bad and it takes so long. It is a pity that the rail services were not further developed since the past sixty years. It would have been much easier to go by rail sometimes, but we do not yet have speed train services here. And going by air is safe, but it is not always so very safe as casualties are almost 100 percent if anything happens. For instance, I will go to Kuveri this weekend, and sometimes, I feel quite apprehensive about these air travels."
A few more discussions about acquisition of land and real estate followed. But the phone kept ringing from Chief Suleiman's several lines. He had sent out his secretary during the discussions with his son. He now felt he should take some of the calls.

"I now have to excuse myself. Some of my business associates are waiting."

Chief Suleiman told his son.

It was Wednesday afternoon and father and son rescheduled another meeting for the following Wednesday. Neither father nor son had any reason to suspect that the scheduled meeting would not hold.

Chapter 16

WAS IT VENGEANCE BY COLLABORATORS OR AN ACCIDENT?

On the same Wednesday evening after he held a meeting with his son, Chief Suleiman held a meeting with the *National Executive Council of Patrons of The Chambers; NECPC*. This was the highest governing council of all the top-secret societies in Konganoga. The Chambers in Kuveri, where Chief Suleiman was initially a patron, was only a small arm of the larger body.

The meeting was attended by all the patrons from all over the country. There were also observers from sister fraternities and sororities from overseas. Chief Suleiman had been serving as the overall national boss for just over a year. He had, during that period, because of his new position, multiplied his wealth many-fold. At the same time, however, he had become a more dissatisfied man than he had ever been.

Since after his discovery that his son was no longer in school and that he had indeed joined *The Chambers*, Chief Suleiman had never again found peace, especially after he discovered that his son had also known about part of his sources of wealth. He had been weighing in his mind how best to disengage himself from the clutches of the fraternity without incurring the wrath of the disciplinary wing of the organization. He knew that the latter wing could go to any extent to eliminate "fleeing members", as members who unilaterally decided to quit, were called.

Ironically, Chief Suleiman, some thirteen years earlier, was the head of the committee that prescribed the death penalty for all fleeing members. The idea behind such severe punishment was to deter people who might expose the activities of the secret societies. The organization had hatched and fully developed hit squads from within its ranks. The hit squads would usually act independent of directives from the leadership of the organization once it was established that a member or some members had committed serious "deviant behavior."

Chief Suleiman had only hoped that his stature and standing in the society would be too intimidating for any actions against him from the hit squad whose members he had, at one time or another, tutored.

Again, many of his former boys, like Chief Unafefe, had been fully entrenched into the hit squad by Chief Suleiman himself. He had felt that with such people, who he often addressed as his boys, in the forefront of the organization, his safety was guaranteed even if he wanted to quit.

He, nevertheless, still had some premonitions about the possibility of the "mad dogs" that he had trained turning loose on him when he would have been out of power. It was that fear and persistent doubt that was primarily responsible for Chief Suleiman's bad mood. It was for that reason that he had bared his mind to his son earlier on that day.

Chief Suleiman informed his national executive members that he intended to relinquish his position as national chairman of the Chambers as well as all its affiliate bodies.

"I intend henceforth to retire into a quiet and peaceful life. It is my desire to avoid all links with this life of crime." Chief Suleiman announced to his benumbed members.

The explicit reference to "life of crime" must have particularly piqued the gathering as audible hisses of disapproval were heard from many corners of the room as soon as that reference was made.

In spite of the hisses of disapproval of his address, Chief Suleiman continued: "I want to devote the rest of my life to making amends for my half century of iniquities. I have a family that looks up to me for moral guidance. My twenty-two-year-old son abandoned his medical school education to join this group. My life and my heritage have been thrown into shambles, and I feel a sense of hollowness even with my swimming in wealth and financial abundance. I want to retrace my steps, and I appeal to you all please, to help rescue me from this bondage by allowing me to go in peace."

When Chief Suleiman concluded his speech, there was utter silence in the hall for more than two minutes. It took one courageous member from among the group to open up a floodgate of questions and concerns.

"Oshimiri, this club made you, and you, as captain, want to abandon this ship midstream. Why did it take you so long to recognize that this group was ruining your family?"

Before Chief Suleiman could articulate an answer, another questioner asked to know whether the chief still remembered the penalties for the action that he was about to take.

"Do you remember Sir, that you are one of the architects of the penalties that accompany the action that you are about to take?" The bold member asked from the floor.

The floodgate having been opened, the questions and challenges could no longer be controlled at a certain stage. Even Chief Unafefe, who was one of the beneficiaries of Chief Suleiman's goodwill through *The Chambers,* was one of those who threw questions laced with angry words at Chief Suleiman. Chief Unafefe whose English had slightly improved, wielding his massive frame and in a rare effrontery and uncharacteristic challenge of his benefactor raised his voice and said:

"Oshimiri, my Chief, Sir, what fate go befall your boys like me, when, you who be the captain come abandon this ship for the middle of the ocean? You want make we sink for ocean and die?" Chief Suleiman looked on in utter surprise as his subordinates who prior to his notice of abdication dared not look him straight in the face. The latter suddenly needed no prompting to challenge him. He repeatedly adjusted himself on his seat, utterly dumbfounded. Tempers appeared to be rising. With the all-powerful Supreme Commander on his way out, things appeared to be spiraling out of control.

The gavel came handy and the meeting was adjourned for a fortnight during which time it was believed that tempers would have cooled. But that was not before the outgoing Supreme Commander of *The Chambers* had regained composure and announced solemnly on the microphone: "My fellow Chambers, it is not my wish to do anything that would jeopardize the interest and good name of our revered Organization. I shall for as long as I live keep the secrets of this honorable body and ensure the respect and reverence with which we all hold our fraternity." As Chief Suleiman uttered the words "Honorable" and "good name", they sounded sour in his mouth knowing what he knew about the body.

But it was obvious that Chief Suleiman had been eating with the devil for twenty-five years without forging long-enough spoons. Even when the *Supreme Chambers* Chief Suleiman had assured his members that he intended to step away "without jeopardy as a member of the organization," obvious doubts about his sincerity still were visible on the faces of the members present.

By Saturday morning, Chief Suleiman was at the VIP wing of the airport on his way to Kuveri. He wanted to have a quiet weekend in his Kuveri mansion after a turbulent midweek meeting with members of the governing council of his organization. He also wanted to meet personally with the regional branch executives of his organization to inform them of his intention to step down from the top position in the organization and as a patron of *The Chambers*.

After Chief Suleiman checked in to the first-class preboarding area of the airport, his Karuja chauffeur had driven back to town. It was to be a ninety-minute flight from Karuja to Kuveri. Chief Suleiman regularly made this trip weekly or every other week. Two assistants who always traveled with him, were in the open hall of the economy class waiting area, also waiting to board.

The first-class passengers were soon asked to board, and Chief Suleiman boarded with his newspapers and a few personal files that he wanted to look through in flight. It was a small plane on domestic flight and formalities were not much. Apparently too, security was not tight even though people were still screened for metal detectors. But movement of crew and other airline staff to and from the tarmac did not appear to be very well scrutinized. Chief Suleiman took his seat as a first-class passenger in the plane and took up his newspaper to read.

There had been a departure delay of about thirty-five minute, and Chief Suleiman and the other passengers were already getting anxious because of the people who would be waiting for them at the Kuveri airport.

The announcement just came on for the economy-class passengers to queue up for boarding.

Then the unexpected happened.

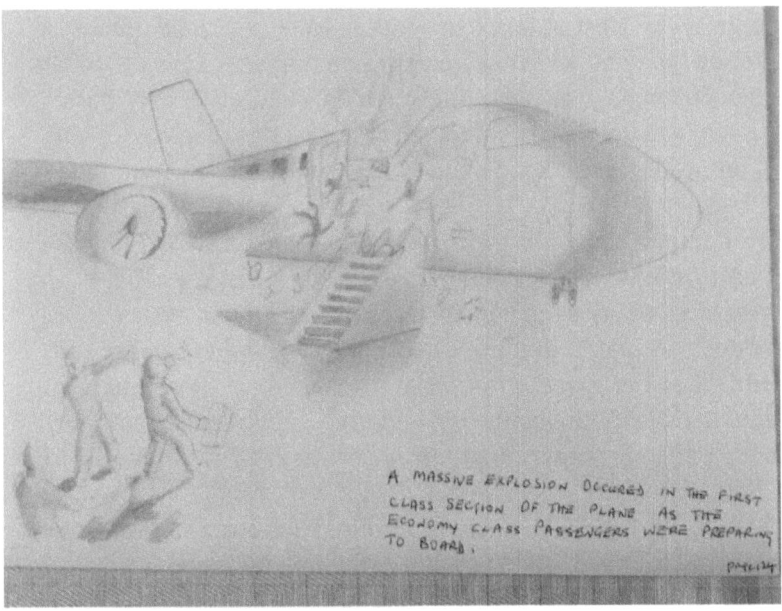

(A massive explosion occurred in the first-class section of the plane as the economy class passengers were preparing to board.)

There was a massive explosion in the plane.

The explosion occurred just between the cockpit and the area of the plane designated as first class. The explosion was so massive that it tore apart the entrance door of the plane that had not been closed. White smoke filled everywhere, and the ensuing fire sent even people in the boarding area of the building running out and fleeing in all directions, towards the security check area and even with panic up to the adjoining road.

By the time the fire truck got to put out the fire, a good part of the plane's anterior end had been completely destroyed. A few of the first-class passengers and the crew who were already in the plane and who were not blown apart scrambled to escape through the rear door, but that area was not open. When the fire was finally put out, eleven people lay dead in the plane—either badly blown apart by the blast or burnt to death before they could escape. Among the dead was the Supreme Commander of the Chambers Chief Suleiman, Oshimiri I of Umudioha, eight other first-class passengers, and two members of crew. Six people escaped with different degrees of burns. Just five people escaped completely unharmed.

The cause or source of the explosion was unknown. Preliminary investigations yielded no immediate evidence of the cause of the explosion. Many people believed that it was foul play. It was indeed speculated that the explosion was timed to correspond with when the plane was in the air. Fortunately, there was a thirty-minute delay. If the plane had departed on schedule, a lot more, if not all, the passengers might have perished.

Not a few people who knew of the Chief Suleiman saga believed that it might have to do with the explosion. But nobody was sure. Could Chief Suleiman have been the target? Could some extremist members of the Chambers have played a part to avenge a violation of the oath of "loyalty-or-death", or was it a mere coincidence?

Was it an accident or was it foul play? Nobody was certain. Neither the airline nor the National Aviation Authority could proffer any credible explanations. But one thing was certain: foul play could not be ruled out especially since the plane was still on the tarmac and not in the air. Nobody heard the details thereafter. Investigations were said to have been commenced. The investigations went on for many months. Many people of power and influence might have been involved.

The stakes were too high. Nobody was certain of anything anymore.

Chapter 17

THE POST-SULEIMAN ERA

If Chief Suleiman lived a life of controversy and publicity, his death and burial generated even more publicity and controversy. Hours after the identification of the body of Chief Suleiman in the local hospital, some members of the Chambers showed up to claim his body. They presented papers to support a prior declaration by the deceased that "the Chambers should take charge of everything in the event of a member's death or disability." They declined request for an autopsy and declared their intention to enforce their decision in court.

Elaborate burial arrangements were planned and organized by *The Chambers*. His family was allowed to play only minimal role even after they had contested the apparent usurpation in court.

The widow Mariama, her son Ade and Mariama's two stepdaughters literally watched from the sidelines. The consolation for them was that their loved one ostensibly made his peace with himself and with his core family before his tragic death. It was only after her husband's demise that Mrs. Suleiman got to know the full extent of her husband's involvement with, and indebtedness to *The Chambers*. The family nursed its emotional wounds with equanimity and mourned their departed husband and father quietly and with all due reverence.

(Members of "The Chambers" assembled from far and near and took over the funeral ceremony, relegating the Suleiman family to the sidelines.)

The same afternoon after Chief Suleiman's interment, the national leadership of *The Chambers* posted its men to take charge over all the deceased's offices and other properties with the exception of his core residence in his home village and his residence in the provincial capital, Kuveri, and his new mansion in Karuja.
Apart from these, all his business outfits were occupied by representatives detailed by *The Chambers.* In every case of such occupation, the organization displayed papers to prove that they had the mandate to take over.
Mrs. Suleiman and her family after consultation with their lawyer decided not to contest any of the claims from *The Chambers.* They realized that the organization had, in its possession, documents akin to a will to back up their claims. All in all, they decided to keep away from the public eye especially after Ade had narrated to his mother and her sisters the details of his last meeting with his father. It looked as if Chief Suleiman suspected

that he might be hit by The Chambers after quitting, hence he uplifted his family adequately before his demise. His two daughters also testified that he had made some good checks available to them weeks before his tragic death. Nobody was sure what he had made available to Mariama under those circumstances. But it was obvious that he had prepared himself and fairly adequately taken care of his family materially in the event of the worst.

Three months after the burial of Chief Suleiman, his personal lawyer delivered a package to his family. It was the documents for a trust fund for two hundred million dollars that Chief Suleiman had specified should be utilized through AMEND Incorporated, specifically for a fight against cultism and other social ills and for helping victims of cult-related activities. Those funds had been carefully tailored by Chief Suleiman to be outside the reach of The Chambers. It was another very welcome relief for the Suleiman family as they daily got convinced that their late patriarch and tycoon "did not die in vain".

Because of the decision of the Suleiman's not to contest *The Chambers*' usurpation of most of their late patriarch's assets, what would have made the headlines about one who might have ranked as one of the world's wealthiest men was nipped in the bud. The family was spared the heartaches of endless litigations, especially in a society where societal ills like *The Honorables* and *The Chambers* were in virtual control of almost everything.

Officially, Ade was still a member of *The Chambers*. The organization's maxim of "once a member, always a member" still applied to him. But his saving grace was that he had not risen high enough in the hierarchy of the organization. He was still within the ranks of the people that the organization called colt members or *the colts*. Those were mainly students who, out of youthful exuberance and adventurism, often joined the organization within their student days only to run away soon after graduation.

It was known within the ranks of the organization that over 75 percent of colt members would run away. The organization rarely bothered them thereafter provided they had not held high office or benefited immensely from the organization and provided they kept their mouths shut.

"Colts" in *The Chambers* often played the roles of spearheading car snatching, kidnappings, disruption of gatherings during elections where *Chambers'* interests were jeopardized, robberies, and hired killings. Often, they were compensated on the spot after each "successful operation" so that they would not come back later to start making bigger demands. The on-the-spot compensation was the ground on which Ade was paid two thousand dollars after he successfully delivered his first and only snatched Mercedes-Benz car.
As long as colt members did not start opening their mouths too wide after leaving the organization, they were often left to depart in peace. There was a reward for every service rendered to the organization and a price to pay for every favor received.

Indeed, the top hierarchy of the organization did not encourage all colt members to remain with the organization so that there would be space for other new members. If every colt persisted, the organization would become too unwieldy.
Even in the numbering of the members in the official register of the organization known as *Inner Temple* Register, the year was usually attached to the number code of the member. Ade, for instance, was 146B/06. The 06 indicated the year of admission. If there was another 146B present, then the last two digits of the year of admission would be added to differentiate one from the other.

Occasionally, however, if a long-gone member rose in society to become very rich or very famous, even if he or she had not been an active member for many years, the organization might reach out to the estranged member and ask for favors. Again, if a long-gone member was running for high office, members of the organization might again rally round to offer help. If the help was accepted, of course, there would be a price to pay later.

In the case of Ade, he became inactive soon after the car-snatching episode and after he played the role of an usher during the party in honor of his father. Thereafter, he got so disgusted with himself and his father and found solace in alcohol and drugs before he was rescued by his father. Indeed, only few people in the organization still remembered that he was once a member of the group.

Ade could easily have taken advantage of his membership of the organization to rescue for himself and his family part of his father's assets. But he chose not to. He knew the implications. He knew that there was a price to pay. He did not have the long spoon with which to eat with the devil. Not even his late father, with all his fame and wealth, could fashion out such a spoon. He readily remembered his father's last speech. He knew that he could still be a tycoon in his own right. He was already on the path to becoming one and purely from clean and honest business.

Ade was soon to put the issues of his father's property behind him to face his business.

He got more resolved ever than before to succeed. He wanted to prove that he could still succeed and become a tycoon and even successfully get into politics without resorting to evil.

He immediately incorporated a huge charitable organization—the Suleiman Foundation—which, like the earlier AMEND Incorporated was geared toward helping to eradicate cultism in schools and colleges and which gave grants to individual existing cult members to help them rebuild their lives and fit back into the society.

Suleiman Foundation concentrated on rehabilitation while AMEND Incorporated concentrated on prevention of involvement in cultism by lectures, seminars, workshops and teaching school children the evils and dangers of cultism.

Both organizations opened offices in both Kuveri and Karuja, but

Suleiman Foundation later established offices nationwide.

It did not take long before some members of *The Chambers*
started visiting offices of Suleiman Foundation, asking for ways
whereby they could help to reclaim their lives and rebuild.
The number of those who visited and sought genuine help
increased by the week. Many earnestly sought advice and
assurance that it was possible to reform without necessarily
paying the ultimate price. Even some of the leaders of the
organization who hitherto had thought it impossible to back out
soon found an escape route. They were encouraged not to accept
help from an organization that would in future demand a pound of
flesh.
A few who sought loans to start small businesses were given the
loans with no interest charged. Others who sought advice on
overcoming some social problems were advised and aided.
The most surprising was yet to come.
Eight months after the death of his mentor and friend, Chief
Unafefe surfaced at the headquarters of Suleiman Foundation. He
did not come alone. He drove in, in a convoy of eight other cars all
occupied by top notches of The Chambers. Their arrival appeared
to have been timed for the day and hour when the chairman of
the Board of Trustees of Suleiman Foundation was holding his
monthly briefing with the Press.
The visitors sought to meet with the chairman and the Press
Corps.

It was not a scheduled visit and was most unusual. The
receptionist who happened to recognize the ruthless Chief
Unafefe and some of his notorious companions, fearing that the
visitors were out to foment trouble, quickly alerted the Suleiman
Foundation chairman, Ade. They also alerted the police in case of
any eventuality.

The visitors appeared impatient and had opted to stroll around the
premises instead of taking their seats in the reception. Ade,

observing the movement of the visitors through the closed-circuit television monitors, also personally alerted the police. He also deliberately delayed ushering in the visitors until the police arrived.

In less than one hour, the premises was up filled with cars and anxious passersby. The atmosphere appeared tense. What could Congressman Chief the Honorable Dr Sir Unafefe, Oyinatumba I of Umudioha, and eight other well-known and notoriously rich and dreaded businessmen and politicians and a convoy of armed policemen be doing in the premises of Suleiman Foundation on a day that the foundation's monthly briefing was being held?
It certainly would not be anything short of evil. The crowd grew by the minute. Other Pressmen soon joined.
When the place was swarming with people, Ade then came out with the other members of the Board of Trustees to welcome his "guests" for whatever their mission was.
He expected that Chief Unafefe would ask for privacy, but he did not. He rather asked for a public address system. One of the Pressmen immediately provided one. Ade was apprehensive. He had always associated Chief Unafefe with nothing but evil even while he was *The Honorable's* Personal Assistant in Karuja.
He was certainly apprehensive but having long relinquished his evil associates he was prepared to counter whatever Chief Unafefe had up his sleeves. He felt that nothing could be worse than the death of Chief Suleiman his father and the circumstances under which the latter died. He knew that *The Chambers* and whatever they stood for would have little powers over him and Suleiman Foundation, which was a duly incorporated body. On his own part too, he was on solid financial grounds and would be prepared to face the forces of Chief Unafefe if the need should arise.

One of the members of the Board of Trustees of the Suleiman Foundation moved up to Ade and whispered into his ear not to let Chief Unafefe have the microphone and the floor without a prior ascertaining of what the latter wanted to say and what his mission in the property was. Another member of the Board of the Foundation indeed audibly labelled the visitors as invaders and trespassers and demanded that they be arrested or ordered out of the premises. But Ade overruled the member and loudly said, "We are fighting an evil system and encouraging good. We will do so in the marketplaces. We will do so in public parks. We do not hide our identity." Then remembering a statement that he had read many years from his favorite high school novel, John F. Kennedy's Profiles in Courage, he loudly declared: "Let any assassin fire!" After he said this, Ade turned to Chief Unafefe and said, "Ladies and gentleman, please let us hear Chief Unafefe."

There was no clapping of hands at the introduction of Chief Unafefe. Rather, hearts pounded loudly as Chief Unafefe adjusted his overflowing garment and cleared his throat.
He took a quick glance over his shoulders as if to ascertain that his team was still with him. And, in his baritone voice and in the fullness of his poor barely-comprehensible English which many wrongly believed would have greatly improved with his long stay and exposure in Karuja, he stated:
"Chairman of the Board of Suleiman Foundation, ladies and gentlemen, from what we de see, it be like you get some apprehension about my presence here with my group of distinguished friends and honorable. Here with me today are Chief Amos, Chief Oti, Chief Ekeh, Chief Unakoja, Chief Etim, Chief Sule, Chief William, and Chief Dagogo. For those of you who no know me, my name be Congressman Chief the Honorable Sir Dr Joshua Unafefe, Oyinatumba I of Umudioha Kingdom.
For make we avoid doubt, I wish make I state for categorical say our visit na peaceful one it be. We come here as friends, not as enemies. We come make we state for open say we wan be members and co-sponsors of Suleiman Foundation. Our speech go be short. We want make this one be surprise visit. Na him make we no inform your Board Members before we come. We come here as friends, not enemies or rivals.
We want quit cult. We don tire for cult. Cult it no good. It no good

147

for us. It no good for our *childrens.*
We like the kind thing way Suleiman Foundation them de do. We
come here to support Suleiman Foundation with this small check
of one hundred million dollar. And this amount go be only a
beginning. This one be our all talk. Thank you, Mr. Chairman.
Thank you, ladies and gentlemen."

There was subdued silence for a while. It looked as if the audience
was not sure of what they heard. Chief Unafefe spoke in his
characteristic pidgin English. But most people present got the kind
and generous message of cooperation which he conveyed. But
they appeared to want to ascertain that they heard the
Oyinatumba right.
It was not many times that anything good would be expected to
emanate from Chief Unafefe even when he would repeatedly
"win" elections. Then the thunderous applause followed. It lasted
so long that it looked as if it would never stop.
The unthinkable had happened! The backbone of the cult was
about to be broken! What was it that could have prompted the
sudden change of heart for the better on the part of Chief
Unafefe? The suspense in the atmosphere around the reception
hall of the Foundation building was palpable.
With the kingpins of the cult led by one of their emerging leaders,
Chief Unafefe, and eight other notable leaders of the organization
quitting and donating to further the cause of Suleiman
Foundation, the demise of the notorious *Chambers* and their
affiliate bodies was only a matter of time. Something must have
gone seriously wrong with the top hierarchy of the organization.

Ade was stunned. He did not appear to know where to start to
show appreciation. He merely accepted back the microphone from
Chief Unafefe and said, "Ladies and gentlemen, you have heard
this from the horse's mouth. Chief Unafefe, I cannot thank you
enough. Thank you, thank you, thank you." As a renewed round of
applause started, a scarcely audible voice could be heard in the
loud speaker, saying,

"Wetin him say? Him de call me horse?"

The voice was talking to one other *Honorable* member of Konganoga's legislative House who was among the visiting team. Apparently, the speaker was not aware that the microphone was not switched off. It was Chief Unafefe speaking.

Chapter 18

A DREAM ACTUALIZED; A SILENCE BROKEN

Ade's security and car-distribution business grew rapidly after the mass exodus from the Chambers of Chief Unafefe and his group. With the permanent exit of Chief Suleiman, the subsequent withdrawal of Chief Unafefe and many former acolytes of the deceased Supreme Commander the car-snatching business in Konganoga especially in the Karuja and Kuveri areas dropped drastically. People felt more confident to buy new cars. The roads became safer and drivers paid more attention to avoiding the rampant pot-holes than to worrying about car snatchers and kidnappers along the highways. There was greater feeling of general security. The "big masquerades" had jumped ship, and it was easier to apprehend the smaller fish who were essentially unpracticed robbers who had no godfathers to protect them. Ade expanded the Board of Trustees of the Suleiman Foundation to accommodate some of the new converts. Chief Unafefe and people like him were made associate members of the Board with no voting powers. Ade was wary not to flood the Board with the newcomers lest the devils that had invaded the minds of some of them in the past should rear their heads again and overwhelm the good work that had been done so far.

Chief Unafefe and his group of defectors and cult quitters, before their final departure from the nefarious organization, had ensured that they maneuvered most of the late Chief Suleiman's assets in Kuveri back to the project—The Suleiman Foundation. Nobody was sure of what became of their oats never to quit, the violation for which Chief Suleiman appeared to have been taken out. With the exit of the likes of Unafefe who were enforcers of the oat of inviolable perpetual membership, there appeared to be left in the fold, nobody who was strong enough to sanction violators. An implosion appeared to be taking place within *The Chambers* leadership.

The Karuja-located assets of Chief Suleiman however, continued to remain within the clutches of the few topnotches of the cult who were gaining tremendously from crime and who, therefore, persisted in the acts. But things were never to be the same again for the sponsors of evil.

The Suleiman Foundation was soon to become a household name in every institution of higher learning and in high schools as a symbol of battle against indiscipline and reward for the disciplined and well behaved in society.

Many subunits of it were formed and were properly funded. The Suleiman Foundation Annual Lectures were held in Karuja and all the provincial capitals, and handsome honorarium was awarded to the distinguished guest lecturer at every stage. It became a big honor to be appointed a Suleiman Foundation Guest Lecturer for any year.

The Suleiman Foundation scholarships were awarded each year to deserving students who had distinguished themselves in academics and in character. It became about the most highly treasured scholarly event in the entire Republic of Konganoga with endowments in several faculties of the nation's top universities. People in academia and public life were not left out.

The Suleiman Foundation Awards were made annually with huge cash value and beautifully carved plaques made from ebony wood that were presented annually to deserving individuals from all over the country.

It was a thing of great joy to be selected as a Suleiman Foundation scholar. The scholarships were not only prestigious; they were also worth a lot in material value.

Heads of schools and colleges struggled to prepare their students for the competition.

They would usually publish the names of such honorees as the names of their schools in many pages of their college journals. The Foundation gave a lot of publicity to its activities nationwide.

The name Suleiman came to symbolize dignity, hard work,

compassion patriotism, and good behavior. The headquarters of the foundation in Karuja was a very imposing edifice, and a bust of the late Chief Suleiman adorned the expansive lobby, which also did regular displays of the activities of the Foundation both in Karuja and in the provinces.

It was a big irony that such respect and honor was being bestowed on an individual whose activities in life were laced with blood and all that was antisocial and repugnant. The only happiness for Ade and the few who knew the details of Chief Suleiman's past was that he repented fully and made atonement before he died. Happily, it was only Ade and select members of *The Chambers* like Chief Unafefe, who knew the details of how the late Supreme Commander lived a terribly devilish double life. Only a handful knew the details of the hundreds if not thousands of people who lost their lives as a direct consequence of his criminality. To most observers, Chief Suleiman lived a life of sterling philanthropy. But the fact remained that the source of the philanthropy was from car snatching, kidnaping, murders and multiple antisocial activities from which he sponsored candidates into the nation's highest legislative and executive positions, reaping many-fold from such sponsorships from the nation's loose treasury coffers.

(Sister Mercy, the former flight attendant, confesses and embarks on street penance with a Bible and a Cross.)

As was usual with most investigations into tragedies, crimes, and other related events in the country Konganoga, the findings of the investigations of the cause of the explosion that killed Chief Suleiman and eight others were never published.
But three years after the tragedy, "The Eziokwu", one of the local newspapers in Karuja, carried a story titled "A Courier's Confessions?"
The story narrated how a thirty-six-year-old lady, who said her name was Sister Mercy, walked into the premises of the newspaper carrying a small wooden cross and a Bible in her hands.

Sister Mercy went on to narrate to one of the editors of the newspaper how, as a cabin crew member in the services of a local airline three years previously, she had been given a small but rather heavy package by a man whom she met in the VIP section of the waiting section of the airport. She said that she was paid fifty thousand dollars to deposit the baggage under a certain seat in the first-class section of the plane. She said that the man had assured her that the material was some harmless but treasured material that the owner said he did not want to be subjected to further rigorous airport inspections for some personal reasons. Sister Mercy had further told the newspaper that she confirmed that the man was a ticketed first-class passenger before accepting the package, which she felt was, at worst, drugs since the man was also a ticketed passenger and had apparently passed the initial screening process.

She said that she had realized that the material might have been explosives only after the event had occurred especially since the seat number of the passenger was apparently still vacant as of the time the explosion occurred. Miss Mercy the cabin crew member as she was as of the time, was one of those who escaped the explosion with minor injuries.

Sister Mercy further stated that since after the explosion, she had never had peace of mind but that she had been too afraid to narrate her story for fear of reprisals and the law. She lost her job after the airline laid off some staff after the accident. Miss Mercy who on conversion became known as Sister Mercy stated that she had "found solace only by carrying the cross here on earth to atone for [her] sins."

Further questioning of Sister Mercy about the man who handed her the package revealed that the man was heavily-built and unusually bulky and Pidgin English. She further stated that the man had a prominent dark mark on the ala of the right nose. Even though she looked at the man's boarding pass before accepting the passage, she could not remember the man's name. Miss Mercy also confirmed that the man had not boarded the plane before the explosion. Some first-class seats were still vacant, but boarding of economy-class passengers was about to commence before the explosion occurred. Again, poor investigative facilities in Konganoga and the fact that investigative personnel there had a penchant for accepting "kola" (bribes) to overlook certain aspects of their duties made it impossible for the true identity of the man who must have masterminded the explosion to be confirmed even after the confessions of Sister Mercy.

Congressman Chief the Honorable Dr. Sir Joshua Unafefe was a very bulky man. That quality had made him a one-time very treasured bodyguard to Chief Suleiman. He did not speak good English even though that did not bother him in parliament where he rarely opened his mouth. Also, he had a scar on his face from chemical burns to the ala of his nose some years previously. On one of the evenings during the years that Joshua Unafefe was faking a blind beggar in the passenger trains, he had asked his guide to procure him a bottle of some grease remover so that he could more readily remove the Vaseline that he used to seal his eyelids every early morning before the day's begging business for effective simulation of a blind beggar suffering from possible conjunctivitis. He did not want to continue with the nightly arduous task of using soap and plenty of water to wash off the Vaseline. Water was not always available, and the process of washing off the thick layers of Vaseline was often laborious. After the purported grease remover was procured, Unafefe had decided to first try the liquid on the skin of his face before trying it on his eyes. The liquid turned out to be very corrosive and had given Unafefe a burn on the side of the nose. This burn had turned very dark with time. Unafefe had accused his guide Mr. Okon of attempting to make him permanently blind so that he would no longer be able to count the money donations collected at the end of each day's begging.

"I know your plans," Unafefe had told Mr. Okon, his guide, after the burning incident.
"You want make I become blind so you go de steal the money wey people de give me. This your greed go kill you one day. You no go school. You no fit preach Bible. You no fit preach Koran. You even no fit beg. But you fit get me something to make me blind. You no

go see better, and you go get big trouble one day." Unafefe had cursed his guide.

The face-scarring incident was the beginning of the long-drawn disagreement between Unafefe and his guide—an event that ultimately led to accusations of stealing, the threat of exposure, and ultimate flight of Unafefe to his hometown, Umudioha, before he was hired by Chief Suleiman.

Even though Sister Mercy's descriptions matched one man, the man was "The Honorable". He was a chief. He was a sir. Above all, he was an untouchable sacred cow, a member of the revered club of the Chambers with nation-wide if not world-wide connections! After Sister Mercy's confessions a number of people strongly linked Chief Unafefe to the explosion that killed Chief Suleiman. The description was almost unmistakable. No other person that had the capacity of inflicting such damage was known in Karuja and environs. Besides, Chief Unafefe had felt strongly aggrieved after the exit of Chief Suleiman from the Chambers. Again, Chief Unafefe was a member of the hit group that had been placed under oath to deal with defecting Chambers without warning or authorization. Ironically Chief Suleiman was a strong advocate of severe measures against "defectors and saboteurs", as people who opted out of the organization and "opened their mouths widely" were labeled.

Chapter 19

THE BARON ON THE RUN

Chief Unafefe was seen more frequently in Kuveri after his
renunciation of his membership of the Chambers. He only visited
Karuja when he had special committee meetings in parliament.
Even though the organizations, which he announced his
extrication from, were still
operational, they were no longer quite as strong as they used to
be.

Besides, since he was the virtual leader of the hit group that dealt
sometimes fatal blows to fleeing members, Chief Unafefe, in flight,
had left a serious vacuum which was difficult to fill.
It was even rumored that before he fled the organization and
planned its disintegration that he and a select group of the leaders
had looted a great deal of the assets of the organization including
those recovered from the late Chief Suleiman.
The confessions of Sister Mercy sparked off renewed inquiry into
the airplane explosion that claimed the life of Chief Suleiman and
eight others. The earlier enquiries were inconclusive and were put
in the cooler as were most similar enquiries in Konganoga.
The precise description of the probable mastermind of the
bombing appeared to be zeroing in on one man whose standing in
the Konganoga society had slowed down the speed of
investigations. The probable suspect might not have been very
educated. He might not have been a particularly knowledgeable
individual. But he was very smart. He knew when to hold his
ground and when to run. He knew that the grounds beneath his
feet as a Chambers member were quite shaky. That must have
been part of the reason for the donation of scores of millions of
dollars to The Suleiman Foundation.
That was what appeared to have necessitated Chief Unafefe's
sudden absconding from the cult so as to be seen as an upright

man, much as he knew that the protection that he obtained by being in the cult and in the top hierarchy of the secret society would be lost if he left. But he had weighed the benefits of remaining in the cult against the benefits of appearing to the general society as a reformed man. He had opted for the latter.

The decision to put on the appearance of a reformed man by Chief Unafefe was informed partly by the reverence that he saw being heaped posthumously on someone whom he found had benefited tremendously from the organization before reforming. That person was the late Chief Suleiman.
But Chief Suleiman's reform was not forced on him by any circumstances. It generated from within him. It was genuine. It was almost all-encompassing and was done with the best of intentions. It was laced with remorse. It did not seek to repair one wrong with another wrong. It was a decision made with good intent; one that was prepared to undergo suffering and sacrifice if need be. It was true.

Chief Unafefe's reformation was forced on him. It was no genuine reformation. It was false. It was not prepared to undergo suffering and sacrifice. It had the intention of destroying *The Chambers* house because it no longer appeared capable of offering shelter to him as an individual.
But it was already too late. The noose was closing in on the culprit. Sister Mercy's confessions stirred the need to take renewed look at the manifest of the passengers on the ill-fated flight that never took off.
Chief Unafefe's name was not in the manifest. But accusing fingers were being pointed. It was relatively easy to use a false name. And, in Konganoga where bribery and graft were rife it was relatively easy to obtain and use false identification for internal flights in Konganoga.

There were not many wealthy men who had a distinguishing very black scar on the nose and who spoke pidgin English and were

bulky and lived in Karuja and were capable of getting to the airport to bribe a flight attendant with fifty thousand dollars. The bribe sum was revealed by Sister Mercy as part of her confessional statement after she became "a born-again Christian."
There were no other men that fitted all those descriptions perfectly. The one man who fitted into these qualities however, also possessed enough financial muscle to cover up or indeed largely obliterate his paths and abandon a first-class ticket which he or she had purchased. Chief Unafefe had little or no formal education. But he was a chief of Umudioha, a knight of his new-era church, a doctor of letters and above all *The Honorable* congressman representing a constituency which he hardly ever visited and whose boundaries or population he scarcely knew.

Attempts were made by agents of a certain individual to get Sister Mercy to change her statement and declarations but with no success. Sister Mercy's statement appeared to indict a certain highly-connected individual who had links to *The Chambers,* one who had a high profile in the political circles in Karuja. Sister Mercy had spoken and would not accept two million dollars to refute or withdraw the statement.
She would not even touch that amount to feign temporary insanity even if the law enforcement people accepted money to parade her before the press to feign insanity.
She clung tenaciously to the Bible and the cross in her hands and, even under torture, had declared that she would stand by her description of the man who had bribed her at the airport on the morning of the bomb blast in the airport. Sister Mercy said that she was already prepared to die. Killing her mysteriously would make her an instant martyr. So, it was better to ignore Sister Mercy and let her alone so that she would not continue to be in the news.
Therefore, the people who masterminded the plane-bombing were in panic, and they had good reasons to be.
It became advisable for Chief Unafefe, the Oyinatumba of Umudioha to get out of the country for a while to let investigative

and judicial tempers cool. He had once planned a vacation in the United States but had not actualized it because he could not readily obtain a diplomatic visa. But he had decided to use an ordinary visitors' visa if need be, more so as it would enable him to travel incognito. The money to spend in any overseas vacation, no matter to which country and no matter for what duration, was no problem. No, not when one was an Honorable, from the Republic of Konganoga.

Chief Unafefe had completed the forms for interview at the American Embassy in Karuja.
He had heard that it was difficult to obtain visas at the American Embassy in Karuja. He had earlier learned that if people had plenty of money in their accounts and had visible means of livelihood and ties in their home countries that they were more likely to obtain the visas.
Chief Unafefe had also heard that some public servants, who had too much money in their bank accounts but who had no visible explanations about how such huge bank accounts that did not match their income, were denied visas. He heard of one of his friends who was told that his extremely fat bank account could be "public funds".

Chief Unafefe did not want to face any of such uncertain or embarrassing situations.
He sought alternative ways of obtaining a US visa. Ready suggestions easily came his way. He was told that if he provided ten thousand dollars in cash for the embassy officials and paid one thousand dollars to the agent, he was certain to secure a visa. That was "petty cash" for a fabulously rich Unafefe who was prepared to part with up to one million dollars to suppress detection for complicity in a multiple airport murder case. Chief Unafefe discussed briefly with his American Visa Advisor. The latter was an unofficial visa procurement tout who apparently had ties with a few lower cadre embassy staff within the embassy.
Through the agency of the recommended Visa Advisors, visa

procurement had indeed in the past been facilitated for some applicants. In a few other cases the Advisors had turned out to be scams. Chief Unafefe immediately paid twenty-five thousand dollars to the agent who was recommended to him even when the recommended Advisor was said to have demanded only eleven thousand dollars as total charges for the official fees and unofficial facilitator charges.

"Make you give the embassy man twenty thousand, make you take two thousand and keep three thousand for official visa fee and contingency," he told the thoroughly surprised agent. The latter immediately proceeded with utmost speed to process the application papers for the scarcely literate Chief Unafefe. A large sum of money having exchanged hands, even in an apparently corruption-free process, an interview date was obtained and the necessary bank statements and other documents were assembled. The agent reviewed the documents and was greatly surprised that his fellow Konganogans could have so much money in their bank accounts—so many hundreds of millions of dollars in several bank accounts.

When the form was being filled, Chief Unafefe insisted that all his titles must appear on the form. "My full name be Congressman Chief the Honorable Dr. Sir Joshua Unafefe, Oyinatumba I of Umudioha Kingdom."
There was not enough space in the name column to accommodate all that Chief Unafefe wanted included. But he insisted that everything must be included "You must include all my titles. You fit make the letters very tiny so all my titles go enter" Chief Unafefe suggested. On being told that the number of available boxes, not the size of the letters, was what mattered, Chief Unafefe proffered a solution. "Add more boxes and make them small, small boxes. You must add all my titles. They no give me my titles for free. Me, I pay big money for each of them." Chief Unafefe insisted, his English fluctuating between his normal pidgin English and the much of good English that his private coaches had been teaching

him.

The stunned agent had to fill the form by himself after series of failed attempts by Chief Unafefe. The latter's writing was not only illegible but was also bore no relationship to the required questions.

"We may have to drop some of the titles to ensure that your actual name is accommodated," the agent had suggested.

"Even if you go drop anything, you must not drop one thing—*The Honorable!*" Chief Unafefe had insisted. "You must also not drop the sir and the Dr. I tell you before say I no steal those titles. I been pay well-well for them," Chief Unafefe emphasized.

At the end of the day, Chief Unafefe had his way, but only partially. Virtually every word of his titles had to be abbreviated, sometimes beyond recognition. The Honorable was abbreviate simply as Hon. Doctor was already abbreviated to Dr. and Congressman was abbreviated to Con. The agent was worried that "Con." Would tend to suggest the word con-man. He thought of abbreviating the word to Col. But on second thought he realized that Col. would suggest Colonel a far cry from what his client was.

A week before the scheduled date of interview, the agent who had started regretting why he charged so little to a man who had so much, came back to Chief Unafefe.

"If you pay fifty thousand dollars, VIP interview can be arranged for you. You will be collected right from your house to the embassy by embassy officials in embassy vehicle. The queue is usually long, but you will not have to wait at the queue. You will be placed right in front of the queue when you come to the embassy, and you will he interviewed first. You will need to obtain a second passport. That one is easy with Konganoga's Passport Office. You will go in for the interview with the first passport, and I will have the second passport sent in directly in advance. Your interview will be a formality as your visa will be ready in the second passport. Everything will be arranged. It will not matter what the interviewing officer decides when you see them inside. Your visa will be ready with me on the second passport."

Chief Unafefe was exhilarated. "Embassy man, him go collect me for house? Him go give me VIP treatment? Then him go give me special visa? Fantastic! I go give them hundred thousand dollar instead of fifty thousand, if them go do that!"
The heavy sums of money being bandied about by Chief Unafefe might sound fabulous for any individual who was not conversant with the deep pockets of Konganoga's congressmen and women. Their wardrobe allowances for six months far outweighed the annual salary of an American President.

With one hundred thousand dollars in his kitty, it was easy for the agent to arrange for a well-washed minibus with thoroughly refurbished upholstery to come early on the appointed morning to collect Chief Unafefe from his house to the embassy. Special uniform had been made for the minibus driver and a false plate number with the sign of the American flag with the bold inscription USA Embassy overhung over the rear plate number. Printed news-magazines, bearing the American flag on the front cover were conspicuously displayed on the rear seat and a chaperon, an African albino lady neatly dressed as an American Embassy official with an emblem of an American flag sewn to the left breast pocket was in the passenger's seat to welcome Chief Unafefe into the fake American embassy minibus. The fake embassy chaperon had greeted Chief Unafefe profusely in a feigned American accent as the latter clambered into the vehicle with all dignity and air of importance. She had to twist her tongue properly to fit with the foreign accent and phonetics of an embassy official.

Very early that morning, the agent had arranged for a tout who would stand in the queue right in front and who would give his space to Chief Unafefe as soon as the latter arrived at the queuing section of the embassy building.
Chief Unafefe was clutching a small purse which he had stuffed with one-hundred-dollar bills.

He continuously put on the air of the very polished and revered honorable gentleman who was being led to an exalted podium to accept his prize for some well-deserved achievement. He was neither smiling nor frowning. He donned a rich black three-piece suit that he had bought specially for the occasion. Over his neck, he hung a glittering gold chain which he had also bought specially for the occasion. Over the dangling gold chain, he had hung a prominent multicolored fluffy garland. His fingers were adorned with two thick gold rings, and an expensive gold watch adorned his wrist. He was clutching three different types of cell phones even after he had been told by the agent that cell phones were not allowed inside the embassy building.

Just before he climbed out of the car in front of the embassy building, he dipped his hands into the purse and pulled out a bunch of one-hundred-dollar bills that he handed over to the chaperon sitting in front. He did not count the money. As he dipped his hand again to pull out more notes for the driver, a security man attached to the embassy who ensured that vehicles did not spend more than a few seconds in front of the embassy, approached the minibus.

"Hey, driver, move! Move!" the security man yelled at the driver who had already stretched out his hands ready to receive his own dollar bonuses from Chief Unafefe.

"Drop your passenger and move or I go flog you!" the security man yelled again as he approached the vehicle and pulled out a horsewhip.

Chief Unafefe slid back the money he had intended to give to the driver and hurried out of the vehicle. He nearly fell down as the driver moved on even before Chief Unafefe had fully stepped out of the vehicle. The frightened driver had to drive off almost as he his dollar-spraying passenger stepped out.

The embarrassed Honorable sighed heavily and said: "Don't this police know that this one it be embassy vehicle?" As Chief Unafefe stepped out of the vehicle, the agent ran up ready to receive him. He was surprised at how gorgeously and outrageously Chief Unafefe had dressed. He was afraid that his dressing would attract undue attention. He immediately took Chief Unafefe to the front of the queue where the paid tout, who had been holding the space in the queue, immediately made way for Chief Unafefe. As he did so, Chief Unafefe again unzipped his purse and gave the tout ten pieces of one-hundred-dollar bills.

The eyeballs of both the tout and the other people in the queue almost popped out of their sockets. The tout, who was obviously a devout Christian, accepted the money and knelt down in front of Chief Unafefe and made the sign of the cross in gratitude to God. As he got up, he kept making the sign of the cross in disbelief, as he hurried away from the scene. He was earlier paid ten dollars to queue up and surrender his space for a stranger who in turn had paid him one thousand dollars in gratitude! The lucky tout would not need to work for a couple of weeks.
Chief Unafefe's agent, notwithstanding all the money he had received from Chief Unafefe, kept looking jealously at the tout as the latter hurried away. It was obvious that the agent wished that the money had been passed through him so he might have his cut.

Notices were placed in conspicuous places outside the embassy, warning that cell phones were not allowed within the premises of the embassy. Chief Unafefe ignored the notices.
For the much that he knew, such notices were not for people who wore the tag of "The Honorable. In his opinion they were certainly not for special visitors who were brought to the embassy in embassy vehicles." Those notices were probably meant only for ordinary visitors and lesser men to obey. After all, in Konganoga, *The Honorables* make the laws. Lesser mortals obey them.

Chief Unafefe was clutching his cell phones very conspicuously. He immediately stated making calls to one of his friends as he approached the first security check point at the gate of the embassy. He wanted to announce his presence at the embassy. He wanted to describe the VIP treatment that he received to another Honorable in Karuja.

"Honorable Chief Omego 1, It is me, your friend Honorable Chief Unafefe, speaking from American Embassy, ..." Chief Unafefe started in a conversation with his friend.

Ever before Chief Unafefe could say more as he approached the first security check point a smartly-dressed embassy security man approached him.

"Sir, didn't you read the notices? Cell phones are not allowed within embassy premises," Chief Unafefe was told as he got to the gate with its crowd-control devices.

"My name be Congressman, Chief the Honorable . . ."

Chief Unafefe told the security man, still holding the cell phone to his ear. But the gorgeously-dressed *Honorable* was not allowed to complete the self-introduction.

"Sir, cell phones are not allowed within the embassy premises!"

"But I be the Honorable . . ."

"For the final time, sir, cell phones are not allowed within embassy premises!"

Chief Unafefe looked around for the agent. It might be necessary for the agent to come and remind the officers that he was the VIP who was brought down earlier that morning in the embassy minibus.

But the agent was nowhere in sight. People not going for visa interviews were not allowed that close to the security gate.

It might be necessary to do a little settlement, a little "softening of the ground" a little greasing of palms as was widely practiced in Konganoga.

"May be this police wants some tip", Chief Unafefe mused.

He reached for his wallet, unzipped it and pulled out a large bundle of one-hundred-dollar bills. The amount pulled out must have been well over fifty pieces.

The eyes of the officer popped out in surprise. His reaction in private in a country with endemic corruption could not be predicted, but the offer was in the full glare of the bystanders and most likely in the full glare of dozens of cameras.

The officer sternly responded, "Sir, we don't accept money here, and again, cell phones are not allowed within embassy premises"

Chief Unafefe was *pissed* off. Nobody had ever treated him that way. Maybe those people did not know who he was—

Oyinatumba, the chill that can catch a community, a former leader of *The Chambers,* the Honorable, a Knight, a Doctor of Philosophy; "Certainly, these people do not know who I am!" Chief Unafefe said, almost in a whisper.

"Officer, make you call my agent. I be the Honorable VIP who your drivers bring from my hotel suite earlier this morning. Call my agent for outside there, him go explain better."

The officer was hardly listening but he allowed the applicant to complete his sentence before again informing him that cell phones were not allowed within the embassy premises.

Chief Unafefe found he was helpless. He thought of leaving the queue and abandoning the idea and going for a diplomatic visa. But he had already been promised a VIP treatment. He had already been brought in a VIP "embassy minibus". Maybe the VIP treatment would recommence inside.

When Chief Unafefe found that he would certainly not be allowed to go inside the embassy compound with his cell phones, he again tried to deposit them with an embassy staff at the gate.

"OK, Officer, make you hold my phones for me. Me, I be Congressman, Chief the Honorable Dr. Sir Joshua Unafefe, the Oyinatumba of Umudioha. I want go America. Make I rest small there. Na my money I go carry go there go spend. So, make una no delay me much for this visa thing."

After the one minute of self-adulation statement Chief Unafefe looked around in surprise that nobody appeared to have been taken in by his self-declared high opinion of himself. Then in a humbler voice he turned to one of the security staff and said:

"Officer make you hold these phones for me. Make sure you don't call anybody with *The Honorable's* phone. I go give you plenty money when I come back after collecting my visa."
But nobody seemed impressed. Instead, the officer's order again came on more forcefully: "Take those phones out of this place otherwise we will get you arrested or cancel your interview."
On hearing the unbelievable words "arrested" and "cancel" Chief Unafefe tossed the three cell phones to the side of the door. But the firm order still came.
"Sir, you cannot leave those cell phones there. You can take them and hand over to somebody outside and get back to the line from the back. Sir, step out of the line for the next person!"

Now sweating profusely with all his overdressing, Chief Unafefe stepped out of the line and collected back the three cell phones and walked across the road to a kiosk where he saw a sign: Deposit Your Cell Phones here for $5. Chief Unafefe hurriedly dropped his three cell phones on the counter and dropped one-hundred-dollar bill for the man manning the counter.

Since he was already at the front of the queue, he walked straight to the front to take up his former turn in the queue to enter the embassy. But the order came on sharp and strong: "Sir, we don't allow people to jump the queue."
"But I dey for front of the line before. I only go out of the line to deposit my cell phone." Chief Unafefe attempted to correct.
"Sir, please take your turn at the back of the queue. The notices are clear on these."
As Chief Unafefe kept standing at the front of the queue and obstructing other officers,
two massive embassy police officers walked up to him and grabbed him by both armpits and led him to the tail end of the queue.

Chief Unafefe was dumbfounded. Again, he looked around for the agent. The agent was nowhere to be seen. But he was indeed around a short distance away from the queue where he and other visitors and escorts of visa applicants were waiting.

For the second time, Chief Unafefe thought of leaving. But he decided that having gone that far that he would see the process to the end. He decided that he would lodge a formal report of his being mistreated, later
"I go report these urchins at the gate to the embassy chiefs who I before, before pay twenty-thousand-dollar through my agent. Those senior people for inside them go understand better than these rude messengers here." Chief Unafefe said.
By the time Chief Unafefe got into the embassy and had his turn at the interview stand, it was well after midday.

The interview did not last long. Chief Unafefe felt that it was because it was only "for formality purposes" as he had been assured by his agent. He remembered his agent's assurance that his visa would be on the second passport which was in custody of the agent. Allegedly, the passport in his possession was only for formality during the interview.

Chief Unafefe could not fully explain what he intended to go to the United States for. His inexplicit and poorly expressed answers were a complete contrast to what the agent had filled in the form. Chief Unafefe could not understand most of the questions. He kept saying in response to every question, "I be Chief Joshua Unafefe, Oyinatumba I."

"Is *Oyaii Trumbaa* your surname?" ("Is Oyinatumba your surname?") The interviewer asked, trying to pronounce the jaw-breaking title "Oyinatumba" as best as he could.
"I be Chief the Honorable Dr. Sir, Joshua Unafefe, Oyinatumba I of Umudioha Kingdom!"
"Sir, you filled Oyaii Trumbaa as part of your name, and it is not the name on your passport.
Is Oyaii Trumbaa your last name? I mean, is that your father's

name?"

"You dey ask for my father? My father him don die for long time. My name be Congressman Chief the Honorable Sir Dr. Joshua Unafefe, Oyinatumba 1 of Umudioha Kingdom. You no see that there for my form?" Chief Unafefe said angrily, almost getting crude and insulting.

"I am sorry, sir, but you have not explained any definite reasons why you want to enter the United States, and there are many inconsistencies in your application documents."

Chief Unafefe's passport was quickly marked with the visa rejection stamp and returned to him. Chief Unafefe collected back the passport and raising his hand to his face, he saluted the consular officer:

"Thanks Sir Madam!" He believed that he had gotten the visa.

It was on his way out that another visa applicant explained to him that the immediate return of his passport signified a denial of visa. Chief Unafefe could not believe his ears.

"Wetin that Oyibo woman mean?" he exclaimed.

"E-fit be say him no know say na me be the person wey them driver come collect this morning for house".

He turned to get back to the counter to explain himself again to the consular officer. But the latter was already attending to some other applicant. Chief Unafefe was promptly escorted out by the stern-looking security man.

As Chief Unafefe got out of the embassy fuming, he told the first inquirer who asked him whether he was successful,

"That small girl she know not what him de talk. In any case that one be only a formality. I believe say, my visa go be for the other passport which my agent hold."

The agent was at hand to reassure Chief Unafefe with the second fake passport apparently fully done with "an American visa". He immediately collected back from Chief Unafefe the first passport on which the visa denial was stamped.

The agent's plan was that Chief Unafefe would have proceeded with the genuine visa if that was granted. But in the event of the visa being denied (which was the case), there were alternatives—even if they were not genuine alternatives. The apparent fulfillment of the deal with a passport bearing a fake visa ensured that the full amount of the agent's fees was paid.

"Thank you very much. I for no need see that ye-ye small girl in the first instance sef," Chief Unafefe told the agent as he collected the second passport bearing the fake visa. He unzipped his purse once again and emptied half of the dollar contents into the agent's hand in appreciation.

He then turned around and headed for the kiosk where he had deposited his three very sophisticated cell phones. He was the last person but one for that day's interview, and he had spent so much time at the gate of the embassy. He also had spent quite some time with the interviewer who could not understand him.

When he rushed out from the queue to deposit his phone at the kiosk, Chief Unafefe had dropped his three cell phones and one hundred dollars as advance payment for custody of the phones. He thereafter had rushed back to take his place in the queue. He did not wait to collect his receipt, which the kiosk owner had detached and dropped for him on the counter. A smart tout who stood by had walked up and collected the receipt as soon as Chief Unafefe walked off from the kiosk.

With the receipt, the tout had returned a short time later. He promptly claimed the three cell phones as soon as he noticed that the depositor was safely within the embassy premises.

"I wan claim back my phones," Chief Unafefe had told the kiosk owner after he came out from the embassy.

But the kiosk owner had only one more cell phone left unclaimed and it was not Chief Unafefe's.

"Let me see your receipt sir?" the kiosk owner requested.

"Which receipt?" Chief Unafefe replied.

"Where is the receipt which I gave you when you deposited the phones?" the kiosk owner asked while bringing out the lone remaining cell phone, believing that Chief Unafefe was the owner.

"But you no give me any receipt. What kind question be that?"

As the surprised kiosk owner kept staring at Chief Unafefe, the owner of the one remaining cell phone walked up to the kiosk and deposited her receipt for the phone, which the kiosk owner promptly delivered without further question after confirming that the tag on the cell phone matched the receipt.

"Make I get my cell phones immediately or I go deal with you!" Chief Unafefe shouted at the kiosk owner.

"Please, sir, make you carry your trouble *commot* from me. Me I no get strength to argue", the kiosk owner replied.

The rage of the former tout in Chief Unafefe was stirred to fever pitch.

"You, rat, you want steal my expensive phones," Chief Unafefe yelled as he jerked his massive frame forward and reached for the neck of the beleaguered kiosk owner.

A cry of "Help! Help!" rang out from the kiosk owner.

Within a minute, other kiosk owners, who hawked wares and other hawkers on the other side of the road in front of the embassy building, street urchins and all, rallied around in aid of their colleague. The first grabbed Chief Unafefe by the waist. The other two grabbed him by both hands. The third pulled the gold chain off his neck. The next one grabbed the gold watch and tore it off Chief Unafefe's wrist, wounding him in the process. The others threw him to the ground. They overpowered him and pummeled him, kicked him, and tore his expensive jacket off his back.

"Agent! Agent! Where you be? Them wan kill me-o-o!", Chief Unafefe yelled on top of his voice.

But the cry did not bring the agent to Chief Unafefe's rescue. The latter was smart enough not to rush to his client's rescue in the midst of such an angry mob. The agent rather ran up to the gate of the embassy to request the help of the embassy police in defense of his client.

(The touts and street urchins beat and stripped Chief Unafefe naked and left him on the road and fled at the sight of the police!)

But the embassy police said they were not authorized to leave their duty posts. They however radioed other policemen nearby. By the time the cops arrived, Chief Unafefe had been stripped naked to the undergarments. He was also bleeding from the corner of his mouth. Everything he had on him had been snatched away by the angry mob.

Only the passport with the fake visa that the agent provided was found some distance from the kiosk. It fell off one of the attacking hawkers as he ran away from the police. The rampaging mob dispersed at the sight of a siren-blowing police vehicle. Even the kiosk owner in whose defense the other hawkers had assembled had also run away at the sight of the approaching police vehicle.

Chief Unafefe was thus rescued from the mob, but he was certainly not in one piece.

He had a shirt donated by the agent tied around his waist to cover his nakedness before the police vehicle drove him back to his residence. They had wanted to drive him straight to the hospital because of his multiple bruises and the bleeding on his lips. But Chief Unafefe had opted to be driven straight to his house. He did not want the publicity, which his going naked to hospital would generate.

As the police vehicle came to a halt in front of Chief Unafefe's massive mansion one of the officers, apparently the youngest and most junior of the three asked Chief Unafefe,

"Chief, you own this fine house?"

Chief Unafefe even when he was still deeply engrossed with the events of the previous five hours could not ignore the eulogy. He immediately replied,

"Yes this one it be only one of my many fine houses. You no know say I be The Honorable?"

The inevitable request for hand-out then came from the young officer,

"Chief, you go find something for your boys?"

Apparently, the officers had forgotten that they were not at one of Konganoga's scandal-ridden airports or at a toll-collecting road-block. They forgot they were dealing, not with one of the poor wretched of the Earth along the poorly-maintained roads, but with one of the country's *Honorables*. The latter would hear no evil and see no evil for as long as their gargantuan salaries and allowances were paid in Karuja and the state capitals.

The meanness in Chief Unafefe immediately manifested. He had been rescued and taken to his house with a borrowed shirt tied around his waist to help cover his nakedness.

As soon as the police car conveying the beleaguered and badly traumatized Honorable pulled up in front of the latter's house, Chief Unafefe immediately opened the door of the car and without as much as a word of simple courteous appreciation, he banged the car door and disappeared into his mansion.

Obviously, he did not want to create a scene by being seen almost naked by passers-by.

But it was not in his reckoning that a word of appreciation to officers who rescued him, would certainly not have done him any harm.

Chief Unafefe had never had it so bad as an *Honorable*. He had never been so humiliated all his life, not even as a road-side beggar.

"That me Oyinatumba who even big people fear for everywhere go get naked by street urchins, people who no qualify to be my driver, cook or steward it no fit happen," Chief Unafefe lamented. He felt that that kind of humiliation was not possible. But it had happened. The negative publicity that Chief Unafefe was trying to avoid was about to come in monumental proportions.

Chief Unafefe spent the greater part of the night trying to figure out what to do to avenge his humiliation.

The police had not made any arrest at the site of Chief Unafefe's attack. It was an open place, and before their arrival, the attacking mob had dispersed. None of them could be identified. Only a few press photographers, who often lurked around the embassies hunting for newsworthy events, were still lurking around. Chief Unafefe only wished that they did not snap images of him naked as the policemen helped him into the police vehicle.

"I go deal with that kiosk man who steal my phones and who cause those *agbero* (hoodlum) useless boys to come attack me. I go teach him say power pass power. I go lock him and him kiosk up for police cell till him produce my cell phones and till him go produce all those *agbero* boys who come attack me. I go show them pepper. I go get police make them beat them and torture them till them mama no go know them again," Chief Unafefe kept threatening the kiosk owners and swearing to himself.

About 3:00 AM, it occurred to Chief Unafefe that since some Press men were around the embassy that afternoon that he needed to see them so that they would not carry the news.
He did not want publicity about his going to the embassy, and that was why he went as a private citizen and not as *The Honorable*. He felt that if he did not see the press boys, one of them might carry the news of his attack. That would be negative publicity for him—a congressman, an honorary doctor of philosophy, a knight, and a chief!

It was already too late into the night for Chief Unafefe to start making contacts and sending emissaries to the media houses. But he was so weak and had pains and bruises all over his body from the beating that he had been given. His lips were swollen, and his eyelids were bloated. He decided to wait until morning.
He had planned to buy up all the print runs of any newspaper that carried the news. He decided to send his boys to buy up every copy of any newspaper that carried the story. That way, he would ensure that not many people would read the story. Chief Unafefe did not reckon with the radio and television.

"I go get the newsboys to take photographs of that thief in the kiosk who stole my cell phones. His kiosk go disappear forever after tomorrow morning. After that, everybody go know say I no de answer Oyinatumba for nothing. Before now I don deal with bigger people till them talk truth, not to think of that little brat. And when I finish with that kiosk man, I go get Parliament make we pass law say nobody go carry business go for front of America embassy again. That way those foolish boys no go get work again. After that, them go know say na big man wey them beat. After this one those street urchins no go take eye see America embassy again"

Chief Unafefe did not sleep most of that night. He took repeated doses of pain-killing tablets to suppress his pains to no avail. The pain in his mind was much more than the pains from his swollen eyes and lips. He did not know which one was the more important loss to lament about. His costly gold watch and the raw gold chain that he bought for half a million dollars were stolen. Even the ring for his wedding with his estranged wife and another costly gold ring, which he wore to the interview, had been pulled from his fingers and stolen. His two fingers were traumatized in the process of forced pulling of the rings. In addition to all that, he had the beating of his life.

The agony surpassed what the former train-commuting Unafefe felt on the morning that he discovered that his guide had stolen all the money that he had collected for many weeks from begging in the trains as a feigned blind man. Hitherto the latter incident, the disappearance of his money in the hotel room had been the worst experience of his life. He remembered that he had to flee from a lucrative begging job for fear of being detected as fake. This time, he had to hide in his house from the press because of the beating he got from some street urchins and beggars. Chief Unafefe tossed around in his bed most of the night, planning how to avoid unnecessary publicity and how to avenge the humiliation that he suffered.

About 6:05 AM, when he was just about to fall asleep, his home phone rang. It was Bode, his friend.

"Oyinatumba, this one be you? Thank God you still de talk!" That was the frantic inquiry from the caller, an old friend of Chief Unafefe. The latter was another former motor park tout who Chief Unafefe had helped to set up a motor transport company for, in Karuja.

"Bode, what happen?" Chief Unafefe asked with pains from his traumatized lips. The pain increased with every word.

"I just come hear for news say it be like they kill you for embassy yesterday," Bode added.

For a while, Chief Unafefe who could tell a lie at the drop of the hat, thought of denying the attack. But he didn't know the extent which the story had gone. Also, he was not sure whether or not some photographs had been taken of the scene by the ever-present *Press boys*. He, therefore, decided to admit the occurrence of the attack but to play down the story.

"Yes, my brother, I just go embassy go see the US consul general, and on my way back, some of these area boys come embarrass me small. But nothing to worry. They no harm me. I bring my hand out for motor, and they only come snatch away my wristwatch. No problem. I don lock them up for cell. Everything now be OK," Chief Unafefe falsely boasted, attempting to diminish the magnitude of the assault. He did not want people to ever know that a chief of his stature was so humiliated.

"Thank God. Them announce for news say them beat you till them tire. They also say them strip you naked and leave you for dead till police come take you to hospital. Na him make I worry come phone you." Congressman Bode said. Like Unafefe who helped install him, Honorable Bode was a crooked poorly-educated and looting legislator. And so, he correctly fancied that Chief Unafefe was not telling the truth. But he felt relieved that his comrade in treasury-looting was safe.

All the sleep disappeared from Chief Unafefe's eyes. Even the aches and pains appeared momentarily suppressed. He jumped out of bed and made his way to his sitting room.

He turned on the radio and the television. That was it! All the news media had gone to town with the news: "Chief Unafefe Mobbed," "The Honorable Chief Unafefe Stripped Naked at US embassy," "Oyinatumba Humiliated," "Chief Unafefe Beaten and Left for Dead," "Congressman Attacked at US embassy."

The headlines of all the dailies were about how Chief Unafefe was stripped naked in front of the American embassy.

News channel after news channel carried different versions of the story. But one thing was common with all the versions— Congressman Chief the Honorable Sir Dr. Joshua Unafefe, Oyinatumba I of Umudioha Kingdom had been beaten up and stripped naked in front of the American embassy in Karuja.
Three of the newspapers and two of the television networks had vivid photographs of the Honorable Chief Dr. Unafefe, in underwear, being led into a police vehicle.
One of the newspapers had described the chief as "a sparsely literate man who previously had no visible means of livelihood, but who had recently become stupendously rich."

It was a terrible day for the Oyinatumba. The chill that was in consonance with his chieftaincy title, Oyinatumba, appeared to be catching the title-holder himself!

Chapter 20

VENGEANCE AND THE HONORABLE ROBBER

Chief Unafefe's several travails in life had greatly prepared him for taking up challenges even at short notice.

Immediately after he learned that all the news media were awash with adverse news about his unfortunate experience at the embassy, he got out of bed, and despite his pains and his multiple bruises, he stepped out of the house and attempted to stem down the circulation. He knew that there was little that he could do about the news that had already left the electronic media. But he was determined to minimize further circulation of the news from the print media.

He got his chauffeur to take him straight to his office in the congress building. There, he issued a rebuttal of the story that he was beaten up at the American embassy. But true pictures didn't tell lies. People who knew Chief Unafefe already knew that even when he was caught in the act in any situation that he could go on denying.

"I wan make it be for record that the story about my beat-up no be true. Na my political opponents and enemies of progress de spread that lie", Chief Unafefe told the press men on being questioned.

After the lie, which he told with careless abandon, the pain on his lips reminded him of his swollen lips. He, thus, was constrained to modify his story.

"This swelling you see for my lips it be one small accident I been get for staircase yesterday," Chief Unafefe lied.

When accosted by one of the reporters and shown the photographs after his official denial of the story, Chief Unafefe simply stated, "It fit be me it fit be another Unafefe." Then turning to the reporter, he said, "For your place, only one man de answer Unafefe?"

"But is the photograph yours?" the reporter had asked Chief Unafefe.

"Na only one man de look like this for your place?" Chief Unafefe had denied his own photograph with a question.

There was no pinning down of the former thug who could lie and swear that a chicken which he was caught stealing was not a chicken but a wild goose.

Having literally brushed aside all direct answers to questions, Chief Unafefe planned his vengeance against the kiosk owner, whom he said was responsible for his travails at the embassy.

Despite the fact that the police had come to rescue him from the wrath of the hawkers, and in spite of the fact that it was actually Chief Unafefe who initiated the attack by grabbing the kiosk owner, Chief Unafefe had returned to the front of the embassy two days after the incident with a busload of twenty thugs who he had recruited from the local motor park. He had come looking for the kiosk owner. But the latter had earlier been warned about the possibility of such an attack. He had therefore decided to shut his doors to the public for some days. When Chief Unafefe arrived at the scene and did not find the man, the thugs had proceeded to destroy the kiosk with hammers and clubs. Chief Unafefe had been used to taking the law into his hands. He had also been used to getting his way after such incidents by massive bribing of law enforcement personnel.

He had his way with such incidents. He would plan and finance the event but would ensure that he was not seen in the premises of the crime. He would ultimately stay in the background and arrange legal defense or settlement for the involved personnel. In this particular instance, however, things had worked a little differently. He had taken personal charge in directing of the reprisal attack against the property of the poor kiosk owner.

Because of the publicity given to the beating up incident that occurred two days previously, the authorities of the embassy had requested that security around the embassy be beefed up. More policemen in mufti had been deployed to the area.

As soon as the thugs started knocking down the kiosk, therefore, the embassy security, who had sighted the goings-on, alerted the police stationed nearby. Within minutes, in a rapid response that was uncharacteristic in Konganoga, the police were at the scene. They swooped on the thugs and arrested seven of them. The others fled.

Unafefe was remotely directing the thugs' activities from his office. He was on telephone contact with the leader of the assault team when the police swooped on them. He was still communicating with Ebuka who was also called Titus. Ebuka was leading the thugs when the police sirens were heard some distance away.

Ebuka, whose nickname was "Strangler", was a very massive and ruthless thug. He was known to be the points man for all daredevilry kidnapping and muggings, which were masterminded by Chief Unafefe. During election times, he led all the disrupting of the opponents' campaign rallies. During such campaign disruptions, he had on two previous occasions been seen to hold the chief bodyguards of the opponents by the neck until they were choked to death. He had had very visible red tattoo marks of skull and crossbones all around his neck and had been in and out of jail several times. He was indeed on bail with many criminal charges outstanding against him as of the day that Chief Unafefe sent him to organize the embassy kiosk raid.

In the chokehold death as well as in most other cases that led to his arrests, Strangler had been bailed either by Chief Unafefe or by a surrogate of the latter.

At the time of Strangler's arrest, he was still on the phone with Chief Unafefe, who was indeed still issuing instructions to him over the phone.

"Listen to me, Strangler. I no want make that man escape. Him go be around his kiosk. Fish him out and wring his neck. No use of guns. Strangler, Strangler, are you there?
Hello. Hello . . ."
Chief Unafefe could not easily procure the release of the thugs. Reports had it that many of the arrested men had reported that they were "recruited by one *Honorable*" by the name Chief Unafefe."

The involvement of Strangler in the case made it the more dramatic. Virtually everybody who ever listened to the news or had followed crime reports in Karuja must have heard Strangler's name mentioned several times. In bank robberies, kidnappings, car snatchings, politically motivated murders, almost anything that was evil and barbaric, the name Strangler would, one way or the other, be associated with it.

In one particular incident, after robbing a particular popular bank, Strangler had the street leading to the bank strewn with one-hundred-dollar bills from his vehicle as he drove away. He had targeted the bank as they were loading money into bullion vans to deposit with the central bank. The money, which he scattered along the streets, ran into tens of millions of dollars. But he escaped with many more millions. As his escape vehicles deliberately scattered the money along his escape route, thousands of people, including some law enforcement men in uniform, flooded the streets and struggled to gather the free money, thereby obstructing the streets and making police chase more difficult and hazardous.

It was on the twentieth day of December that year, and Strangler, as he sprayed the money, also sprayed printed leaflets with the inscription "Merry Christmas, from your friend Strangler."
After that incident, Strangler became an instant friend to many. Despite his notoriety, the money-spraying incident made Strangler very popular. Many people, who had never owned five hundred

dollars for Christmas, collected as much as fifteen to twenty pieces of the one-hundred-dollar bills, which Strangler sprayed on the streets.

Most of the people who collected the money were jobless people, beggars, and street urchins. Strangler made the Christmas worthwhile for hundreds of families. Many families who could not afford a chicken for Christmas in corruption-ridden Konganoga republic were able to slaughter a goat or a ram for the festivity courtesy of Strangler's "magnanimity". Not even Unafefe who represented the people and participated in the financial brigandage at the nation's capital city, had ever remembered his constituents the way "Strangler the gangster" appeared to have put smiles on people's faces that Christmas, albeit with criminally-acquired funds.

During the Christmas sermon in a church in Karuja that year, the officiating minister had condemned people who stole. His listeners did not stir. But immediately, when the preacher said that "thieves like Strangler will not smell the gates of heaven," there were loud boos against the minister in the church. Some people walked out in protest. During the tithe offering that followed, not up to fifty people out of the more than one thousand celebrants went forward to give tithe, all in protest against the allusion to Strangler as one unworthy of heaven.
During the following Sunday service, which was the New Year's Day service, the officiating minister had to apologize to the congregation for preaching against one who the officiating minister now had to address "more correctly" as "the people's friend—Titus Ebuka, alias Strangler." .....
Thereafter the offering queue once again elongated.

Chapter 21

A PEACOCK HUMBLED

After the embassy-beating incident, Chief Unafefe did not want to get into any more negative publicity too soon. The publicity that was brewing over the arrest of Strangler and the other band of thugs was not fun for Chief Unafefe. He had tried unsuccessfully to bulldoze his way as usual through the security agencies to no avail. The fact that the assault was directly in front of the American embassy made it a little more difficult for the culprits to be treated with kid gloves by the public safety officials. All the officers that Chief Unafefe gave money to ensure Strangler's release collected the money but did nothing.

The culprits were charged to court but were released on bail. The bail was guaranteed by Chief Unafefe even when he had earlier not wanted to get involved in that case after the very negative publicity, which he had received not too long previously.

All eyes were on Chief Unafefe on the first day that he came to his office in the National Assembly building after the beating incident. Every member of congress wanted to take a look at his face to confirm the report that the member, who was very popular because of his very bad English and his usual belligerent attitude to even innocuous statements from other members, was indeed taught a befitting lesson.

Every member wanted to have a chat with him to hear his version of the conflicting reports. Many wanted to see him to confirm whether indeed the boastful chief was given a black eye as was reported.

It was not fun at all for Chief Unafefe. He did not want to answer so many questions especially on an issue that was so unpleasant for him. Because of the barrage of questions and in order to give time for the story to die down, Chief Unafefe decided to bring forward his proposed travel date to the United States. He decided to travel almost immediately. He readily changed his booking and prepared everything for the trip.

"I want go America go rest small," he told his friends. "Life in this Konganoga Republic has become too monotonous. It be too much money-money, too much thief-thief" Chief Unafefe said.

Having now made it public that he was traveling out of the country, Chief Unafefe felt that there, being nothing more to hide, that he might as well have obtained a diplomatic passport instead of the problematic regular passport and visa.

He mentioned his intention to one of his friends, and the friend agreed completely with him.

Chief Unafefe, therefore, proceeded to process a diplomatic passport and visa. He was asked to submit all previous passports containing recent visas, which he already had. It was in the process of reconciliation of records that it was discovered that the visa that the agent had procured for Chief Unafefe was indeed a fake visa.

When this information got to Chief Unafefe, he was extremely furious. His fury was partly because he lost so much money and valuables in the process of procuring the visa. He was even angrier because of the fact that he was subjected to the greatest beating of his life in the quest for that visa. He immediately sent for the agent. Of course, the agent anticipated that there might be problems and had closed shop and relocated. He had collected from Chief Unafefe more money for a single transaction than he could have made in a lifetime of visa-faking and visa-agency business.

Chief Unafefe swore that he would deal with the agent appropriately. He threatened hell and brimstone and sent out his boys in search of the agent. But it was all futile.

The man had collected so much money that he could afford to relocate to any city of his choice away from the reaches of the man who he jokingly referred to, among his friends, as "Crooked

Honorable and money miss road."
Eventually, diplomatic strings were pressed, and Chief Unafefe was given a diplomatic passport and visa. It was so straightforward that chief Unafefe kept blaming himself for not toeing that clean line of action from the beginning.

A team of five assistants had accompanied Chief Unafefe to the airport. As usual, he was thoroughly embroidered in a three-piece suit with a new set of gold chain and rings and gold watch to match. He carried a small swagger stick and even though he hardly ever wrote anything because of limited literacy, he always had three or four expensive gold pens sticking from the breast pocket of his coat.

As was usual with him, he had a completely shaved head. He had fallen in love with the pomade Vaseline petroleum jelly since the days when he applied this jelly to his eyes to feign blindness. His clean-shaved head shining with the applied Vaseline petroleum jelly against his massive frame, large jaws, and small head gave him the look of one of the large prehistoric animals that had gone extinct. He had purchased a first-class ticket and was given VIP treatment at the checking in counter.

At the screening point, he had initially resisted removing his shoes. He felt that as an Honorable Congressman and a chief that he would be afforded a waiver of that requirement. It was only when he saw shoes being removed by all expatriate passengers, many of whom he viewed with much awe, that he consented to remove his own shoes. He had never traveled out of the country and had felt that the "big man" status that he enjoyed in Konganoga—a status which carried him through many obstacles and which placed him above the law—would equally carry him through a circumvention of international airport regulations.

At the duty-free shop section of the airport, Chief Unafefe was so fascinated at how nice things on display were. He moved from counter to counter admiring the trinkets, the cosmetics, the different types of wines and carvings. Since he had never traveled out of Konganoga and all his flights had been limited to local airports in Konganoga, virtually everything fascinated him.

"If this kind thing dey here for Konganoga, how much better it go be for America?"

He did not see many people buying freely at the gift shops, so he only descended on the colorful magazines and purchased bundles of them. As he sat down in the VIP waiting area, he crossed his legs and kept admiring the photographs since he could not read fast. He felt very satisfied with himself.

As Chief Unafefe sat in the assigned first-class seat, he reclined back on the seat and heaved to himself, "Chei! Unafefe him don arrive proper! (Yes, Unafefe has finally arrived!)"

First-class passengers were feted and pampered by the airline. They could ask for any type of wine and any type of meal that they wanted. They were given a wide choice. They had much wider room and leg space. They had unlimited access to music, and news magazines were provided freely for them.

As Chief Unafefe sat and watched the economy-class passengers enter, he felt such a sense of importance that he promised himself that he would begin to travel every three months. He said within him,

"This one it be like proper heaven. Even sef, these ladies wey de serve food for plane, them look like proper angels too. If man fit marry angel, perhaps them go allow me marry one of them, That one, I go know say I don arrive proper heaven." (He likened the first-class facility to visit to heaven and the cabi crew to angels. He wondered how great it would be if he were allowed to marry one of the angels, the female cabin crew members! So depraved in thoughts and crude in utterances was the near-illiterate and rustic Umudioha *Honorable* ex-robber!

Chief Unafefe was not a good family man. In his depravity coupled with his very limited exposure, he was of the opinion that money, the billions of dollars which his outrageous Konganogan legislator's salary and allowances had provided him, he had believed that he could purchase anything. He had married four times and had ended up divorcing in each case. He was weak in morals and was very lustful. Nothing interested him as much as looking at the legs of young ladies and muttering silly comments. As he sat there in the first-class section of the plane, he could not take his eyes off the ladies who were doing their legitimate in-flight duties.

Chief Unafefe called for red wine, and shortly after that was supplied, he called for white wine. Then he called for juice. And in each case, he felt that he was obligated to exhaust the quantity supplied. After taking so much fluid, he felt very uncomfortable. As one of the female flight attendants was walking past Chief Unafefe raised his hand in the manner of a timid school boy who wanted to ask a question: "Fine lady," he shouted "I beg, come. Una get any medicine for this una place? E-bi like my belly wan burst." He was requesting for medication that would relieve his abdominal bloating.

The flight attendant did not quite understand Chief Unafefe. But as the latter kept rubbing his palm over his abdomen, the attendant felt that he probably wanted to use the toilet.

"The toilet is over there, sir."

Chief Unafefe understood and headed for the toilet. Before he could get to the toilet, he regurgitated and vomited massively on the floor of the aisle!

He created quite a scene, and the situation was compounded by the fact that not many people could quite comprehend his pidgin English. None of the flight attendants could understand him.

The saving grace was that there were many Konganogans in the plane. One of them, who apparently was a nurse, helped pacify the obviously agitated Chief Unafefe.

Having emptied his stomach after the vomiting, Chief Unafefe felt very much relieved and went back to his seat a much more humbled man. He did not ask for any more food or drink for the remainder of the flight.

By the time the plane reached Atlanta Georgia, which was the flight's first port of entry in the United States, Chief Unafefe felt he was in another planet. He had always boasted to his other former thug friends, whom he left behind in Kuveri on his elevation to Karuja, that Karuja was like London. He had never been to London, but he often described Karuja in very glowing terms.

"That place it be like London and New York," Chief Unafefe often told his bewildered friends who would usually gather to listen to his stories at the early stages of his entry into Konganoga's congress.

After he had stayed in Karuja for about three months and gathered hundreds of millions of dollars in salaries and allowance, it became more difficult for him to accommodate all his friends—most of whom, he felt, had become far below his status. He, however, never forgot some close ones even as he did not have too much time for them. He, indeed, had initially collected one of his close friends as his Personal Assistant and another as his Secretary. It was later that it became obvious to him that he could not succeed with two virtual illiterates in control of his Constituency Office. He had then to hire a properly educated assistant and secretary. That was before he made Ade his Personal Assistant at the request of Chief Suleiman. He had, at that time, converted the previous Personal Assistant to a personal guard. That was a role he had performed for the late Chief Suleiman.

Chapter 22

SIGHTS AND SOUNDS OF THE BILLIONAIRE *HONORABLE*

The first one week that Chief Unafefe stayed in New York was like a dream to him.
His nephew, in whose house he stayed, lived in the Long Island area of New York.
For the first two days of Chief Unafefe's visit, his nephew had taken time off work to entertain him and show him around the place. After that, the poor young man had gone back to his postal services work which he supplemented with security work at the week-ends.

After the first two days of staying indoors, Chief Unafefe decided to take a walk around his neighborhood. His nephew lived in a multiple apartment complex of more than one hundred units. When Chief Unafefe came out of the room, he could not see anybody along the corridor. He walked up and down the corridor, and everywhere was so quiet.
He wondered whether all the other people had packed out or whether other people actually lived in those apartments.

His nephew had left for work and had directed his uncle, Chief Unafefe, on how to warm the food in the microwave oven whenever he was hungry. For more than five years since he started making money from *The Chambers* and related high-profile criminal activities, Chief Unafefe had never had cause to enter the kitchen. He always had one kind of steward or cook or some other attendants and servants to attend to his needs. Even when he was still Chief Suleiman's thug, he always had his meals from "mama put" the roadside food vendors.
He did not have as much as a cooking pot in his house. It was only after he started marrying his series of wives that he had some cooking utensil at home. After he moved to Karuja as a

191

congressman, all meals were from five-star hotels all expenses paid by government.

In his nephew's house in New York Chief Unafefe wondered how a chief, an *Honorable* and a big Sir Knight like him, would be expected to go to the kitchen and prepare his meals. He started wondering whether it would not have been better for him to check into a hotel as he had contemplated doing before his nephew urged him to stay in his apartment with him. Little did the billionaire Konganogan Honorable imagine that he was going into a one bed-room apartment with his nephew. Apart from the company he would have in his nephew's house Chief Unafefe was afraid that if he stayed in a hotel he might neither understand the English nor would his Pidgin English be understood by the hotel staff.

In Karuja he could use any combination of tenses and any admixture of words and he would still be understood. But there in New York Chief Unafefe's near illiteracy stared him in the face and he did not want to make a laughing stock of himself if he could help it.

Hence, he had opted to stay with his nephew.

But going to prepare his meals in the microwave, was a lot belittling for Chief Unafefe.

"What kind country be this one?" Chief Unafefe muttered to himself.

"What kind *oversea* be this wey rich man no get cook and steward? Even for Konganoga we get them for plenty. Even small rich man for government service get small cook for house. For Konganoga this my nephew Mark, who be graduate, him go get cook or steward or both. But look at him for this place him de cook him own food. Him de do three different work yet him no get enough money for to hire cook and steward. But, no way for Congressman Chief Doctor, Sir Unafefe the Oyinatumba of Umudioha go come here come cook him own food," a disappointed Chief Unafefe said in exasperation.

By 5:30 PM when his nephew came back, Chief Unafefe had not yet had his lunch.

He told Mark his nephew, that he should hire a cook and that he was prepared to pay the monthly salary of the cook.

"Look here Mark, I go pay the cook's salary even if it be double what I pay my cooks at home," Chief Unafefe said. When, however, the Chief was told what it would cost to maintain a cook in New York, he added, "Then everybody should go become cook."

"Look here Mark, me I get plenty money, but no way I fit pay common cook that kind money which you talk." Chief Unafefe said when he was told what a personal professional short duration chef would cost.

An arrangement was struck for home delivery of his choice foods from an African restaurant in the city.

On the morning of his fifth day in New York, Chief Unafefe phoned his nephew at work. "Mark, make you send your driver to come carry me go town. I don tire for stay watch this television all day. I want go barb my hair and see how Oyibo barber be."

Chief Unafefe's nephew had a hard time explaining to his uncle that it was not usual for people to have drivers in America. "Uncle, you can't afford to keep a personal driver here. Not even the wealthy people can always afford to maintain full time chauffeurs," the nephew told Chief Unafefe. You have Uber and Lyft drivers and numerous taxis who you can readily call to drive you wherever you wish to go to. And they are inexpensive and readily available." Mark reasoned with his uncle.

Chief Unafefe was stunned.

"Mark, you forget say me, I be *The Honorable*. I be Chief and I be *Chambers* stalwart. Big money for ordinary cook, I no go fit pay. But money for personal driver and personal car no go be problem for me. How you come say that somebody for America him no afford a chauffeur when ordinary traders for Konganoga fit pay two or three drivers? Even ordinary P.A's to *The Honorables* in Konganoga parliament fit afford to keep chauffeurs who drive them to work and drive their wives to the market and to the hair salons. And every senior civil servant get "driver" who washes his or her car and does other small chores for them including taking the children to school and often doing some domestic assignments for them. How come that for America where people get more money them no fit get drivers?"

Chief Unafefe paused for a while and fixed a straight gaze on his young nephew. Then with a countenance of genuine surprise he continued, "Again, if it be because of money, look, Mark, I get plenty money. I want rent car, and I want make you help me get personal driver. I go de pay am well-well. Any amount him want as salary I go pay. I want take photo with my American driver. Later, I also go want make I get beautiful American girl friend like those ones I see for plane who dress smartly and look like angels. We go talk about that one later. I go show the photo of my American car and driver to all those my friends for Karuja to show them say, na me be proper *Honorable* and proper *Oyinatumba*. You know, say many of my friends for that parliament, them be afraid to even travel because them no fit communicate or interact. But me, The Honorable Chief Unafefe, Me I come refine well-well. I no fear for any situation. Na him make them call me Oyinatumba."

As Chief Unafefe persisted with his request for a driver (chauffeur), his nephew had to advertise for one. At Chief Unafefe's request, also a limousine was rented for a full month. "I want make you get me that long car wey long like airplane. I also want make you get me the kind driver wey go de wear uniform for drive me around the town. I see say that for this America them like big things well-well. For me, money no be problem, I get am plenty-plenty, perhaps even pass your President for this your America. Even sef, how much them de pay your driver here." Personal drivers on short term basis may charge as much as twenty dollars per hour or even a little more. And, they will ask for a minimum of twelve hours engagement for a minimum of 3 to six months duration since it is a short duration employment" Mark said

Chief Unafefe surprised his nephew when he offered to pay fifty dollars an hour for his chauffeur. Mark wished that his uncle would have hired him for that assignment.

"Twenty dollars per hour? Get me one and I go pay him fifty dollars per hour or even more. Look, even one hundred dollar per hour I go pay!" Chief Unafefe offered.

"I would readily have taken leave of absence from my job to drive my uncle around for any length of time." A perplexed mark quietly stated.

The hired chauffeur was very excited about Chief Unafefe's offer. Since he emigrated from the Philippines to the United States three years earlier, he had never had it so good. He phoned his friends to tell them that he had landed "a bonanza from an African king." Chief Unafefe offered to retain the driver for ten hours a day inculcating two hour paid break time for every day of the week including weekends. He paid the driver double for hours in excess of the forty-hour week. Mark's eyeballs were almost popping out as Chief Unafefe dipped his hands into his large wallet and pulled out twenty pieces of one-hundred-dollar bills and dropped on the table for the chauffeur. He then said, "This one it be advance payment. I go do you well if you drive me well-well for this New York. I hear say this your New York it get plenty thief-thief like some part of my country. Before-before, I know no say Oyibo people also de thief. I beg you, I be Chief for my country. I be *Honorable* too. Even now I also be doctor and sir.

"So, I no want make you take me go for any kind place wey those una New York thief them people dey. Na him make I come tell this my little brother say make him get me personal driver. Like I been say before, I go do you well-well if you drive me safely until I go back home. You hear?" (I don't want you to take me to where your New York thieves operate. I didn't know that your white people also have their own share of robbers. For my own protection I instructed my nephew to procure me a good personal driver. I will compensate you handsomely if you drive me safely).

195

Chief Unafefe's past and his experience with his part of the world had made him come to believe that he needed to pay handsomely to purchase the loyalty of an employee who ordinarily would see himself as doing his job. Coming from a society where bribery permeated almost all facets of society, Chief Unafefe felt that he needed to bribe his hired chauffeur before the latter would do his job.

I wonder what kind of money my uncle made in Konganoga that enables him to spend so lavishly and so carelessly." Mark mused as he listened to his uncle who had not offered even a dime to his nephew to enable the latter to finance the *Honorable's* sometimes ridiculous domestic demands and lavish lifestyle.

Chief Unafefe insisted on travelling to as many places of interest as possible. He traveled from New York to California to see Hollywood.

"I want make I see that place where them stay make many of those big cinema. I also want see that famous town which them de call *Lassa Vega*. The day I come watch Cassius Clay come knock out Sonny Liston for boxing, I come swear say I must one day come visit that town where that fight come take place." Chief Unafefe said with an air of strong expectations. He painted the image of a seven-year-old who was greatly looking forward to unwrapping of his birthday packages. He obviously was looking forward to visiting the city of Las Vegas In Nevada as well as many other places of interest, which he had often watched in movies. He had heard so much of Las Vegas and admired so much of Mohammed Alli's boxing that he had come to believe (though wrongly) that the then Cassius Clay's so called 'Phantom Punch' that floored Sonny Liston, took place in Las Vegas instead of (correctly), in Lewiston Maine.

Unafefe had paid the flight for his New York driver to accompany him to Los Angeles California.

He also rented a hotel room for the lucky driver who often helped Chief Unafefe navigate through his language and other communication problems. As Chief Unafefe was driven round the bus that took tourists round Hollywood, Chief Unafefe was so fascinated by what he saw that it immediately occurred to him that it would be big business if he could replicate some of those things in his home town Umudioha.

"If I bring some of these things for Umudioha, I go make plenty money and Umudioha go become known all over the world." Chief Unafefe said.

Even with all his crudeness and his poor academic background, Chief Unafefe was a very bold and determined man. He was very daring and would never feel shy to go for what he wanted. Unfortunately, he would always ride the waves irrespective of any infringement of the legitimate interests and the fundamental rights of other people.

If the likes of Unafefe had a good education and were to channel their ingenuity into more progressive things, his country Konganoga would probably have benefited greatly.

Unafefe had approached the bus driver a black American and had said to her, "My sister which town you come from? Me I be Chief *the Honorable* Sir Dr. Joshua Unafefe, Oyinatumba I of Umudioha Kingdom. I know say you don hear of Umudioha. Na me be the Oyinatumba 1, the number one kingmaker for that place. I wan make I buy these machines come put them for Umudioha. My people go like them well-well."

The bus guide did not quite understand what Chief Unafefe said. But she could pick up the words buy and machine. So she politely told Chief Unafefe, "You can easily check in the Internet, sir."

On hearing the word sir used in addressing him, Chief Unafefe's face brightened up.

"So even people in America don come know say I be sir?" Chief Unafefe said to himself.

"It fit be them also know say I be chief and doctor. Even sef them fit know say I be the Honorable." He continued. Then, raising his voice a little more in self adulation the elated Chief Unafefe declared:

"Unafefe don arrive-o-o!" ("Unafefe has arrived now!"), he

shouted to the utter consternation of other passengers.

As soon as the bus tour came to an end, Chief Unafefe walked up again to the bus guide, who was now busy checking in a fresh set of passengers into the bus.
He brought out his wallet and pulled out five complimentary cards each with the coat of arms of the Republic of Konganoga and his name and array of titles boldly printed. He also pulled out ten pieces of one-hundred-dollar bills and thrust both the cards and the money into the hands of the bus guide.
"I want make I remind you say me be Chief the Honorable Sir Dr. Joshua Unafefe, Oyinatumba I of Umudioha Kingdom. My phone number dey for these cards. I want make you phone me tell me how much I go pay to buy this machine come put am for my town Umudioha. I even fit make you the manager. In that case I go pay you well-well pass the thing wey them de pay you here. Me, I be very happy say, women them de drive big machine like this one. I go be happy if you fit come for some months come teach my people say, woman's place it fit pass kitchen work. It go help us well-well. Thank you. You do well."
The bus driver was hesitant. But, Chief Unafefe thrust the cards and the money into the palm of the rather embarrassed bus driver and in a moment, he disembarked and was gone. He immediately headed back to the rented limousine that brought him to Hollywood, leaving the bewildered bus guide wondering whether the sudden gift of one thousand dollars was for good or for bad.

As Chief Unafefe stepped into the Northridge Center shopping mall in California, he kept wondering whether he was seeing a mirage or whether it was all real. When his limousine driver told him that there were even bigger and more beautiful places in town and in other cities in America, Chief Unafefe found it difficult to believe.
"Which kind people build all these things? Which kind brain them get?" He mused.
"It be like them get double brains. The wonderful thing here be

say, the Electricity people no de take light. Any time you touch switch, light go come. I also hear say them Police no de take bribe for road. *Poto-poto* pot hole no day for highway. Everybody de mind him business. Oyibo country fine-o-o!" Chief Unafefe shouted to himself. Even with all the man-made rot and decay in the social fiber of his home country, Chief Unafefe greatly appreciated decency and finesse. Within him he knew that his people seven thousand miles away possessed the talents that would have replicated what he beheld in America. He knew all too well that it was people like him, *Honorables* who were anything but honorable, who were responsible for the continuing decay. For one split second of introspection, he admitted that it was the likes of him who were responsible for the rot and decay. But it was only for one split second!

It was soon time for Chief Unafefe to leave for home. One month had passed by so quickly.
Chief Unafefe had already started feeling home-sick. He had started missing the homage that people paid him daily in Konganoga. He had started feeling lonely in spite of the many fascinations that New York City and the City of Los Angeles presented. He stopped short of proceeding North to see his much desired city of *Lassa Vega* (Las Vegas). He had been too absorbed by the fascinations in Los Angeles to make time for further exploration up North.
On getting back to New York, Chief Unafefe had felt that it would not be right if he spent one month in America without even knowing who his next-door neighbor was. The restless and pompous Chief was wondering why everybody seemed to mind their own business. He wondered why people did not talk loudly or hug themselves when they met in the streets. He had wondered why the people who lived adjacent his nephew in the apartment had not come to greet them in the mornings, or at least why they had not come knocking on the door to enquire about their welfare.
"How come your neighbors never come to greet us or at least

come to know how we are doing?" Chief Unafefe asked Mark. He had often asked his nephew what the names of the people who lived in the adjacent apartments were. Mark however, had simply replied that he did not know. He did not imagine how important it was for his uncle that he should know and possibly get into contact with the people who were his neighbors.

"You have been away from home for a long-long time, Mark. And so, you fit don forget say our people in Konganoga, we fit join in breakfast or dinner for our neighbor's pot without invitation. All neighbor know every other neighbor like him brother or sister. We always talk say that your neighbor always be your brother. But it be like say, for this America neighbor no de know him neighbor. It appear say, every one for himself. That kind behavior it no good." Since Mark did not seem to be moved by Chief Unafefe's view of friendly neighborliness, Chief Unafefe decided to check out for Mark's neighbor. He decided to extend show of good neighborliness to the occupants of the apartment to their right since that apartment showed more signs of human presence than all others.

"I fit go tomorrow go salute our neighbor. It go good if them come know say human being been live here. How man go just stay lock him door for day and for night against all neighbors. It be prison you dey so? Chief Unafefe queried.

On the next day, after his nephew left for work, Chief Unafefe decided to take a walk around the long corridors of the expansive apartment complex. Just as he shut the door to start his walk, he heard soft music coming from the adjacent apartment. Chief Unafefe was happy that, at least, his neighbors were indoors. "Thank God, these our neighbors them dey for house today. Make I go say good morning to them. At least them go know say we be good neighbors."

Chief Unafefe, therefore, walked up to the front door of the adjacent apartment to the right. He knocked loudly on the door and then called out, "Good morning-o-o! Na me your neighbor Chief Unafefe de greet you. Good morning! You sleep well for night?"

In the practice of his Konganogan people it was not unusual for neighbor to go wake up neighbor in the morning if only to show good neighborliness. Neighbors randomly check out on neighbors with no invitation and no warning and irrespective of the time of the day or night. And that is Konganoga!

As Chief Unafefe greeted at the top of his voice after knocking, the music from the room appeared to die down. When the music stopped, Unafefe felt that the loud music had not allowed the neighbors to hear his greetings earlier. He then knocked again and once again shouted, even in a louder tone:

"Neighbor, it's me. I come greet you-o-o. Good morning! It's me your neighbor, Chief Unafefe, it's me de greet-o-o."

Somebody appeared to have peeped through the door hole. Chief Unafefe waited, and on not hearing anything further, he again shouted, "Good morning, na your neighbor de greet so-o."

There was a gentle opening of the door and a middle-aged lady peeped out through the partially opened door.

As soon as Chief Unafefe saw the face of the lady, he smiled broadly, and thrusting out his hand as a show of courtesy. He wanted to shake the lady's hand while saying, "Ah! na mama baby. How you dey, Ma? (It's a baby's mother, how are you Madam)?"

In Konganoga, it was most unusual for neighbors not to know, or regularly greet themselves. A new entrant to the neighborhood was expected to go around calling up other neighbors and greeting them. People were more outward and warmer, and they did not have to give notice before bumping into their neighbor's houses. Oftentimes, people did not even have to be invited to celebrations before they would join. It was usually a thing of great joy for celebrants to see many faces of people who were not personally invited to marriage ceremonies, burial ceremonies, naming ceremonies, housewarming ceremonies, and so on. Chief Unafefe felt that it would be in bad taste if he was not to greet the neighbors who lived in the adjacent apartment in the same building. He did not reckon with the individualistic culture and the greatly varying backgrounds of the society in which he, indeed, was only a passing visitor.

When the lady neighbor who was being greeted by Unafefe saw an unknown man at her front door thrust out his hand at her and shout a language she did not understand, she was frightened and immediately shut the door with a bang. She thought the intruder at the door had evil intentions and that he wanted to grab her. She quickly made for her phone and dialed 911.

Meanwhile, Chief Unafefe, who was still outside, muttered a curse in disappointment.
"Well, if this foolish neighbor no want make I greet her, I go go give my greetings to the neighbor to our left. Perhaps the latter fit be more polite. I hear say some Oyibo people de fear when stranger de greet them. I hear say it even be worse if the stranger be black person. But me, Unafefe, I be the Honorable. I get money. I get power. And so, what else do I want from them. Na only to show good neighborliness."
Unafefe paused for a while to reconsider the wisdom of knocking on more doors.
"This kind neighbor woman, she be wicked neighbor. Common morning greeting, she begin to run away." Chief Unafefe muttered. He then made up his mind and moved to the door of the next apartment. He leaned forward and repeated the knocking and the greeting. As he was still standing at the door shouting "good morning," he heard repeated sounds of the siren outside the building complex.

"These *oyibo* people dem too de die. Every now and then, siren go de blow and ambulance de carry dead body de make loud siren noise as it de run for road." Chief Unafefe mused as he waited for a response to his loud knocking and greetings on the door of the second-floor apartment.

In Chief Unafefe's Konganoga community, the sound of sirens almost always signified the conveyance of a long-embalmed body in an ambulance for burial. Hardly did ambulances get called to convey the sick to hospitals. Of course, even if they were called, the indiscipline on the roads would make it impossible for them to get to their destinations in time. Invariably any siren-blaring ambulance seen on the road was either dashing down to convey a dead body to the morgue or to convey a long-embalmed one for burial. Hardly would an ambulance be seen conveying the needy living to the emergency room. Sound of a siren alternatively signified a drive through the chaotic traffic by one *Honorable* or one *Excellency* or another or some police officers rushing, not to respond to an emergency situation but perhaps to assist or supplement their colleagues in one extortion police check point or another. As the roads get more chaotic, the *Honorables* will better be served by air ambulances which only the likes of Honorable Chief Unafefe would be able to afford.

As Chief Unafefe mused and waited in front of the second neighbor's door, three bulky and fully armed policemen rushed up in his direction from one end of the corridor.
'Chei! Which time my country Konganoga go fit get this kind police! See how nice and neat and well kitted these policemen be! For policemen in my country the money for police uniforms will be readily embezzled at source. Oyibo good-o-o!"
As Chief Unafefe was still silently complementing the police and their smart uniforms the officers rushed towards him and made for their pistols! Chief Unafefe felt that the policemen might be mistaking him for a thief. He immediately thrust his hand into his pocket in an attempt to get out his passport to show the officers that he was a visitor. He had earlier been advised by his nephew to ensure that he carried one form of identification or another anytime he was leaving the room. Since he did not have a driving license, the only acceptable form of identification that he had was

his international passport. And he had wanted to get it out to show to those policemen.

But Unafefe's thrusting of his hands into his pocket sent a wrong message. He might be reaching for a gun!

"Take up your hands into the air!" The order came from the distance. The young lady who called them must have reported an attempted break-in in progress.

The officers obviously suspected that the bulky man with clean-shaven head was reaching for a weapon. That he did not fire was a miracle. If he had fired perhaps, that would have been more in consonance with the once-held belief in a society where Chief Unafefe's skin color would have been synonymous with felony or some form of mischief. If the officers had fired, they would have been exculpated, for fear for their lives!

The officers quickly closed in on the perplexed Chief Unafefe and immediately grabbed him by the shoulders and arms and forced his hands behind his back. They forced him to the ground and put him in handcuffs.

It happened so quickly that Chief Unafefe's protestations were scarcely heard. The loud shouts of,

"I be Chief Unafefe I no be thief " made little difference. Chief Unafefe was quickly searched.

"I be Chief Unafefe!" indeed sounded as "I be thief Unafefe!" especially in the ears of suspicious officers responding to a call.

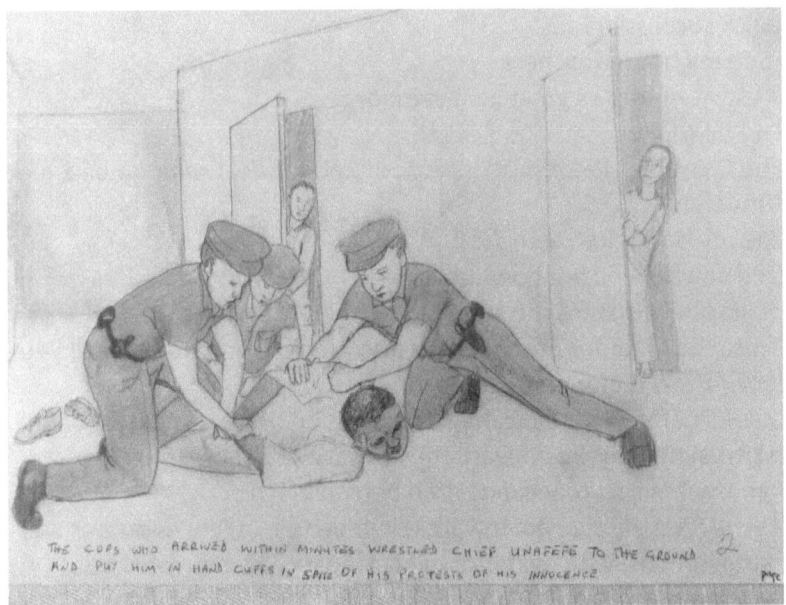

(*The cops who arrived within minutes wrestled Chief Unafefe to the ground and put him in hand cuffs in spite of his protests of his innocence*)

Chief Unafefe continued to shout,
"Chineke! Chineke! Chineke!
My God, my God, my God)
I no be thief-o-o
Na only greeting I want make I say-o-o!
I just want say good morning to our neighbor-o-o!"
"I beg, no kill me-o-o!"
Brisk and rigorous searches yielded no weapons. Only the apartment keys and an international passport and two long chewing sticks were found on Chief Unafefe. One officer quickly turned through *the suspect's* international passport. Then the manhandling became milder. Then the interrogation started.
"Where do you live?"
"What's your mission in this apartment?"
"Did the apartment owner invite you?" The questions followed in

quick succession.

"See my house for there.

I just want make I greet my neighbors.

I no be thief.

I be Chief the Honorable Sir Dr. Joshua Unafefe, Oyinatumba 1 of Umudioha.

See my house for there . . ."

'Did you say you are honorable thief?" One officer asked. He obviously misheard the suspect.

"Yes, I be Chief for my country. I also be the Honorable. Make you look for my diplomatic passport!"

Chief Unafefe kept indicating the direction of his apartment with a protrusion of his lips toward the relevant direction as his two hands were securely handcuffed behind his back.

As they led the suspect towards their vehicle, a few questions and protestations, with evidence of his innocence confirmed the erroneous arrest.

The officers became more polite as soon as they realized the error. They subtly apologized to Chief Unafefe for the rough handling. But they advised him to be wary of how he went around "looking for who to bestow unsolicited good mornings to."

"You are obviously but unintentionally violating the peace and privacy of your neighbors. But we will only issue a warning this time." The officer cautioned.

The excitement that was still building up in Chief Unafefe suddenly took a nosedive. It had not quite reached a crescendo before the sudden nosedive.

Chief Unafefe had scheduled to stay for one full month and had bought his return ticket accordingly. But now he suddenly needed to go home.

"I must go home immediately." Unafefe told his nephew as soon as the latter returned from work. I seriously de consider hopping into the next available flight back to my country. This your Oyibo country , it no good! These people, them nearly for break my bones. Which one be my offence? Only morning salute to my neighbors. No, no, no! This place it no good. Them no get respect! Them fit do this to chief for them place? Them even no get respect for the Honorable! Mark, make you hurry go rebook my flight. I go pay whatever it costs. I beg, make our people no come hear say these mad Oyibo officers come handcuff me! Oyinatumba him big pass that." Chief Unafefe kept lamenting.

Yes, Chief Unafefe needed to get back to his fiefdom before further humiliation would come his way. He was diligently pacified to a little extent by Mark.
"Such mistaken identity is not unusual especially if you are a black man in America." Mark told Chief Unafefe.
"But the good thing be say that those policemen never asked me for bribe. They apologized after they discovered their error. For our Konganoga country even when police make mistake, them go begin demand bribe from you before you go become free. The big man in the office him go ask for account of every operation. He go think say him boys collect bribe and set you free. And if you no give bribe, them go manufacture crime put for your head. That one be the very bad aspect of the deep-seated corruption for our place." Chief Unafefe said.

Even though he had spent so lavishly, Chief Unafefe was still very much loaded with cash. His diplomatic travel documents had waived a number of financial restrictions for him.
But even with the earlier mounting excitement about what he saw and the general orderliness, the neatness and the civility in the system, Chief Unafefe had started getting bored and was getting disenchanted with the lack of recognition, which he was getting. Nobody came in the mornings to pay him homage and hail him by his titles. He yearned for the shouts of "Oyinatumba! Oyinatumba!" which he received wherever he went in Umudioha and even in Kuveri the state capital and Karuja, the national capital.

Chief Unafefe yearned for the appellation of *"The Honorable"* and "the chief" and "sir," which emanated from every lip at the mention of his name.

He missed all the vain glory of titular embellishments, which he had been used to for quite a while.

He needed to go home.

He needed to go back to the empire where vanity was hailed, and criminality and unbridled corruption had been elevated to an adored art in governance.

He needed to get back to the land where stealing of public funds by public office holders was not only condoned, but was also expected and was eulogized.

He needed to get back to the land where justice was not expected unless it was paid for, and even after that, it often went to the highest bidder.

He needed to get back to the empire where the likes of him would steal the electoral mandate of the people, dismantle it, and install themselves as *"The Honorable."*

He needed to get back to the land where evil people had converted the once noble appellation of *"The Honorable"* to something to be viewed with disdain and have rapidly made it synonymous with theft, embezzlement, looting of public funds, and subversion of the will of the people.

He needed to go back to Konganoga—a land blessed by the gods but cursed by evil men like him.

Chief Unafefe needed to go home.

A decent society would have little place for people like him.

Chapter 23

ANOTHER *HONORABLE* COMES ON BOARD

Chief Unafefe did not slip in quietly back into Konganoga. He ensured that a sumptuous party was thrown to welcome him back from "a historic tour of North America." The State capital was awash with bill boards that displayed Chief Unafefe standing beside his rented limousine in both New York and Los Angeles. Other billboards showed him standing in the midst of other tourists who he falsely claimed were his "admirers and assistants." By so claiming, the Konganogan Honorable had told his listeners that "even in America, them know say I be *"The Honorable* and a very important man.

One of the attendees to the Chief Unafefe's Kuveri and Karuja welcome parties was Chief Unafefe's chief hit man Mr. Titus Ebuka Nweke. The latter ensured that on each occasion he signified and indeed dramatized his presence with drummers and dancers. He also paid for the blaring of his name on the microphones that were stationed in strategic corners of the welcome arena. By ensuring that his name was loudly announced on the microphones Chief Nweke ensured that his principal Chief Unafefe, noticed his goodwill and loyalty.

Titus Ebuka Nweke, alternatively known as Strangler, might have been a robber. But he was not a fool. He knew when his popularity waxed, and he was not the man to miss the opportunity of utilizing his fame to get some favors. He had been Chief Unafefe's chief hit-man and bouncer for nearly three years. One week after Chief Unafefe's heavily advertised and celebrated return from America, Strangler approached his boss Chief Unafefe with a rather strange and unexpected request.

When he came to Chief Unafefe, Strangler prostrated before him.

Still in the prostrated position, he hailed Chief Unafefe by his most-cherished title which he repeated over and over again: "Oyinatumba1, Oyinatumba 1, Oyinatumba 1!

"Oyinatumba 1, my big Oga and master. Sir, you know say I be your loyal servant. You know say, I go do anything wey you say make I do, even if it be to strangle any enemy. You know say I don serve you well well. You be like father to me. You know say people don begin de like Strangler well-well after the money which I been give them on the streets for Christmas period. I even come hear say many family wey never chop chicken for many Christmas come chop Chicken from my Christmas largesse. Many come de thank me, but I come tell them make them thank you, Oyinatumba my master.

Them talk say, one big turn deserves another. Na him make I come to you today for that *another*.

Strangler paused for a while, apparently to allow his master to fully assimilate the heaped eulogies. He then cleared his throat and then slowly and with calculated words said:

"You know Sir, that local government council election don de come. I come ask you for some kind favor. I wan make you make me one of *the Honorables*. I wan make you help make me become *The Honorable Local Government Chairman.* This one it be my only request." Strangler paused again to observe the obviously-surprised countenance of his principal, Chief Unafefe.

Undaunted by the obviously surprised look on the face of Chief Unafefe, Strangler boldly continued:

"If you make me become local government chairman, you go control all the money and all the appointments for my cabinet. I go be only the local *Honorable*. I still go de serve you well-well even as Honorable Local Government Chairman. I still go de strangle anybody wey you wan make I kill for you. I still go de kidnap for you. I still go de snatch car for you. Anything that you wan make I do, I still go do. In fact, I go do them better since I go be *Honorable*, and that title of The Honorable go help me pass through many obstacles. I go get government car, government pass, government money and government everything. And if you wan be governor, senator, or even the over-all boss of everything for State House Karuja, I go fight better for you as an Honorable. I go use my Honorable title come clear all the way for you. I only de request for Local Government *Honorable,* not the kind big *Honorable* for center in Karuja, the kind which you, my master be. Oyinatumba, this one it be my only request–o-o."

Chief Unafefe was completely stunned by Strangler's request. Mr. Titus Ebuka alias Strangler, a motor-park tout, a known robber and bouncer, a stark illiterate was requesting for sponsorship as *The Honorable* Local Government Chairman of his community. A practicing robber and killer, had promised if manipulated into office, to surrender control of the entire purse of the Local Government and all appointive portfolios to the sponsor godfather. It had never crossed the mind of Chief Unafefe who himself was another semi-literate *Honorable,* that a man who had never gone to school, who was never home-schooled or who did not go beyond the second year in the primary school could have such a high ambition. Here was a man who, all his life, had been into crime, a man who had been in and out of prison, a man who could not sign his name, a man who was associated with everything that was evil and barbaric seeking to be rigged into high office. Here was the man who unabashedly wanted to be sponsored to present himself to the people to ask for their votes, however rigged and falsified, to govern them. Chief Martin Amannaya Suleiman and Chief Unafefe after the latter were complete misfits that taunted the title of "The Honorable". But here in Mr. Titus Nweke alias Strangler, in all its glory, was the full personification of a would-be "Honorable robber".

Chief Unafefe knew that he too was not academically qualified enough to belong to Konganoga's Federal House of Representatives. He knew that he had to forge credentials to make him eligible to contest the elections, which Chief Suleiman cheated to make his crony win. But Chief Unafefe felt that, at least, he attended school up to the middle primary school level. He knew that he could express himself enough to be understood in Pidgin English. He knew that he was smart enough to know when to concede, when to use his brains, and when to employ his brawns. He knew that he was articulate and only rarely irrational with his muscles and his guns.

But here was a man, this Strangler, who, like his nick-name, suggested, could strangle a man for no just cause—a man who could not distinguish between right and wrong and who could make no single correct sentence in any language other than his native tongue.

Here was Strangler who, even his colleagues in the tout business, did not trust and who could hardly negotiate anything with anybody without threatening to fight. Here was a man who could not sign his name properly or even spell it. Here was Strangler requesting Chief Unafefe—himself an impostor in academic eligibility—to sponsor and recommend him for the position of the chief executive officer of a local government!

The request from Strangler put Chief Unafefe in a difficult position. If he acceded to the request, it might reopen debates during the campaigns about his own eligibility for the position that he occupied. It would confirm the allegations that his part of the country relished in sponsoring half-literate people for political office.

On the other hand, if he refused the request, it would expose him to Strangler's anger and possible rebellion. Strangler was some kind of a man Friday for Chief Unafefe. He did the dirty jobs for him and was prepared to obey his commands to the letter.

Again, Unafefe feared that a rejection of the request might make Strangler want to blackmail him. He already had enough problems to want to be involved in that kind of fresh credibility problem.

Again, he was subtly beginning to get worried about Strangler turning into some kind of Frankenstein monster.

He however decided to pass back the onus on Strangler. He promised to back the latter if he would succeed in procuring a high school certificate—even if a forged one. He also told Strangler that he would sign an agreement with him confirming that he, Strangler, as local government chairman, would hand over to Chief Unafefe half of the monthly revenue accruing to the local government from the federation account. A third condition was that he, Chief Unafefe, would be responsible for appointing all the principal supervisory councilors for the various functionaries of the local government.

Again, Chief Unafefe had added that Strangler must promise in writing that he would immediately commence night school for adult education classes so that he would at least know how to sign his name and write some basic words.
For other things, he could always choose to speak in the vernacular and bamboozle everybody with uncouth native idioms, which he was very good at.
Strangler knew neither what was meant by monthly revenue nor, indeed, how to get about forging a high school certificate. He only kept nodding his head as the conditions were being spelt out.
At the end of the spelling out of the conditions, Strangler, still nodding in the affirmative, rose from his prostrated position. He stood at attention before Chief Unafefe, and holding his outstretched palm over his forehead as in a saluting position, he said, "Oyinatumba I agree to everything!"
He then said, "Just write whatever you want make I sign. I go sign am now-now."
As he said this, Strangler held out his right thumb as if in a ready position to thumbprint any available document.

Chief Unafefe was torn between his wishes. For a brief moment he reflected on how his erstwhile master the late Chief Suleiman got him into the Federal Legislature all with forged documents and in spite of his absolute lack of qualification. He remembered that he too was in the same situation as Strangler was. But he considered himself more educated and more experienced than Strangler who could not as much as spell his name. Somehow, he had wished that Strangler would reject the conditions especially the one dealing with the appointment of the supervisory councilors since that would be tantamount to making Chief Unafefe the de facto chief executive in addition to his legislative position in Karuja. On the other hand, he was excited at the idea of his installing somebody who would be so inept that he, Chief Unafefe, would control the government.

By that evening, after Chief Unafefe had gotten his private lawyer to draft the agreement, Strangler was summoned to sign the documents in the presence of the lawyer in the latter's office. Strangler came to the signing ceremony dressed fully in three-piece suit which he had gone to purchase as soon as Chief Unafefe told him that the documents were ready.
He looked so trim and respectable in his six-feet-four-inch height, clean shaven and looking every inch corporate.
When that evening Strangler met with Chief Unafefe and the latter's lawyer, the lawyer mistook Strangler for a fellow lawyer and asked him, "Is your practice in town?" He could only imagine that it was somebody of the status of a lawyer who would be considered for the exalted position of a Local Government Chairman. But in answer to the question "Is your practice in town?" Strangler, who could only make meaning out of the word "town", thought that the lawyer was asking him whether he lived in town. He therefore immediately replied, "Yes, I live for town." The response somehow was appropriate as a reply to the question. But never in the lawyer's wildest imagination did he imagine that a complete illiterate could be sponsored to the high post of a Local Government Chairman.

It was only during the agreement signing incident proper, that the legal gentleman was shocked to the marrow. He came to realize that there still existed within the ranks of humans who wore suit and who, in the twenty-first century world, had the audacity to want to govern when they could not as much as read or write.

When the lawyer gave the document to Strangler to read through before signing, the illiterate Mr. Titus Nweke simply said, "I think say that one it be Oyinatumba's agreement? No need to read it. Chief Unafefe na him be my Oga, my big boss. Bring the agreement, I go sign am." ("Is that not Oyinatumba's agreement? It is not necessary to read it through. He is my boss. Bring the agreement and I will sign it").

As the lawyer was still pondering over what manner of lawyer would sign an agreement without as much as reading it through, Strangler collected the pen from the lawyer and started to rub the ink on his right thumb. The lawyer was amazed. He thought that the gentleman was testing to ensure that the ink flow was OK. "The ink flows well. You can sign with it. But if you want another pen, I can provide another." The unsuspecting lawyer said.

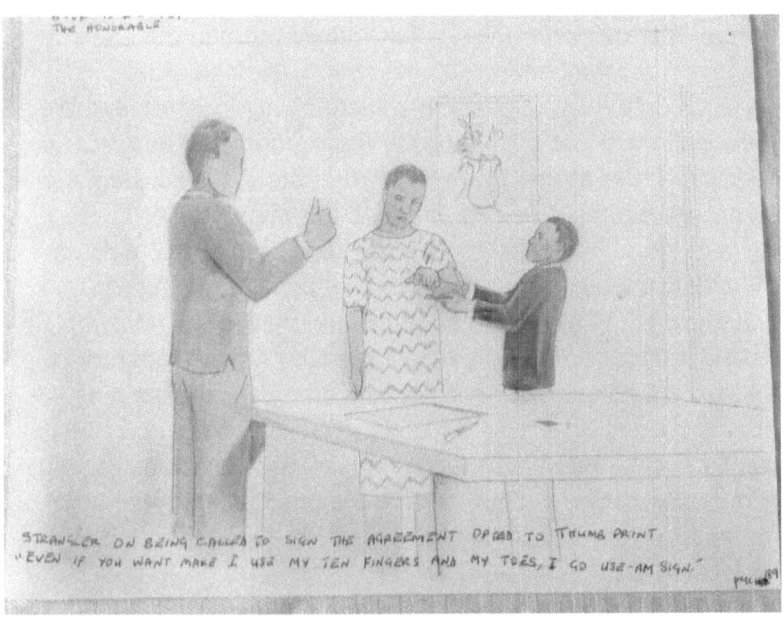

(Strangler on being called upon to sign the agreement, opted to thumb-print. "even if you want make I use my ten fingers and ten toes, I go use them sign", he said.)

Chief Unafefe, who was watching was very happy that there was, at least, somebody who he was more literate than, aspiring to leadership.

He felt very happy that he was not alone as a near-illiterate legislator.

"Me, I be semi-illiterate. This Strangler man, him be complete illiterate." Chief Unafefe said. "We fit begin form Association of Honorable Illiterate Legislators of Konganoga. We go de call am AHILK for short. Me I go be them president. This Strangler man him go be provost or Chief Whip. Him go de whip any noise makers for meeting. I go propose am for next House meeting for Karuja."

Chief Unafefe truly felt convinced that his proposed "AHILK" as an Association would do very well. He truly believed that the illiterate or semi-literate *Honorables,* would indeed out-number and out-maneuver the well-educated ones among the legislators.

"AHILK members, we go be more brazen and more ruthless. We go silence all them book people wey de shout for radio and newspapers, all of them wey de call us looters. We go chop all this surplus government money finish. All this mineral wealth wey them de shout about, them no go see one drop of it. We go tap them finish. We go tell them say no be them put am for underground. When we come tap am finish, them fit go complain to God if them wish. By the time Strangler finish for him big thumb, him go come use him big toe come sign all remaining mineral money agreement. And after ten years from now, we go come deny say them get anybody wey de answer Strangler as him name or surname." Chief Unafefe concluded as he joked audibly, taunting his mastery of Pidgin English to the consternation of the on-looking Attorney.

Yes, the educated but docile Konganogans might have read somewhere about the possible consequences of wholesale looting, or what history would say about the looters. But Chief Unafefe's AHILK members would read no history and even if they were lectured about the judgement of history, they would have so starved Konganogan historians of resources that the latter would all be suffering from dementia and would never get to document what they witnessed before they would all retire and die in penury.

As Strangler kept struggling to rub enough ink on his thumb from the pen, Chief Unafefe intervened on his behalf.
"Barrister, make you give my friend an ink pad. Him go sign by thumb printing. Him no go school. But I am sure him go make very good and very honest Honorable Chairman."
Strangler immediately concurred. "Yes. ink pad go better pass this rubbish pen. With ink pad, even if you want make I use my ten fingers and my ten toes, I go use them all sign."
"What?" the lawyer screamed in disbelief. A stark illiterate was about to run for the Chairmanship position of his Local Government!
But the Attorney quickly recollected himself. He quickly realized that even his client the Chief and Honorable Federal Legislator in their midst was barely literate.

The lawyer retreated to his seat. All that came to his lips was the involuntary exclamation: "God save Konganoga!"
As he searched for an ink pad in his drawer, the lawyer continued silently: "I feel very sorry for Konganoga and most of all for the people of Umudioha Local Government Area."
But he suddenly remembered that he must not show his surprise. He needed the continued patronage of Chief Unafefe the Honorable Congressman.

The documentations for registration as candidate were soon over with. Virtually all of Strangler's documents were false. But after lots of money had exchanged hands, they were all accepted as correct. The electioneering campaigns soon commenced. These were games in which both Chief Unafefe and Strangler were experts.
Strangler, through the assistance of Chief Unafefe, had gotten the

traditional ruler of Umudioha to confer a chieftaincy title on him. Strangler had taken the title of Ochemba, which meant "the shield of a people." He had purposely taken that title to partially neutralize his other terror-connoting nickname of Strangler, which tended to suggest that he could strangulate people. It did not take time, with very massive infusion of funds and aggressive publicity, for the name "Ochemba" to become a household one for Strangler in the community.

Chief Titus Ebuka Nweke, alias Strangler, the Ochemba I of Umudioha, with the massive financial backing of Chief Unafefe, became the favored candidate to win the chairmanship elections. But that was only for, as far as the suborned press and paid agents could go. The people, even the ordinary ones among them, still knew that Ochemba 1, even with all the pent-up publicity and eulogies being poured on him, was the same murderous and thieving Strangler who they used to know. A few went a little further back to voice the observation that even the acknowledged chief backer of Chief Nweke, Chief Joshua Unafefe, the Oyinatumba I of Umudioha, was also himself a well-acknowledged armed robber, cult patron, a car snatching kingpin, and a murderer. It did not take long before people started ridiculing Chief Nweke and his sponsor, Chief Unafefe. They nicknamed them as *Ogbu ara obara* 1 and 2 of Umudioha. The term *Ogbu ara obara* signified "the one who kills and sucks up the victim's blood." The appellation, which was widely used during the electioneering campaigns, was an eloquent testimony of the acknowledgement by people of the ignoble roles that Chief Nweke and his sponsor Chief Unafefe were playing in the society.
The derogatory but popular title of *Ogbu ara obara* was bestowed on the two ignoble friends and titled chiefs of Umudioha, but it was never used openly by any person unless the person was predisposed to being a martyr and had made up his or her mind to disappear forever.

The local government Election Day was soon at hand. Because of the rampant malpractices and distortion of election results that obtained with the secret ballot system in elections, an ingenious though apparently crude system whereby all supporters of any candidate lined up behind the photograph of the candidate in all polling stations was employed. That way, the total number of voters who cast their votes for any particular candidate would be seen by everybody present, and the numbers would be counted and announced publicly in every polling booth.

The results would then be collected from all the polling booths and summed up for each of the candidates, and the final result would be announced. That was supposed to make for transparency.

(The queue for Mr. Onuoha elongated and curved several times but only a handful of voters queued up to vote for Chief Nweke)

Before the elections, the principal opposing candidate to Chief Titus Ebuka Nweke was a well-educated and highly revered retired high school principal who was called Mr. James Onuoha. Mr. Onuoha was a highly religious and highly principled man. Strangler was no match for the latter. Virtually every campaign organized by the opposing candidate, Mr. Onuoha was disrupted by agents of Strangler and Chief Unafefe. But people were still determined to elect the retired principal. The latter had promised a progressive, educationally focused, and people-oriented government.

Chief Titus Nweke, the newly crowned Ochemba I of Umudioha, had little to say during the electioneering campaigns except to continually remind voters that he was the favored candidate of Chief Joshua Unafefe, the Oyinatumba I of Umudioha.

On Election Day proper, in every polling station—including the polling station located in Chief Titus Nweke's village—the queue for the retired school principal elongated and curved several times. Very few people stood behind Chief Titus Nweke's photographs.

The many people who had been given money through agents to queue up behind the photographs of Chief Nweke would stand behind his photograph for a minute or two and then suddenly move across and queue up permanently behind the retired principal's photograph.

By initially standing behind the photograph of Chief Nweke, the people said that they had satisfied the oath which they swore to, when they collected money to stand behind the photograph of Chief Nweke. The oath did not specify that they must stand permanently behind any photograph!

The results, as announced publicly in all the polling booths, indicated that the retired school principal Mr. James Onuoha won the elections in all the wards in spite of occasional disruptions by some thugs and hired miscreants in some polling stations.

There was jubilation everywhere in all the communities of Umudioha Kingdom. An attempt at imposition of another scoundrel as the Honorable Chairman for Umudioha Local Government had been averted.

The will of the people had triumphed over the will of scoundrels, unrepentant killers, kidnappers, and dealers in dismembered human parts. Sanity and the rule of law would gradually return to the polity.

As the people danced and rejoiced and carried branches of trees in jubilation all over the villages, the electoral Returning Officer for the local government area was holed up in a secret location where he had been housed by Chief Unafefe. He had, as early as the previous night, signed the final result sheet, which was supposed to be a compilation of the results from all the polling stations as were supposed to have been announced in the polling centers. The results, signed by the chief electoral officer, were in the possession of Chief Unafefe who, as soon as the elections were over, ensured that the electoral officer, whose bank account and secret cash caches had been fattened by some hundreds of millions of dollars, was safely driven to the central announcement center to declare the official winner of the elections as decided by the fake results that were in his possession.

Before the multitude of pressmen, reporters, party stalwarts and all at the Local government Headquarters, the Returning Officer tapped at the microphone, cleared his voice and with the signed result sheet in his trembling fingers read the cooked-up figures and announced as follows:

"The official winner of the elections for the position of the Umudioha Local Government Chairman, as declared by me Chief Longinus Opigo the duly-appointed Electoral Returning Officer for this local government, is Chief Titus Ebuka Nweke!"

So declared the thoroughly-suborned Electoral Officer.

The elections were over, and the official results had been announced. The announced winner Chief Titus Nweke (alias Strangler), Ochemba 1of Umudioha would, in a few days, surely assume control. And he would begin to be addressed as *The Honorable*.

Another dishonorable *Honorable* had come to power, and the party would continue. The loser Mr. James Onuoha the highly-qualified retired high school principal could spend his money and go to court if he so wished. Tons of more bribe money would be doled out by Chief Unafefe. And at the end of the day the highest bidder in bribe-giving would still win the day. And the highest bidder, without doubt would be the self-acclaimed Oyinatumba who everybody knew to have tons of ill-gotten cash to throw around.

The tribunals would sit, but the government would not be disrupted. The announced "winner" would immediately utilize government resources at his command and control his way further through, and legitimize his purchased victory.

The will of the people had been subverted and the loser had but one choice: to go and spend his or her money at the Election Petitions Tribunal and appeal court which though stated to be independent, was almost always manipulated by the government of the day.

While the stated loser spent his or her money on legal and other fees, the declared winner even with obvious falsification of results would sit back in government house and utilize government resources to fight the stated loser.

The allocations would come from the center and would be spent by the scoundrels. They would use the people's money to subvert the will of the people. By the time the wrongs were righted, if ever they were, monumental damage would already have been done. There was no punishment for the scoundrels, and they would escape with their loot. It was the law of the jungle where might was right.

Chapter 24

THE BATTLE ROYALE

The electoral battle had been lost and won. A victor, albeit the real loser, had been announced, and he was soon sworn in. The true winner had been condemned to seeking elusive justice at the law courts. The motor park tout and acclaimed scoundrel "Strangler", by the grace of another bigger tout Chief Joshua Unafefe, had been sworn in as *Honorable Chairman* of Umudioha Local Government Council.

The true winner of the elections the retired school principal Mr. James Onuoha, had been compelled to resort to the electoral tribunals and the law courts. He had been a very honest man while he was in service. He had not stolen school funds or embezzled any government grants from his school.
It was obvious that he would not have enough funds to fight the case. Chief Unafefe knew this. He and his protégé, Strangler, Chief Titus Ebuka Nweke, were fully aware that by the time the case would have undergone all the legal rounds, that they would have controlled the local government treasury for a year or two.

Again, Chief Unafefe and Chief Nweke knew that winning or losing most cases in the electoral tribunals was largely dependent on the amount of money each of the involved parties was prepared to part with. It was hardly ever based on facts or justice.
Chief Unafefe had tons of cash to part with, and he knew that he would recoup whatever he spent in installing Strangler within the first few months of Strangler assuming chairmanship of the local government.
Strangler was neither literate nor did he have the slightest idea about what it meant to be in governance. All his life, he had been a bouncer to one wealthy businessman, a political thug or a personal guard.

223

His massive body, large jaws, and clean-shaven small head made him look like one of the frightful figures in children's storybooks.

Chief the Honorable Titus Ebuka Nweke, the Ochemba I of Umudioha, had been sworn in as the new Chairman of Umudioha Local Government. The case instituted against him by the acclaimed winner of the election, Mr. James Onuoha, was in court, but the declared winner of the election was in charge.

The godfather of the entire episode, Chief Joshua Unafefe, was calling the shots from his palatial house in the village. He had made it clear to all those who cared to know that the political appointments in the local government council were for sale to the highest bidder.
Anybody who was able to pay him five million dollars would be eligible for a cabinet position in the council. Those who wanted positions in the assistant capacity would be required to pay him two million dollars. He was gracious enough to leave the other positions to his protégé, Strangler, to fill.
Strangler fixed his own fees, but often, he changed these at the spur of the moment. If he liked the face of any lady who came to his office seeking for a teaching appointment or for promotion in status, he could lower or even waive the fees. If he felt that a person seeking elevation in status or revision of the terms of a contract with the local government was wealthy enough, he could hike the fees.

Under Strangler, there was no time schedule for office hours for the chief executive.
The office hour started as soon as the *Honorable chairman* came on seat and ended when he left the office. He always wore a gold wrist watch but time for him, was completely irrelevant. The relevant time of the day revolved around him.
Morale and discipline plummeted.
One thing Strangler was good at was in his sartorial excellence. He always came to the office in impeccable three-piece suit and

brilliantly polished shoes. He commandeered a fleet of six cars, which accompanied his official car to work every morning. Each of the cars had a chauffeur and a security man attached to it.

As soon as Chief Nweke, the chairman, assumed duties as the new Local Government Chairman, he signed an interim executive order, seeking a loan of two hundred million dollars from the banks for the purposes of running the local government, pending the formation of the legislative arm of the government. The bank reserves of the previous government had been cleaned out by the previous administration before they left office.

The local government was indebted to the banks to the tune of over five hundred million dollars.

The two hundred million dollars that was freshly borrowed was immediately shared out between Chief Unafefe and Chief Nweke in the ratio of 2:1. Chief Unafefe, borrowing from his experience at the center, had advised Chief Nweke to borrow the money on behalf of the Local Government immediately after he got into office.

"You no know what go happen tomorrow. Some bribed tribunal or greedy judge them fit remove you tomorrow. So, you go begin de borrow and begin de chop the money today, today!" (You cannot predict what will happen tomorrow. And so, you must start to borrow and embezzle right from the onset, preferably from today). Chief Unafefe had advised Chief Nweke.

In keeping with the terms of the agreement under which Chief Unafefe sponsored Chief Nweke—the former would after the initial 2:1 ratio for sharing the initial revenue—continue to take 50 percent of the subsequent monthly allocations accruing from the federation account for the Local Government for as long as Chief Nweke remained Local Government Chairman.

The agreement was silent on what would be each party's share of expenses that would be incurred to sustain the position of chairman or what would happen in the event of a sudden loss of the position. Also, the agreement specified federation account without reference to debts that might have been owed that would need to be subtracted as soon as the revenue from the federation account arrived. The money accruing to the local governments varied from month to month as it was dependent largely on the amount of minerals that sold t the center.

For most months, the revenue accruing to the Umudioha Local Government averaged close to two hundred million dollars. For the first three months, Chief Unafefe went home with disbursements of about one hundred million dollars each month. That was apart from large sums of money that he collected from people that he put in as supervisory councilors and in top executive positions.

As soon as the month would get to an end, Chief Unafefe would drive to his village home, and the homage and sponsorship allowance (as the money from those sponsored was called) would arrive in large envelopes and boxes.
Of course, Chief Unafefe's main source of official income as an *Honorable Member* of the Federal Legislature, with the several allowances and committee sitting entitlements, would have been lodged directly into Chief Unafefe's bank account.
Then, of course, the huge payments from Chief Unafefe's several criminally oriented outfits would pour in hundreds of millions of dollars each month. The *Honorable's* sources of income were multiple and humungous.

As Chief Unafefe sat in the patio of his village mansion, he nodded his head as the phone alerts for lodgment of money into his bank account poured in.
"This country good-o-o," Chief Unafefe said repeatedly.
Yes indeed, life was good for both Chief Unafefe and his surrogate, Chief Titus Nweke. Their respective bank accounts were swelling in leaps and bounds.
Chief Nweke was so corrupt that he was said to collect bribes even from schoolchildren who wanted transfer certificates for change of schools. He had collection agents in every ward, in every school, in

every office.

He was also said to be so morally bankrupt that he was said to have been seen dating underage teenagers. Of course, in a society where the chief executive was seen as being above the law, no charges would ever be brought against him. Eight months after the elections, the elections petitions tribunal looking into the petition brought against Chief Nweke by the allegedly defeated school principal was still sitting despite the expiration of the stipulated time frame. One or two legal loopholes were easily discovered. Chief Nweke had, through some emissaries, sent the sum of fifty million dollars to each of the three members of the tribunal with a view to receiving favorable judgment. It was all Local Government money. As expected, the verdict came out in his favor.
There was much sadness in the entire local government area.
 Chief Nweke threw a large party to celebrate his victory. On the ninth month of Chief Nweke's ascent to power, the monthly revenue accruing to the local government from Karuja was two hundred and twenty million dollars.
At the month end, as usual, Chief Unafefe was home to collect his "entitlements." All other payers fulfilled their obligations to Chief Unafefe promptly and correctly. Chief Nweke, the Honorable Local Government Chairman however sent down only the sum of thirty-five million dollars to Chief Unafefe. Most of the chairman's financial transactions while in office were done in cash rather than check.   That was because of the Chairman's difficulty with dealing in checks and documents. Sometimes the Chairman would lock himself up in his office with one or two aides, physically counting bundles of money. Because of his literary handicap Chief Nweke often preferred to count large monetary transactions by himself.

The first sign that there was a shortfall in the cash flow from the Local Government Chairman to Chief Unafefe was the unusually small size of the cash box as it was being delivered. Chief Unafefe immediately noticed that the monthly delivery was unusually small as it was conveyed to him. After the boxes of cash from the Local

Government Chairman were dropped in front of him, Chief Unafefe immediately inquired to know how much was brought. "How much money dey for those boxes?" Chief Unafefe asked pointedly. He was told that it was thirty-five million dollars.
"What? Did you say thirty-five million or one hundred and thirty-five million?" Chief Unafefe inquired.
When it was confirmed to him that it was thirty-five million, Chief Unafefe burst out,
"Is that all for the month, or do you have more in the car?" Chief Unafefe barked.
"That is all from Ochemba, Honorable sir." Chief Nweke's driver replied.
"It be like Ochemba wan play chicken games with me? Where is Strangler now? I been check for Karuja before I came down and what him receive for this month be two hundred and twenty million. I be entitled to one hundred and ten million. Why him de send only thirty-five million to me? Him think say I be foolish fool? Abi him think say because me I no go school me I no fit do simple arithmetic? Even himself no go school at all, at all. But him know how him go fit cheat Chief Unafefe. Take back this nonsense chicken money to him at once."

Chief Unafefe was very furious and immediately picked up the phone and called Chief Nweke.
"Strangler, it be like you don begin de grow tail. You wan play game with me? Be careful!"
Chief Unafefe immediately banged the phone and continued to muse, in anger:
"Nonsense! Nonsense! Stupid nonsense! Idiot! Nonsense!"

Strangler despite his newfound high position, still recognized his limitations with Chief Unafefe. Shortly after Chief Unafefe dropped the phone on him Strangler called back and in a humble tone replied,
"Oyinatumba, sir, you know say I been give one hundred and fifty million to those tribunal people. We been get two hundred and

twenty million for this month. Na him make I take the one hundred and fifty million repay part of the loan wey we borrow from local government money to do the settlement of the Tribunal judges. I no even add interest. So na him make we remain only seventy million, and your own half therefore be thirty-five million. Me sef, I go add my own money for this month for to pay salaries since internally generated revenue come dry well well. So, sir, make you be patient for me. Next month go be better."

Chief Unafefe, still seething with anger remained silent for a while. Thereafter, in a calculated voice he then replied: "Strangler, listen properly to me. My agreement with you be say, you go de give me half of the money wey them send you from Karuja. You hear me so? Make you go get your friend, that your hungry village lawyer who I hire during agreement signing, only to please you. Make the lawyer read the agreement again for you. The agreement come say half of the money from central government Karuja. It no mention anything like expenditures or deductions. Any expenditures or deductions them be for your head. They no concern Oyinatumba. I know say you no go school at all at all. I also know say you no even fit sign your signature. But them never cut off your thumb yet; the thumb with which you use sign the agreement. When them go cut off your hand for the money that you de steal from everywhere, it be your hand them go cut off not just your thumb.
Listen, Strangler, the thumb that you take thumbprint the agreement to give me half of the money from Karuja it still dey for your hand. You no go school but at least you go school come to calculate say you go send me only thirty-five million out of two hundred and ten million wey come from Karuja.
Me I go school pass you, and me I know say that half of two hundred and ten be one hundred and five million and not thirty-five million!"

Chief Unafefe paused again for a while and then continued:
"Me I never ask you how much bribe money you been de collect

229

from those village teachers and even from village women who de fry *akara* beans-cake for roadside.

Them say you come begin de tax even the poor women wey dey fry *akara* for them to survive. Me I no ask you any of those. Even my poor aunt who de fry *akara* for village say you come send your agbero tax collection people for local government make them come de chase them for tax. Nobody before you has ever disturbed those poor women for tax. Me I no de ask you that one. Better be careful. No mess with me. I want make I get my complete one hundred and five million money before I go back to Karuja on Monday morning."

Chief Unafefe spoke with anger and an air of finality and dropped the phone.

Chief Titus Nweke, Strangler, appeared mystified for a moment after his patron Chief Unafefe abruptly dropped the phone on him. He stormed up and down the expansive living room of the multimillion-dollar house which he had recently built after only eight months in office.

Chief Titus Nweke alias Strangler, who had no house, no job and no savings, after eight months as *the Honorable* Local Government Chairman, had put up a mansion of about thirty-six million dollars. He had described the mansion to his friends as "a modest home." It was all thanks to the nascent culture of unbridled corruption in Konganoga society where any who spoke out too loudly could either get kidnapped or would be eliminated with little or no investigation done.

Chief Nweke picked up courage and wanted to challenge Chief Unafefe and call off the latter's bluff. But something in him counseled him against the measure:

You didn't win the election. You don't have the connections in Karuja. You cannot speak English. You cannot even write. The money that you have is stolen money, and it will fizzle away the moment you are out of office. Oyinatumba is like your "chi", the small god who holds your destiny. You cannot fight your "chi" or else, you will get ruined.

Chief Nweke further counseled himself:

You were only Oyinatumba's chief thug. He put you in the position in which you are. You fight him at your peril. You cannot match Oyinatumba in wealth or in reach. He will destroy you and ruin you forever. He can buy up even your closest confidants with his enormous wealth. You must swallow your pride and satisfy his demands.

Chief Nweke therefore decided to eat the humble pie. He called Chief Unafefe and requested to come to see him.

Chief Unafefe was not the man to joke with when money was involved. He felt that if he started being soft that Strangler would take advantage of him. To Strangler's request for audience, he replied thus,

"Strangler make you come see me if you de come with the money. If you no hold the money, no come."

Chief Nweke understood his man. He knew that there was no need to beat about the bush. He immediately reached out to the bank manager of the bank which the local government did business with.

Even though it was weekend, arrangements were quickly concluded with the local government functionaries and the bank for an emergency credit line of seventy-five million dollars.

Very early Sunday morning, Chief Nweke was on his way to the house of Chief Unafefe with a certified bank check for a total sum of one hundred and five million dollars; seventy-million dollars overdraft from the bank and the previously rejected sum of thirty-five million dollars in cash.

It was only on the condition that he came with the one hundred and five million dollars that Chief Unafefe agreed to see Strangler the *Honorable Local Government Chairman.*

Even though both men exchanged pleasantries, it was obvious that

Chief Unafefe was not his usual boisterous self any longer. On his part, even though he capitulated, Strangler did not feel happy at the humiliation that he was suffering. Both men, however, exchanged greetings and a few fairly strained smiles. The boxes of money were deposited at Chief Unafefe's feet without thanks. The Oyinatumba merely pressed on the call bell on the side table to alert two Personal Assistants to come and take delivery of the month's "homage money". Strangler left *Oyinatumba Lodge* (as Chief Unafefe's massive mansion was called), soon after.

During Strangler's reconciliation visit to Chief Unafefe, unlike the case in previous months, there was no enquiry about the goings-on in the Chairman's office. There was no advice and practically not even the routine pleasantries about the "shenanigans of the opposition." Both parties remained stone-faced and tight-lipped from beginning to end. Chief Nweke the embattled Local Government Chairman had only apologized to Chief Unafefe for the initial shortfall in the monthly remitted funds.

"Oyinatumba Sir, It be bad circumstances that make the original money come short small. But since I no want make my master unhappy, I come borrow money for bank come pay you." Chief Nweke pleaded. But Chief Unafefe appeared unimpressed. The Chairman departed from Oyinatumba Lodge soon after without the usual pleasantries.

Events subsequent to the visit were to make relations even frostier for the two friends.

The state auditors, who Strangler had refused to "cooperate" with and whom he had indeed, on two occasions, threatened with physical assault, had written very adverse reports about Umudioha Local Government accounts to the auditor general.

It was found that Chief Titus Nweke (alias Strangler) Chairman Umudioha Local Government was being indicted to the tune of nearly four hundred and fifty million dollars belonging to the Local Government. He had, on several occasions, been advised by the officers in the local government that he should occasionally share his booty with the bosses at the state and federal levels in keeping with the corrupt 'settlement culture" of Konganoga Republic. To

these illegal though sagacious pieces of advice, Chief Nweke had always replied,
"For this place, I get only one master, and his name be Oyinatumba. After Oyinatumba, it's me and me alone. Apart from Oyinatumba, me I no know any other god."

Strangler did not reckon with the pervasive corruption, which waded through a cross section of the polity of which he himself as *Honorable Chairman* was an active participant.
By the time of arrival of the federal allocation to the Local Government in Strangler's ninth month in office, he found that he needed to urgently cough out about four hundred million dollars for replacement of unaccounted funds whose disappearance were linked directly to him. His allocation for the month was two hundred and ten million dollars.

Thus, it was that when, on the tenth month of Chief Nweke's Chairmanship, Chief Unafefe came for his one hundred and five million dollars share of the two hundred and ten million allocation to the Local Government, Strangler was unable to give even one million dollars. The entire month's allocation was with-held at source to cover part of the unaccounted four hundred million as per the audit report of the Local Government.
But Chief Unafefe had confirmed from Karuja that two hundred and ten million dollars was again the monthly federal allocation due to Umudioha Local Government for the month. Chief Unafefe was therefore again entitled to the sum of one hundred and five million dollars as per the standing agreement of 50% of whatever derived from Karuja each month with the Local Government Chairman.
When he did not receive the month's "homage money", Chief Unafefe phoned, threatening hail of fire and brimstone. "Strangler, I know you again want make you play me. You come try it last month then you come change your mind. This month again you want try it. You think say me go come beg you for my money every month. That one no fit happen. I think time has come for you to

leave that Honorable Chairman job. It is me Unafefe who come put you there. Therefore, me Unafefe go now begin to plan to remove you from there."

Again, Chief Nweke was dumbfounded. This time, he had no answer to the demands. He had exhausted all the goodwill from the banks. They could no longer make further overdrafts since the previous ones extended to the local government had not been repaid.
There were no more places from where Chief Nweke could borrow to satisfy Chief Unafefe's demands.

He felt that there was no point in trying to plead because Chief Unafefe was a hardened and ruthless man. To plead with him often made things worse.
Chief Nweke, therefore, decided to steer the middle course, and he replied, "Oyinatumba, things de-e tough with me. Make you just give me time."
The response provoked tougher words from Chief Unafefe.
"It be like you don forget your past. I come put you for position, now you de wear tie and three-piece suit. And you de drive for convoy of cars wey even Oyinatumba no fit get. Now you come begin know say you need time after you don collect two hundred and ten million dollar. Remember say another election de come. Even this one sef you never free well-well for am. Since you wan make Oyinatumba be beggar, Oyinatumba go fit also make you be the beggar wey you be before.
The trouble be say this time you don be big man before. So nobody go fit lend you money again. And since you don chop belly full before, you no go fit chop mama-put roadside food any more. So make you de chop my money. Na you go come beg me after this. And I go make you pay double. Just dey there de answer *Honorable* until the day wey I decide you no go be *Honorable* again. That time everybody go come know say you be *The Honorable, the Robber.*
With those threatening words of hail and brimstone against his

former bouncer and later Local Government cash cow, Chief Unafefe dropped the phone.

It was obvious that the two friends had fallen apart. It was obvious that the battle lines had been drawn.
Chief Unafefe went back to Karuja without collecting any money from his vassal. He was fuming like never before.
Even Chief Unafefe's lesser surrogates in the local government council had had their money tied up by Chief Nweke to raise funds to cover for his previous excesses. Salaries for the month could not be paid. The fiscal situation was very precarious.
Chief Unafefe decided to start plotting Chief Nweke's removal in earnest.

Chapter 25

THE FIGHT OF THE TITANS

Chief Nweke did not just fold his hands to watch Chief Unafefe destroy him.

As soon as he realized that Chief Unafefe was plotting to have him removed, he decided to stop all arrangements about raising money for Chief Unafefe. He had learned that Chief Unafefe, prior to his travel back to Karuja, had hosted a meeting of the councilors of the local government and had distributed large sums of money to each of the attendees.

He was further informed that Chief Unafefe had thereafter told the councilors that the Local Government "was getting bankrupt because of the reckless and illegal financial activities of Chief Nweke the Local Government Chairman". Chief Unafefe allegedly had warned the councilors that the situation was likely to get worse unless they did something concrete about it.

He further warned them that the state governor might invoke his constitutional powers and dissolve the local government council if the situation did not improve or if they, as councilors, did not move against the alleged principal actor "in the game of waste and graft". In that case, he warned them that all of them would lose their jobs.

Chief Unafefe finally told the councilors that they should act quickly to avert disaster by summoning an emergency meeting of the council and impeaching Chief Nweke and removing him from office.

The details of the meeting and instigation were leaked to Chief Nweke by one of the councilors who had been getting huge contracts from Chief Nweke.

After the revelation, Chief Nweke was very furious. He felt that he had done all that was possible to assuage and pacify Chief Unafefe to no avail. He knew that Chief Unafefe never relented on any issue that he had made up his mind to pursue. He, therefore, felt that being between the devil and the deep blue sea that it was better for him to take a plunge. With the devil, he was sure to be destroyed. But if he took a plunge into the sea, he might either be struck by the sharks or he might swim to safety or get picked up by a rescuer.

Chief Nweke therefore summed up courage and said to himself,
"In spirit I still be the Strangler of old
Strangler, rescue yourself or you go come perish.
Oyinatumba think say I still be his thug or bouncer.
Just because I respect him as my former master no mean say me, Ochemba, 1 be him houseboy.
Him de treat me like I be him property.
I come try my best to beg him but him just de kick me for ass.
I no go try again; me, I am done with him!
Even if I be him former slave, the chains must come off now
These my muscles make him king
These same muscles must defend me now
I go begin defend myself or I go perish forever.
And if him try fast one on me again, I go teach him say people like me be him power.
It be people like me, Strangler be say Oyinatumba de walk safely for road. Yes, it be people like me be say him be Oyinatumba.
Oyinatumba must beware or else me go make him catch the chill."

By the second week after the disagreement between Chief Unafefe and Chief Nweke, the latter conducted a cabinet reshuffle. He completely removed all the supervisory councilors that were appointed by Chief Unafefe and immediately replaced them with his own men. He also transferred all the executive officers who were loyal to Chief Unafefe. He sent the teachers among them back to the classrooms so that they would not nose around in the local government secretariat. He removed Chief Unafefe's photograph, which was hanging in his office.
He did not display any modesty or candor in manifesting his split with Chief Unafefe.

He summoned a general meeting of the senior officers of the local government, all the elders of the community, and all the religious leaders. He had also invited to the meeting all the principals and headmasters of the schools in the local government, including the leaders of the association of market women and the trade unions that operated in the local government. He gave a prominent seat at the front row of the gathering to the leaders of the "agberos," the thugs. In the front row also were three young men in dark glasses who many people in the gathering could not identify. A councilor later identified one of the dark-glasses-wearing young men as one of the notorious persisting *Chambers* cult members in Kuveri, the state capital.

It was a very well-attended meeting. When all invitees were seated with the traditional rulers of the communities seating at the high table, Chief Nweke was ushered in, escorted by the deputy head of the local government police and the head of the local government civil defense corps.

After observing all protocols, Chief Nweke went straight to the point and announced to the gathering that he had broken ranks with Chief Unafefe, the Oyinatumba I of Umudioha.

"Lady and jentru men," Chief Nweke announced, "it be like Oyinatumba de act true to him name by stealing all the money for development in Umudioha and making Umudioha people get economic chill. I come decide to cut all ties with that devil. Him begin think him own me and the entire Umudioha people and all that we own."

There was absolute silence in the council hall as Chief Titus Nweke the Honorable Chairman paused.

Even in his rustic Pidgin English, Strangler was quite articulate. He took a few seconds to look closely into the faces of his listeners. He appeared to have succeeded in whipping up the necessary sentiments against his former boss. He then went more specific:

"Oyinatumba, like you all know, help me make I win election. Yes, and since I become chairman, I de give am all the respect due to a father. Even safe, him de take half of all the money wey them de give us for development from Karuja every month. Na him make you no de see any development for Umudioha. Me too, I know say I be guilty for helping him steal the people-money.

"I want make you forgive me. I be sorry for the wrong wey me I do. It be for the sake of peace I de give him the money and to fulfill an agreement me and him reach before him agree to sponsor me. But now I be sorry for myself and for all of you. I beg make you all forgive me. I now repent. Them born me Catholic. Never mind that me I be bad Catholic now. But I now sing the song our fada for Catholic Church de call "mea culpa". I go be better man after this. I go begin go church again. Please forgive me.

Me, Ochemba I now say *mea culpa!*   But that man dem call Oyinatumba, him no fit repent. Him come soak him hands for blood too much. It be only chills him fit bring for Umudioha. Him no go see good. My old name be Strangler like all of you know. But I no de strangle people no more. My new name be Ochemba, your trustworthy guard of this community. From today I go de guard this community against all bad people especially against any person who go bring chill for this our good Umudioha. I go strangle such people who bring us chills, for the good of us all. This be my promise to all of you. I thank you, lady and *jentru* men."

The Chairman's brief and blistering address, though delivered in bad English was fully understood by all attendees to the widely-attended gathering of Umudioha people.

The address ended as abruptly as it had begun. Everybody present at least understood the what was earlier known but which was only often muted for fear of reprisals. They understood that two devils who were colluding to defraud the community had parted ways. They further understood that one of the devils had confessed and had promised to mend his ways.

There was a thunderous ovation—the type that Umudioha people had never witnessed before. People were hugging themselves as if some very good gift had been given to the city. A sinner had repented and there was joy in the land.

(Shots rang out from the bush and the vehicles in Chief Unafefe's convoy collided with themselves. A hefty man was seen being pulled out from the bullet-proof car and abducted.)

The coalition of thieves that had stolen Umudioha dry was about to get broken.

No questions were called for after the address. But a short closing prayer was called for.

In the closing prayer, the catechist of the local Pentecostal Church had quoted a verse from the Holy Book: "There will be joy in heaven for one sinner who has repented". The catechist probably could not have been more correct.

Light refreshments provided by the local government council followed after the speech of the chairman.

It was Friday morning, and as attendees to the meeting at the local government headquarters were on their way home, they were all full of hope that a new dawn was about to descend on the community.

Chief Unafefe was being chauffeured home from the airport to his mansion in the village as he was wont to do on most weekends. He always came home in a convoy of four cars. But for some particular reasons, maybe not unrelated to the developments in his constituency, he came back for that particular weekend in a convoy of six cars.

Prior to Chief Unafefe's return, there had been unusually heavy traffic of vehicles on the dusty road that led to his sprawling mansion. There was also an increase in human traffic along that road immediately after the earlier meeting at the local government headquarters.

It was about 6:30 PM. Market women were packing back their unsold wares into their baskets. Most of them were apolitical. They only knew when they would be told to go to vote after every two years or after four years. They had come to accept that the person that they voted for would not win the elections.
They also had come to accept that the people who were said to have won the elections would soon get very rich and that they would purchase more cars, which would raise more dust on the roads and chase them into the side bushes as they passed with their sirens.
Some of those market women had heard that the one whom everybody called Strangler, was said to have won the election. But the market women knew that they all had voted for the retired principal who they said did not win the elections. The market women further learnt that the defeated school principal was having trouble with that other one who was called *Oyinatumba* and that Oyinatumba was supporting his former bouncer Strangler.
Most market won did not care about politics or who the political actors were.
"Let them quarrel." Most market women said. "That one is their own palaver. Just make them not raise too much dust on the road this evening when I am on my way home," one of the women told the other. So much was their apathy about events that directed

their everyday lives.

The siren was soon heard in the distance. That must be Oyinatumba coming home for the weekend. Many of the bicycle-riding men and women cleared the road as they heard the sound of the siren. The few cars on the road also parked to the side of the road. If they did not clear well enough, the horsewhip-wielding policemen in the escort cars would *bless* their backs with indelible scars from the horsewhips.

The cars in the convoy were coming at top speed with their headlamps fully on.

The convoy of cars turned the corner that led to Oyinatumba's mansion. The mansion was about a quarter mile away. It was already a familiar event, a routine for every Friday. Nobody bothered any more.

However, this time, something different happened! There was an abrupt stoppage of the sirens.

Multiple shots rang out from the low bushes. Then there was heavier explosion of gunfire. Four other vehicles were seen driving at top speed to the scene from the opposite direction. There was shouting and moaning. All six cars in Oyinatumba's convoy had been grounded with a hail of bullets from some unknown people in the low bushes. The occupants of the vehicles in the convoy had returned fire, but their vehicles had collided against each other in the confusion that ensued.

The four vehicles that headed from the opposite direction had pulled up to the site of the immobilized convoy. A massive man in heavily embroidered dress was seen being bundled from one of the cars in the convoy into one of the four cars that had arrived from the opposite direction. Some people from the convoy were seen lying prone on the dusty road after they had tried to run away from the attacked convoy. The man that was bundled out from one of the immobilized cars was forced into one of the attacker's cars and was driven off at top speed. It was soon all quiet.

The dust on the road easily soaked up the blood that oozed from the wounded as they lay moaning on the sand dunes on the road. Shattered glass littered the road. One of the cars, the one from which the huge man was dragged out, was not very much damaged. Even its glass was not shattered despite the heavy gunfire directed at it. It must have been bulletproofed. It only got stuck after collision with other vehicles. The driver was not hurt, and as he held his hands up in surrender after his master was pulled away from the car, he looked miserable and subdued.

Some two hours later, two police vehicles came to the scene. The wounded that still lay at the scene had been bandaged up by sympathetic people who came to the scene about an hour after the shooting. The blood on the many that were already dead had already clotted.

No vehicles had agreed to drive through that road after they learned of the shooting. Ambulances in the area were used more for people after they were dead than while they were still alive. Again, the sound of sirens was more likely to be those heralding the movement through the town of one political bigwig or another. It might alternatively be from a bullion vehicle or a police vehicle speeding down the road not to forestall a crime but most likely to escort a politician to a party.

The bullet-proof vehicle that was not damaged was later identified to be the one carrying Chief the Honorable Dr. Sir Joshua Unafefe, Oyinatumba I of Umudioha Kingdom. But Chief Unafefe was no longer in the car. His car had been sandwiched between colliding vehicles and he was abducted by the attackers. His whereabouts could not immediately be confirmed.

The incredible had happened! Chief the Honorable Dr Sir Joshua Unafefe the Oyinatumba 1 of Umudioha Kingdom had been kidnapped!

Chapter 26

A VICTOR EMERGES IN THE FIGHT

For many hours after the shooting, fear gripped the entire Umudioha community. Vehicles that were heading toward the site of the shooting quickly turned back. Stories spread quickly that Chief Unafefe had been killed as his bulletproof car was seen standing with its four doors open by the side of the street squashed between two cars in front and three cars behind. The occupants of the other cars—both the security men and others in the vehicles—were either wounded, dead, or had run away. The attackers, both those that had fired from the bushes and those that arrived in the other four cars, had left the scene.
Nobody felt safe. If that sort of thing could happen to Chief Unafefe—the dreaded kingpin, member of Konganoga's parliament, and leader and financier of some of the most notorious cults in town—then who was safe?

All suspicion was on Chief Nweke in view of the meeting, which he had held earlier in the morning with a cross section of the members of the community and in view of the statements, which he had made during the meeting. It was believed that since Chief Nweke was Chief Unafefe's right-hand man and knew all his routine and his movements that he must have been the mastermind of the kidnapping. Besides, many attendees to Chief Nweke's local government council hall meeting remembered vividly the closing statement made by the embattled chairman, thus: "From today I go de guard this community against all bad people especially against any person who go bring chill for this our good Umudioha. I go strangle such people who bring us chills, for the good of us all. This be my promise to all of you."
But Chief Nweke had purportedly left for a meeting in Kuveri soon after he addressed the councilors and traditional rulers and others earlier in the day. Maybe it was a mere coincidence that the attack occurred on the same day as the day that he addressed the

people. On the other hand, the meeting in Kuveri might have been an attempt to establish an alibi.

Whichever way it was, the fact remained that the peace and mutual trust between the different groups in Umudioha had been broken, and things were not to be the same again.

By the following Monday, a small group of people—supporters of the missing Chief Unafefe—carried placards and demonstrated in front of the Local Government headquarters. They demanded for the release of Chief Unafefe "by whosoever is holding him."

Some of the posters read, "Oyinatumba is our leader." Others read, "Strangler cannot strangle the truth." Yet some others read, "Strangler has strangulated our economy."

As the protesters marched around the premises with their placards, another larger group—made up mostly of the local council workers and students—soon assembled and attacked the Unafefe supporters. They tore up their placards and physically assaulted them.

The police had to intervene to stop what might have been a free-for-all fight.

Situation in the town was tense as animosity built up between the few people who supported the missing Chief Unafefe and the greater numbers who supported Chief Nweke.

By Friday of the same week, an announcement came over the state-owned radio to the effect that a state of emergency had been declared in Umudioha Local Government and that the Local Government Executive Council had consequently been dissolved by the state government. A sole administrator was immediately appointed to run the local government.

The newly appointed administrator was a very disciplined and well-educated retired high school principal. His name, to the great joy of the people of Umudioha, was Mr. James Onuoha.

Tension was thus doused but with the non-discovery of the whereabouts of Chief Unafefe, the community was still living in fear. Secret service operatives flooded Umudioha and environs.

Sporadic searches were conducted especially in homes belonging to known supporters of the ousted local government chairman Chief Titus Nweke alias Strangler.

Policemen conducted stop and search operation on vehicles and soon the tragic episode was converted into a bonanza for the men in uniform as it afforded them the opportunity to harass innocent citizens and extort money from passing vehicles especially commercial vehicles.

Even open vans conveying farm products from the village to the local market in the same village were stopped in search of Chief Unafefe! It soon became an object for fun-making as drivers of commercial vehicles would stretch out their arms, clutching twenty-dollar bills as gratification to traffic officers and jokingly saying,

"Officer, na only this small one I hold. I no hold Unafefe."

Thus was fun made of the man who, only a week earlier, had held the aces in Umudioha; a man whose word was almost law; a man who decided who would be the political ruler of Umudioha Kingdom; the man who thrust into his pockets half the monthly revenue allocation of the entire local government.

How were the mighty fallen!

Four hundred miles away in Karuja, where Chief Unafefe was strongly suspected to have been the mastermind behind the bomb explosion that had killed Chief Martin Omenka Amannaya Suleiman, some two years earlier in the plane, news of the suspect's kidnap made the headlines.

It could hardly be believed that a man of such stature could be so easily overwhelmed even with all the security details that accompanied him.

Some people who knew Chief Unafefe intimately and who had prayed secretly for his downfall, indeed, prayed favorably for whoever was able to rid the society of such a monumental pest; a scourge of society who appeared for many years to have been above the law.

Among those who watched the unfolding events with keen interest was the Chairman of AMEND, a fast-growing Non-Governmental Organization, Mr. Ade Suleiman. The latter's father was two years earlier killed in an airport bomb explosion which was suspected to have been masterminded by Chief Unafefe through the agency of the Chambers Secret Organization.

Ade and his family had fervently prayed for two years for Nemesis to catch up with whosoever was responsible for the murder of their patriarch, Chief Omenka Suleiman. Paradoxically, while Ade and his family members prayed, many more prayed in thanksgiving for the Nemesis which appeared to have caught up with Chief Omenka Suleiman. They knew that though he appeared to have repented before he died, Chief Omenka Suleiman was nonetheless the wealthy leader of a savage secret organization that ruined many young lives. They knew that the latter caused the uncountable dispossession of property and violent deaths on the roads by the ruthless organization that was called The Chambers.

That was the state of affairs when the time again arrived for the upcoming senate and other federal elections.

With the dissolution of the local government, Chief Nweke retired to his newly completed mansion in the village. During the interval that he was local government chairman, he had acquired three brand new cars—one of which was a Mercedes-Benz S-Class car that he proudly parked in the elevated and marble-clad car-port in the architectural wonder of a house, which the monthly federal allocation to his local government had made possible.

Chief Nweke continued to live big from the much cash that he had stashed away during his nine to ten-month reign. He had also, during his short reign, converted a lot of local government council properties to his own use. He therefore went on to destroy the documents which would have implicated him. Even though he was not educated, he had employed a strong team of economic advisers who apparently advised him on how best to steal. The knowledge that he lacked, his mentor the missing Chief Unafefe, who had been very thoroughly schooled in the art of stealing from the coffers of the central government, had easily taught him. But it was not to be all so smooth and all so rosy for the disgraced Ochemba 1 of Umudioha.

The new local government administrator, Mr. Onuoha, though a very pious, very educated, and very thorough man, had called for the files of all federal allocations from the center for the previous one year and had set up a panel to reconcile the purported expenditure with the visible projects on the ground.
He had, on his assumption of office, publicly declared,
"We will run this local government with the fear of God and the good of the people in mind. We will not witch-hunt or target anybody. But bygones will not be bygones where any dime stolen from the people has not been accounted for or recovered."
Ordinarily statements like Mr. Onuoha's should have set the thieving immediate past Local Government Chairman Mr. Nweke alias Strangler, thinking or indeed panicking, or trying to make amends. But the crude villain in *Strangler* made him so thick-skinned that he did not appear to understand that the statement was aiming at past embezzlers like him. He continued to live big and boisterous from his obvious loot.

Mr. Onuoha set up a panel of enquiry to trace where all government money for the previous one year had been disbursed to. The panel, after working assiduously for six weeks, was to discover that 88 percent of the money that accrued to the local government council was personally cashed and utilized by Chief Nweke, the erstwhile local government chairman for purported projects that could not be traced at all.
It found that 12 percent out of the remaining 18 percent of the physical cash was plunged into projects that were only started and abandoned.
Accounting for the internally generated revenue was even worse.

It was found that after the payment of salaries of staff that not a single dime of the accruing funds could be accounted for.
The results of the findings were made available to the state government that immediately forwarded them to the centrally established Financial Crimes Bureau, FCB, which was supposed to be a watchdog for such crimes as were committed in Umudioha. The bureau, which was often accused of being a tool in the hands of the federal leadership for dealing with her political enemies, was however known to be occasionally objective in its activities.

Chief Nweke was neither educated nor was he trained for any job. He was more of a professional bodyguard, a bouncer for the now-disappeared Chief Unafefe. He had no job to go back to, and he had grown too big to get back to the bouncer job.

It was amazing how fast the millions of dollars, which he had stacked up in his house, got exhausted.
Not being able to manage resources and calculate, Chief Nweke, who, most people reverted to addressing by his old nickname, Strangler, had continued in his mansion to live a life of parties and carnivals, which he had learned as the boss of a Local Government. The much loot which he accumulated within the interval that he ceased to pay Chief Unafefe before the Local Government executive was disbanded, was enough to last him a life time, so enormous was the weight of the monthly federal allocation combined with the internally-generated revenue in a clime where public servants were not being paid as and when due.
He continued to hold daily expensive parties in which he often sprayed bundles of money to guests. To avoid detection of his loot as local government chairman, he did not bank his loot but carefully kept all his stolen money in cash in his mansion. He had an assistant who managed the "home bank" for him and who pulled out the bundles of cash as Strangler ordered often when he was drunk or when he wanted to impress his guests that he was still Ochemba 1.
At a stage after he sprayed so much money during a party, people

who were present started calling him Omimi ejo (the sea that never dries). The other title, Oshimiri, that connoted a similar meaning had been taken by the late Chief Suleiman when he was alive.

Chief Nweke wanted to demonstrate to everybody present that even though he was out of power that he was still deep into cash. He was also deep in merriment that the person who would have been a thorn in his flesh had been kidnapped and possibly done away with—possibly by him, possibly by some other people.

Chief Unafefe had disappeared as mysteriously as he came into prominence. And the same system which could not unravel the mystery of the plane bomb explosion could equally not unravel the brains behind a daylight kidnap of a prominent member of the community, a member of parliament, and a virtual kingmaker. And the principal undeclared suspect in the melodrama was throwing daily parties as if to celebrate his ouster from governance and indeed from existence.

The keeper of the treasury for Chief Nweke must have seen the treasures thinning down by the day, and he consequently started to help himself to the loot before it would dry up completely and he would lose his job. First, one of the new cars parked in one of the garages mysteriously disappeared without trace.

One of the gatemen had reported when questioned that he saw Nnoli, Strangler's accounts man and keeper of the treasury, loading certain things for a long time into the trunk of the car the previous day.

By the time Nnoli disappeared, virtually what was left of the treasury had disappeared with him.

By the time Financial Crimes Bureau (FCB) people came for Chief Nweke, there was hardly any cash left with him.

Indeed, Chief Nweke had started looking for buyers for his two remaining cars.

The parties had ceased—not out of modesty, but out of

insolvency.

The music had stopped playing not because of difficulty in choosing the tune but because there was little cash left to pay the musicians.

The friends had stopped coming not because they no longer enjoyed the barbecue or the drinks but because the maker of the parties had gone broke.

It was not too long before even the gateman could no longer be paid. The flower hedges could no longer be trimmed. The cooks and stewards all left. Strangler had no wife and had never run a family of his own.

The once ebullient Ochemba I of Umudioha was holed up alone in his house when the order came for him to proceed to Karuja for a date with the FCB.

"How do they expect me to travel? Who will pay the flight and the hotel bills in Karuja? And who will shoulder the cost of litigation?" Strangler said to one of his ever-dwindling visitors.

And as the Ochemba I of Umudioha ruminated on these issues, the order came for his arrest for the kidnapping and eventual murder of the erstwhile congressman representing Umudioha constituency, Chief Joshua Unafefe. Surprisingly the hitherto somnolent public safety Department of Konganoga had woken up from sleep. A few members of the Parliament had kicked at the apparent inaction of the police in tracing the whereabouts of one of their own. Any other Konganogan victim of a lesser public standing would not have been so lucky to have their cases followed up on. Often, affected families would almost go bankrupt in greasing the palms of public safety officers with virtually nothing being done to avail them justice.

It did not take long before the once glittering mansion, which was completed within eight months of the ascendancy into power of a known kidnapper and unrepentant cultist, was overgrown with tall grass.

It did not take long before the fittings in the building were

251

dismantled and vandalized. It did not take long before even the gates were dismantled by bandits and the fittings and furniture in the house were bundled away by thieves.

Even the carpets on the floor were stolen. Only the block work and the marble floors were left intact. The once beautiful building, which was second only to the mansion belonging to the erstwhile Oyinatumba in splendor and elegance, had been left in ruins.

It did not take long before the owners of the best and the second-best houses in the local government were referred to in past tense. The one was kidnapped and his remains were discovered after five months in a shallow grave.

The other was invited for questioning in Karuja, was declared missing from prison custody in an apparent jail break and never returned. He was six weeks later presumed dead by the prison authorities.

They both, Oyinatumba 1 and Ochemba 1, might no longer bring chills to, or for a split-second guard the gates of the great and proud kingdom of Umudioha. They might be singing in merriment with the angels in paradise. Or, more likely and perhaps more appropriately, they might be shielding their faces from the jeers of the other mocking demons from across the gates of hell.

Chapter 27

A NEW EFFORT TO RIGHT THE WRONGS

Suleiman Foundation and its counterpart, AMEND, were waxing strong and making progress in leaps and bounds. The Chairman/CEO of the two organizations, Mr. Ade Suleiman, was being invited by several communities to be honored with awards and chieftaincy titles. He had however persistently rejected these offers. He had come to regard chieftaincy titles as honor that had been too frequently bastardized to be worth accepting. He had seen the likes of Unafefe and Strangler take chieftaincy titles and acquire jaw-breaking names only to continue in their nefarious activities. He did not forget that his own father was honored with the resounding title of Oshimiri ("the sea that never dries"). But Ade was humble and pious enough to acknowledge the nefarious source of that sea, even when the beneficiary before he died, repented and tried to make restitution and amends.

The senate seat in Ade's senatorial zone was up for grabs after the incumbent had indicated his intention not to run again on grounds of ill health. Taking on a chieftaincy title was one sure positive step for stepping into the limelight by any individual gunning for public office. The experiences of Chief Unafefe, Chief Nweke, and even of Ade's own father, Chief Suleiman, even in spite of the latter's repentance, were very sore ones. Those cases had made a lot of people begin to sneer at the appending of the word chief to anybody's name.
The tragic ending for each of these three people who had played politics that were propelled from evil resources were enough to make anybody wish to remain relative nonentities.
But the people hungered for a change. They wanted a clean slate. They wanted progressive minds with good and productive intentions. Many of them individually and collectively had approached Ade to run for the seat despite his complete lack of political experience.

Chief among these was the newly appointed administrator of Umudioha local government, Mr. James Onuoha.

Mr. Onuoha had been doing very well in governance. Within his first three months in office, Mr. Onuoha had literally transformed the face of Umudioha Local Government area. Four of the seven major roads in the local government area had been tarred. Pipe-borne water had been provided for the two secondary schools in the area. Outstanding salaries of staff had been cleared. Teachers, who were retrenched by the Nweke-led administration for the purposes of saving money for a bulkier loot, had been recalled and re-engaged. Classes that were merged for the purposes of having fewer teachers were un-merged. Bonuses were established for teachers whose students excelled in the First School Leaving Certificate Examinations.

A program was established for assisting childless elderly widows and widowers, and a motherless babies' home was built in the local government area. People who never believed that it was possible for the positive impacts of governance to be felt by the ordinary citizens began to take notice.

The morale of the average worker was greatly boosted by the exemplary leadership of the Onuoha-led administration. Mr. Onuoha announced a program of zero tolerance for corruption. The entire Umudioha Local Government Headquarters was given a new look with repainted buildings and flower gardens and beautifully mown lawns. Recreational facilities were provided for members of staff who were on break, and a program of subsidized lunch was commenced for those who were punctual to work consistently for each full month.

Mr. Onuoha himself led by example by ensuring that he was at his desk in the office by 8:00 AM every workday. This was in sharp contrast to his predecessor Strangler for whom time meant nothing even when for ornamental reasons he adorned a gold-chained wrist watch perpetually on his wrist.

Monthly staff meetings were held in the council hall, and a question-and-answer session in which people could throw questions to and get answers from the Local Government administrator directly was commenced.

Satisfaction and joy beamed on most faces as people, who had never believed that anything good could come out from government, began to see the dividends of good governance. Because of the exemplary leadership of the administrator, a lot of people who had been reluctant to invest in the local government area started to change their minds. By the time Mr. Nweke was six months in office, two full-fledged industries and three cottage industries had been attracted to the local government area. Unemployment which was at an all-time high during the Nweke-led administration reduced drastically with the Onuoha-led administration. Crime also reduced dramatically. Sanitation was excellent.

Umudioha had never had it so good. It was such an unprecedented transformation that not only the Governor of the state but also the federal authorities got wind of the marvelous developments and decided to pour in more resources into the Local Government with the full confidence that the resources would be well managed. Mr. Onuoha's administration did not disappoint their hopes.

Press reports were full of praise for Umudioha Local Government authorities. Umudioha Local Government became a symbol of progress and accountability. People from adjoining Local Government area started to claim origin from Umudioha Local Government area. The best was yet to come.

The authorities in Karuja, the national capital, had announced that the presidency would want to encourage accountable and exemplary leadership by instituting yearly rewards in various forms to local governments, which showed evidence of efficient management of resources and exemplary leadership. It was the first time ever that an award of that nature was to be made. An assessment team was set up to visit the four hundred and twenty local governments in the country to inspect and make recommendations. Some local government chairmen were alleged to have started offering inducements to the members of the assessment team to influence their decisions in their favor.

Mr. Onuoha was not the type of man who would make any such offer. He received the assessment team very courteously and conducted them round the various developmental projects, which his administration had completed and the ones that were still at various stages of completion. He did not as much as hold a party for the visitors. He even, at the time they were leaving, gave them the bill for the expenditure which the local government incurred in hosting them in the hotel. "Your office must have budgeted for your visit. You therefore need to reimburse our expenditures on account of your visit." Mr. Onuoha courteously but seriously told the leader of the visiting federal Inspection and Assessment team. A number of Mr. Onuoha's senior staff had earlier suggested that each member of the visiting team should be given at least a small envelope of cash "to make them remember us." To that suggestion, Mr. Onuoha had replied, "They already have a vote for this trip. We must lead by example."

The facts on the ground were overwhelming in favor of Umudioha Local Government area. Six weeks after the visit of the presidential assessment team, the national press was out with the news: "Umudioha Local Government has won the president's "Local Government Council Leadership and Good Governance Prize" in the country!"

The prize was unimaginable. The prize was a project of the winning local government's choice to the tune of one billion dollars to be sited by the Central Government within the victorious local government area.

It was unheard of. It was unbelievable. And the president himself would come to the victorious local government headquarters to lay the foundation stone of the chosen project. The chosen project would have a completion time of not later than one year. The joy of Umudioha people and, indeed, the joy of the whole state knew no bounds.

The governor of the state, to whom also it was a major honor, made an immediate unscheduled visit to the local government area. His choice of the reputable and incorruptible retired school principal Mr. James Onuoha for leadership of the Council area after the sacking of the thieving Mr. Titus Nweke (alias *Strangler*) had been vindicated.

There was singing and dancing in the streets of Umudioha. There was waving of palm fronds in the streets; and the young and the old, the Christians and the Moslems, peoples of all faiths and the traditionalists all thronged to their different places of worship to thank God for the good fortune which had befallen the local government area. The hitherto nonchalant market women seeing the positive developments around them had become interested in the governance of their communities. Patriotism had started taking roots.

People thronged to the local government headquarters in their thousands to welcome and thank the state governor for making the right choice for the administrator's job.

They carried banners that read:

"Mr. Governor, the glory is yours."

Others read:

"Your Excellency, your incorruptibility won the day."

Yet others read:

"Mr. Onuoha, we are eternally grateful."

The big day eventually arrived. Mr. President had made the first ever visit to a local government to announce an award in that magnitude.

Hundreds and thousands of people had thronged the civic center of the local government venue for reception of Mr. President. People came from far and near to catch a glimpse of the president. The state governor was there as well as two other governors from adjacent states. It was the greatest day ever in the history of the local government and, indeed, in the whole state, winning a national honor for accountability and visible development; an honor which was so keenly contested.

The local government administrator had told the people that he would not influence the people on what they would ask of Mr. President.

"Shout to the hearing of Mr. President what you would want the Central Government to invest the prize money of one billion dollars on. Shout and shout it loud," Mr. Onuoha told the mammoth crowd over the microphone.

"Mr. President is listening, and he will hear your voice. Tell it directly to Mr. President what you think will benefit your children and your children's children. The choice is yours, my good people of Umudioha. You have suffered in silence for so long. But today is your day!"

As Mr. Onuoha uttered these words, tears rolled down his cheeks. It was a very touching moment for all that were present.

The Umudioha community had for long been held hostage by a coalition of three robbers two of who had been buoyed on by a later penitent heinous third master robber. Those scoundrels posed as, and bore the revered title of "honorable". This community, nay, the state and to a good extent the entire country was about to be set free from the clutches of the largely non-penitent scoundrels. Even the heavens appeared to nod in affirmation of and jubilation for the impending good tidings.

A very light shower that greeted the onset of dawn was soon to give way to refreshing sunshine and gentle breeze. Everything appeared perfect for the occasion.

Of course, as would be expected in a non-rehearsed situation from a crowd, there was a cacophony of demands: "More roads! More markets! More industries! More churches! More mosques! A cinema house! A supermarket!"

But among the myriad of requests, one request came out the loudest and strongest: "Mahadum!"

Mahadum the local word for a university was what the people wanted. Translated directly into English, Mahadum meant "know it all." Even the market women who did not have the benefit of a formal school education shouted in favor of Mahadum!

Both the loudness and intensity of that request and even the sound of the word itself, which is reminiscent of the sound of cannon fire, appeared to drown every other request.

The sound of Mahadum was soon to take over from every other request as the former advocates of supermarket, mosques churches roads and industries appeared to recognize the wisdom of those who opted for Mahadum.

"Mahadum! Mahadum, we want a Mahadum" soon became the unanimous call.

"Mr. President, you asked for the opinion of the people. The people have spoken. They want a Mahadum, a university. Our request lies at your feet, Mr. President," the local government administrator said.

The president got up. He appeared dumbfounded for a moment or two. It probably was not a demand that he had anticipated. But unlike the biblical request from Herod's daughter for the head of John the Baptist, this request was a very wise one, and the president easily acknowledged this.

"People of Umudioha, I praise you for your wisdom. I congratulate you for your good fortune, and I rejoice with you for your gift of an honest administrator and a wise governor.

"This is not the kind of request that I had anticipated from any group. It is well beyond what we had anticipated or budgeted for. But your wisdom and your hunger for the highest education for your children have been made manifest. People of Umudioha, you will have a Mahadum, a university! "And because you have had the wisdom to ask for a university, I, today, on behalf of the Federal Government of Konganoga, pledge that we will make up for any shortfalls in the required funds for building a first-class university in Umudioha. This is my pledge to you. This is a promise the fulfillment of which will be commenced with immediate effect!"

The crowd went wild with joy. Some people were weeping with joy. Others were clapping. Some did the weird dance of the *Ojionu* masquerade, and the *Mkpokiti* dancers in the distance showed off their fascinating art.

It was a day never to be forgotten in the history of Umudioha. It surpassed whatever any living individual in Umudioha and its environs had ever seen or heard of.

Within a year, the face of Umudioha had been completely transformed. The state government also stepped in to do many more roads to service the increased traffic that was soon to appear in the local government.

Umudioha, the once sleepy little-known local government, had become a well-known university town courtesy of the honesty and incorruptibility exhibited primarily by one man, a retired school principal—Mr. James Onuoha.

Chapter 28

THE TRIUMPH OF GOOD OVER EVIL

The congress seat that was previously occupied by Chief Unafefe had been vacant since after the official obituary announcement of the occupant was made.
Ade had initially been persuaded to join politics with the aim of running for senate. He had however decided to run for the House of Representatives instead, pending the time he would gather enough experience to move up to the senate, which was his late father's initial plan.
The elections were soon at hand. Ade had joined the opposition party since the people who controlled the party in power at the center in the local government were mostly those who were in the same gangs and cults as the late Chief Unafefe and Chief Nweke.

In spite of the fact that he had considered running for the congress post after his monumental success at the local government level, Mr. Onuoha, the incumbent local government administrator for Umudioha, had fully endorsed Mr. Ade Suleiman for the congress seat.
Ade finally agreed to give the congress seat a shot. He summoned a meeting of his senior staff and broke the news to them. He assured them that even with him as a congressman that the interest of the company and the charitable organizations would not be jeopardized. He further assured them that if he succeeded in getting into congress that he would work assiduously to uphold those standards which AMEND Incorporated and Suleiman Foundation respectively stood for.
He gave them his word that he would not do anything that would bring the image of the organizations to ridicule either by personal action or by association. He handed over his duties to his deputy and set off to his prospective constituency to launch his campaigns.

(Electioneering campaigns promise so much but do abysmally little on assumption of office. Winning is ultimately all about which candidate can dole out the most cash to the election umpires, ... and the judges!)

Ade's launching of his campaigns was like a carnival. The same degree of enthusiasm that greeted the emergence of Mr. Onuoha, the retired school principal, when the latter indicated his intention to run also greeted Ade's emergence as a candidate. The people's enthusiasm was fueled more by the emergence in the opposing party of one distasteful candidate. The latter was one of the hit men of the late Chief Unafefe, who also happened to be the latter's nephew and apparent successor since Chief Unafefe never formally married and had no legal children.

This nephew of Chief Unafefe, whose name was Obinna, was another known practicing cult member. He had inherited almost all the vast wealth of the late Oyinatumba. He had ironically also taken up the title of Oyinatumba II, apparently in memory of his late uncle and, perhaps, to draw inspiration from the exploits or notoriety of the late evil genius.

Oyinatumba II, however, unlike his uncle counterpart, was of relatively small stature, and his high-sounding title contrasted very sharply with the actual physical stature of the title's owner. Again, unlike the case with his late uncle, he did not have monopoly of financial power. Ade could match him dollar for dollar, and he did not have the advantage of the support of the incumbent local government political leadership, which had come out openly in support of Mr. Ade Suleiman.

As the campaigns heated up, Ade's opponent, seeing himself losing grounds, decided to go dirty. In an open campaign rally, he accused Ade of being a cultist.
 "I know many people say that they will not vote for me because they say I am a cult member. Yes, Oyinatumba II is a cult member, but I now want to inform you that Mr. Ade Suleiman is also a cult member. I can tell you that his cult identity number is 146B. I dare him to deny that, and I will bring proof of this," Chief Obinna Unafefe said. He had taken a chieftaincy title lately in preparation for the elections.

When Ade got wind of the smear campaign by his opponent, he quickly defused tension in his campaign organization by not refuting the allegation, but by correcting and clarifying it.

"My good people of Umudioha," Ade announced at a campaign rally, "I had always told you that I was a cult member. That was many years ago when I was a much younger man.
I have also told you that I have since repented. Those of you who know me well will testify that I have done daily penance for the sins that I committed as a young man, which I utterly regret and which I do not recommend to any young man. But my opponent is a practicing and unrepentant cult member. He is active and will never repent.
He eulogizes his actions and that is dangerous for Umudioha. It is

dangerous for our young people, and it is dangerous for our community and nation."

It was obvious that Ade's contrite stance made lasting impressions on the people. His campaign slogan of "A New Direction" was in consonance with his repentant stance.

As the election day proper approached and it looked more obvious that Chief Obinna Unafefe, the Oyinatumba II, was bent on replaying the election-rigging game perfected by his uncle, the late Chief Unafefe, Ade and his team added to their slogan the song: "Eternal Vigilance Ensures Liberty, Watch Your Vote, Video Your Vote, Tape the Result."

Ade's campaign team also formulated a song that encouraged and admonished people to monitor their votes at every moment. The song ran thus:
"The rat everyone knows is a thievish animal
The rat we know is also a timid animal
The rat steals your food when you go to sleep
The rat cannot rob the wakeful man."

It was a very useful song that gingered up everybody into vigilance over the conduct of the entire elections in view of the previous sad experience of the Unafefe and Strangler era.

Students of the University of Umudioha had thronged the polling booths. They turned out massively to vote, and it was obvious who their favored candidate was. They would certainly not abandon the man whose organization had persistently and consistently come to their aid through AMEND Incorporated and Suleiman Foundation.

The single name on their lips in every polling booth was Ade. Many of them swore to fish out and tear to shreds any electoral officer who would dare to mess around with their votes.

When the results were announced in every polling booth, the winner was clear—Mr. Ade Suleiman. Of course, with the watchful eyes of the students and the vigilance of the local government apparatus, it would not have been easy nor safe for anybody no matter how heavily suborned to announce as the winner of the election in Umudioha Local Government any other person than the true winner of the election.

And the winner, ... as expected by all, was Mr. Ade Suleiman.

Chapter 29

IMAGE REPAIR AT THE CENTER

With Ade in the House of Representatives, the bad image that Chief Unafefe's greatly tainted reputation had bestowed on Umudioha was greatly salvaged.
During the years while he was the chairman and CEO of AMEND Incorporated, Suleiman Foundation, and his private auto distributorship outfit, Ade had enrolled back into the University in Kuveri as a part-time student of sociology. He had worked very hard and had secured his degree in record time.

During Ade's swearing in, in parliament, many members who knew Chief Unafefe had listened very attentively to know whether his successor would be as crude as Chief Unafefe was and whether he would address the House in Pidgin English.

Much as many of the members sympathized with the family over the loss of Chief Unafefe, especially considering the circumstances under which he died, many of them who knew Oyinatumba more intimately and who were familiar with his activities had felt, all along, that he was a disgrace to the House.

Many of the members of the House, who were indeed honorable, recognized the fact that it was the likes of Chief Unafefe who brought ridicule to the House and who elicited the odious headline on one of the national dailies. The headline, which was captioned "The Good, the Bad, and the Honorable," with a sub caption of "The Honorables are the Robbers" addressed the membership of the House in very scathing language. It equated the honorable members of the House to the ugly in the aphorism "the good, the bad, and the ugly."
Many members of the House felt relieved that one of the principal characters who attracted the ugly image on the rest of the members had at last made his exit from what otherwise was

supposed to be an honorable assembly. The mode of exit was of secondary consideration. Almost the entire membership however did not seem to see ugliness and robbery in the humongous and most unrealistic monthly salaries which the legislators were paying themselves even in the face of the dwindling fortunes of the rest of the populace. They did not seem to see the immorality of the senators and members of the House of Representatives ripping off the rest of the country by way of their unrealistically-high wages and allowances, even when the rest of the country moaned under diminishing national economic fortunes and mounting foreign debt. They did not appear to see the rapid equation of the appellation "The Honorable" to an irresistible scoundrel who would cheat at all levels of government, one who would sacrifice honor and his or her reputation on the altar of expediency; one who like Chief Unafefe and his likes would corrupt young minds by encouraging their enrollment into nefarious organizations like the notorious Chambers fraternity.

Mr. Ade Suleiman did not disappoint his listeners. In his inaugural address to the House. He spoke in very good English, was very courteous, and displayed a very good understanding of current events and of his duties as an Honorable Member of the House of Representatives.

The big applause that followed Ade's inaugural speech to the House members was more out of appreciation by the other members that a more decent colleague had come on board rather than for the actual points that Ade raised.
Ade was immediately put into the House Committee on Youth's Affairs as well as on the committee on commerce, industry, and humanitarian affairs. It did not take him too long to adapt. He read a lot and learned fast.
Within his first six weeks in the House, Ade had individually sponsored three bills. He also cosponsored four other important bills.
Ade's first bill in parliament was one that called for a special

department to be carved in the Ministry of Youth Affairs for dealing with rehabilitation of drug addicts and for more stringent measures to curb drug usage and cult membership.

The bill easily sailed through its first, second, and third readings within two weeks.
When the bill was signed into law, it was a big triumph for Ade and all that he stood for.
He delivered a speech at the University of Umudioha a week after the bill was signed into law and set up a chair in the Department of Adult Education in memory of his late father, Chief Martin Omenka Suleiman. The professorship was for the advancement of adult literacy and human development. It had the highest funding than any other chair in the university.

Ade's tenure in the House of Representatives was very exemplary. He made it obvious and repeated it at every available opportunity that he would not be party to any bribery or misuse of public funds.
His stand won him many admirers. It also won him a couple of enemies from among those who, like the late Chief Unafefe, would like to perpetuate the barbaric culture of graft, embezzlement, and looting of the public treasury. Such people, just like Chief Unafefe, contributed little or nothing to debates. They would doze off on their seats during important debates but would jump up on their feet once money sharing was mentioned. It was noteworthy that Ade's predecessor in parliament neither sponsored nor even cosponsored a single bill in parliament. He, like a number of others with him, was worse than the ugly side of "the good, the bad, and the honorable." They represented the worst of the worst. They extorted money from the executive before they would vote on any executive-sponsored bill. Lobbying to them meant money sharing, and the interest of the people and the country was not part of their agenda.
To the likes of the late Chief Unafefe, anything would go as long as the correct price was paid. On the other hand, anything would fail

if the brown envelopes did not go round.

Ade soon became the symbol of the conscience of the House. He became the pillar of the human rights movement in the House. He was the only member of the House who came openly and declared his assets and gave copies to the press.

"I am a product of a checkered and evil past. I benefitted from evil practices but I am giving all back to the society which was the victim. I have renounced my past and I am forever reformed. I am here and forever determined to make amends and ensure that the ugliness from which I came does not continue to bedevil our country." Ade consistently said. His humility and candor greatly endeared him to his listeners even in a House overflowing with dishonorable people.

Ade was the only member who stated openly that anybody who knew of his involvement thereafter in any unwholesome activities in the House should go to press without fear of litigation for libel. He was the only member who publicly requested never to be contacted in the sharing of any money or patronage or other material benefits that did not conform fully with the regulations or that were not morally justified.

At first the few that represented the very ugly side of the *Honorable Members* condemned him and labeled him as "playing holier than the Pope." But when Ade stood his ground and continued to manifest piety, honesty and transparency in his daily activities in the various committees of the House, both those that hailed him and those that condemned him came to respect him. When there was any issue that needed a trustworthy person, who would not be amenable to bribery, it was usually Ade who would be contacted.

Because of Ade's popularity borne out of incorruptibility, big transformations began to occur in the House of Representatives. By his sixth month in the House, Ade and three other members sponsored an amendment to the standing orders in the House by which every member must publicly declare his or her assets and make copies of these available to the press and to the members of the House before the middle of the month of January each year. Ade said that it was his opinion that any member who felt uncomfortable making such assets public should not consider himself or herself worthy of holding public office. That way, sudden wealth that could not be accounted for on the part of any House member could be scrutinized.

Back in Umudioha, Ade's exploits in Karuja were making waves. The people of Umudioha felt very proud of him. Even his former political enemies began to respect and praise him. He merited everybody's respect.
Ade capped his popularity by the unflinching support which he gave to his friend Mr. James Onuoha in the latter's quest for the vacant senate seat in Ade's senatorial zone.
Mr. Onuoha with Ade's support easily won the seat which once again projected Umudioha and its adjoining communities as a zone that could be looked upon for repairing tarnished images, for healing political and social wounds and for the triumph of good over evil.

Ade did not live ostentatiously. He did not boast about his success. He always admitted to people that he was initially the product of a flawed system, but he always was quick to admit that he would sacrifice every bit of what he had if only to see that society did not suffer undue disadvantage because of whatever evils that he or his ancestors might have committed. He matched his actions with words and never lost any opportunity of helping out victims of drug addiction who were prepared to turn a new leaf. He also spoke at various seminars and symposia that were organized for the education of drug addicts and potential addicts and cult members.

He gave radio and television talks, urging drug addicts and gang members to turn a new leaf.

"Do not hide and feel helpless and thereby sink deeper into cult and drugs."
Ade told the faceless addicts and cult members. He further admonished the victims:
 "Seek help, and the governments at the federal and state levels are prepared to assist you. Do not feel that you are alone or that your sins are too big to be forgiven. I too was an offender as well as a victim. A beloved family member himself was an offender. But thank God we all repented and turned away from crime. Right now, we are deep into the business of making restitution to an injured society. AMEND, as you probably know, is a product of this restitution effort. Thank God, through a strong resolve and dedication, I was able to rescue myself. Therefore, if you need help, do not hesitate to seek it. Do not be afraid. Do not be shy. I am here to help you."

Ade's crusade was soon to start yielding fruit. The earlier exit of his late father, the late Chief Omenka Suleiman some years back from the organization, along with many of his lieutenants, had tremendously weakened *The Chambers* and its affiliated organizations.
The later exit of Chief Unafefe and his team appeared to have dealt a final blow to the central body of the organization. What remained was the skeleton. The flesh and indeed the central nervous system of the organization had been pulled off.
The few adherents who still clung tenaciously to these organizations at the center were soon to find that they no longer had very much following. The few newly recruited members from among the student population only came during the cult's weekly meetings to partake of the free fried chicken and goat-meat pepper soup. They would soon be gone after the feasting. It was no longer fashionable for anybody to say that he or she was a member of *The Chambers* In campus.

Merely visualizing the cult's characteristic tattoo mark, which used to be a status symbol, was enough to put off even the most tolerant person in the society. Many former cult members had to start paying to have the tattoo marks on their shoulders removed. Any sign depicting a person as belonging to a cult in any gathering was certain to bring an unfavorable reception from majority of the people in that gathering. Cult members who were once the celebrities in most gatherings were soon to become pariahs in most societies. Reason was that academic achievement, and decency were soon once again to begin to assume the pride of place in student life in the campuses of the nation's higher institutions.

And even in the different legislative houses, the exit of the kingpins of crime brought about dramatic improvement in the quality of the membership and in the quality of debates and decency among the members. It gradually, once again, became respectable to be addressed as *"The Honorable"*.

Yes, every Tom, Dick, and Harry who had ever run to be a candidate for the post of a local government council member would previously have liked to be addressed as *The Honorable.* Anybody who had put his or her name as a candidate for a party post in his or her ward in the village would address himself or herself as *The Honorable.* Any thug attached to anybody in governance, at any level of governance, would immediately assume the title of *The Honorable.*

Thus, before the advent of the likes of Ade Suleiman and James Onuoha in the scheme of things, evil had held sway over good in every facet of the society, but not anymore.

Either in strategic discussions about the destiny of Konganoga, or in plotting the embezzlement of funds that would have built schools, roads, and waterways; or in discussions about the robbery of a bank or the kidnapping of an oil worker for ransom, the few bad eggs in the system had assumed unimaginable powers and besmeared the rest that were good. But, again, not anymore!

The likes of Ade Suleiman were multiplying. Those that benefitted from evil were still Konganogans. They would not be expected to disappear overnight. But they would be expected to make amends. There must be restitution for justice to prevail. Ade Suleiman's AMEND Incorporated had led by examples.

The bad had started to be sorted from the good, to be discarded.
Waiting for natural selection to do the job was no longer the answer
A people get the government that they deserve
Yes, but the honorable must no longer continue to be a robber!

For the moment, but only for the moment, evil men and evil women hold the aces
For the moment, and only for the moment, they dictate the tune
But time is running out for them with the ticking of the clock
They may still smile to the banks and walk with a swagger
They may still hold a somber society hostage with their treasures dubiously acquired
They may still wield political power but not with the passage of time
The dawn of day holds up the roses only for the good
The last laugh belongs to the men and women who defy the allure of crime
The long arm of justice will ultimately reach even the hidden crevices and dim corners of the earth
The Honorable by day and the robber by night can never in perpetuity conceal their crimes
Under all shades and under all guises, they still will try
Yes, but only for a moment before the dawn of day
And *The Honorable* who is a robber will kiss the dust
And, a patient and rehabilitated society will certainly triumph in the end.

Epilogue

As the light of day follows the darkness of each night
So will the light of day overcome the darkness in all things
And so, will perpetrators of evil only on borrowed time come to live.
And they disregard this fact only at their own peril

For surely as the light of dawn overcomes the darkness of the night
So shall enlightenment and positive change conquer evil and societal rot
For they that sowed the winds in the course of times past
Have invariably, abundantly reaped the whirlwind.

Where a nation's looters repent and seek society's forgiveness
Where there is genuine penitence and necessary restitution
There, hope and forgiveness may yet be availed to a nation.
But where the dispossessed populace, are further humiliated and mauled
And the robbers mock their way down the street in ridicule of the wounded and the oppressed
There, even for a thousand years of deferred justice, will discontent and emptiness continue to trail the land.